Designing Effective Science Instruction

What Works in Science Classrooms

Designing Effective Science Instruction

What Works in Science Classrooms

Anne Tweed

MᴄREL

NSTApress
National Science Teachers Association
Arlington, Virginia

National Science Teachers Association

Claire Reinburg, Director
Jennifer Horak, Managing Editor
Andrew Cocke, Senior Editor
Judy Cusick, Senior Editor
Wendy Rubin, Associate Editor

ART AND DESIGN
Will Thomas Jr., Director
Joseph Butera, Senior Graphic Designer, cover and interior design
Cover illustration courtesy of iStock, photocanal25

PRINTING AND PRODUCTION
Catherine Lorrain, Director
Jack Parker, Electronic Prepress Technician

NATIONAL SCIENCE TEACHERS ASSOCIATION
Francis Q. Eberle, PhD, Executive Director
David Beacom, Publisher
1840 Wilson Blvd., Arlington, VA 22201
www.nsta.org/store
For customer service inquiries, please call 800-277-5300.

LIBRARY OF CONGRESS CATALOGING-IN-PUBLICATION DATA
Tweed, Anne.
  Designing effective science instruction: what works in science classrooms / by Anne Tweed.
      p. cm.
  Includes bibliographical references and index.
  ISBN 978-1-935155-06-5
  1. Science--Study and teaching. 2. Curriculum planning. I. Title.
  Q181.T87 2010
  507.1--dc22
                                    2009028415

eISBN 978-1-936137-95-4

NSTA is committed to publishing material that promotes the best in inquiry-based science education. However, conditions of actual use may vary, and the safety procedures and practices described in this book are intended to serve only as a guide. Additional precautionary measures may be required. NSTA and the authors do not warrant or represent that the procedures and practices in this book meet any safety code or standard of federal, state, or local regulations. NSTA and the authors disclaim any liability for personal injury or damage to property arising out of or relating to the use of this book, including any of the recommendations, instructions, or materials contained therein.

Mid-continent Research for Education and Learning (McREL) is a nonprofit education R&D organization (*www.mcrel.org*) that offers staff development and consulting services to school districts nationwide, including workshops and other professional support for *Designing Effective Science Instruction*. To learn more, e-mail McREL at *info@mcrel.org/desi* or call 1-800-781-0156.

Dedication

This book is dedicated to my parents, Irvin and Jeanette Leerssen. Their hard work, dedication to family, and love of the outdoors has provided me with the inspiration and optimism to pursue science, continue as a learner, and strive to help others. From them I have learned that with planning and preparation, positive results are always possible!

Contents

Foreword

Science teachers everywhere agree: Teaching science, no matter the level, is hard work! To do it well and to be effective requires continuous learning. Not only is the knowledge base that explains science phenomena continuing to increase, research findings that help us understand how students learn are also increasing. The goal for science teachers is to maintain a balance so that it is not about working harder trying to keep up with the new research-based findings, but about working together to implement the best practices in the classroom.

Designing Effective Science Instruction: What Works in Science Classrooms is designed to pull together recent findings from many science education studies and teacher education initiatives. It can be a daunting task for a teacher to learn about each initiative separately and then integrate the new learning within existing instructional frameworks, one initiative at a time. This book presents an instructional framework and includes the separate initiatives (i.e., addressing misconceptions, formative assessments, inquiry approaches) as part of a larger framework of effective science instruction. An individual teacher of science or groups of teachers can use *Designing Effective Science Instruction* to plan and implement changes to his or her science instruction.

Effective Science Instruction: What Does Research Tell Us? (Banilower et al. 2008) summarizes the research foundation for this book. In this report, researchers shed light on possible reasons for poor student performance in science. Most notably, research revealed that in a national sample of science classrooms, science lessons do not often include the features identified as part of effective science instruction. In other words, too many science students are not clear about the learning goal being taught, and they are not being asked to make sense of the content that the teachers deliver. Students cannot, because of this classroom culture and instruction, understand and retain the science concepts they are supposedly learning. If the students are learning, the learning is frequently temporary and often as a response to a quiz or test. The study further indicated that teachers of science are too often unaware of the research that identifies the effective practices they need to implement in their science classrooms.

For the past several years I have worked with teachers of science as they designed and redesigned their lesson plans, examined their craft, and attempted to implement change in their classrooms. The result was often ineffective, with little or no change to the science teachers' overall practice. The reason for this lack of change was simple: Limited information was available to me about effective teaching and I had to turn to a myriad of research articles that had little impact on the teachers themselves. This book will change all that by bridging the gap between research and practice.

The book begins by providing examples of effective strategies that support the development and delivery of science lessons that foster student understanding of the science concepts being taught. It targets one key element found in the (Weiss et al. 2003) research into designing effective lesson plans. The book dives into the characteristics of effective lesson plans, asks teachers to reflect on their current lessons, and then provides strategies for redesigning those lesson plans into even more effective lessons—ones that embody the characteristics of high-quality lessons from the research.

Using the Content-Understanding-Environment (C-U-E) method, this book gives teachers the tools to approach lesson planning with confidence. Teachers will be able to pinpoint aspects of their instructional practice that need improvement. They will understand how to seek out the content knowledge and experiences they need to become more effective science teachers. They will be able to implement changes to their teaching craft, to become effective facilitators of student learning, and to provide their students with rich and active learning environments that allow for successful student achievement.

I know teachers of science will find this book helpful, valuable, and informative. The book will assist as they evaluate science instructional practices, reflect on that practice, and make changes to improve that practice—the hallmarks of being effective science teachers. *Designing Effective Science Instruction* embodies this. Let the journey begin.

—Shelley Lee

References

Banilower, E., K. Cohen, J. Pasley, and I. Weiss. 2008. *Effective science instruction: What does research tell us?* Portsmouth, NH: RMC Research Corporation, Center on Instruction.

Weiss, I., J. Pasley, S. Smith, E. Banilower, and D. Heck. 2003. *Looking inside the classroom: A study of K–12 mathematics and science education in the United States.* Chapel Hill, NC: Horizon Research, Inc.

Acknowledgments

Anne Tweed, principal consultant, would like to thank the following individuals for their support and assistance with the *Designing Effective Science Instruction: What Works in Science Classrooms* book.

Special thanks to Jan Tuomi, who was a major contributor to the instructional framework, and to Judy Counley, who created the figures and tables for this book.

Thanks to McREL staff: Sarah LaBounty, who contributed writing support; Heather Hein, writer/editor; Sue Amosun, administrative coordinator; Linda Brannan, director of information services; and special thanks to Lisa Maxfield, administrative coordinator.

Thanks also to Ceri Dean for her editing and overall project support. And a final thank you to Laura Arndt, Jean May-Brett, Shelley Lee, and Susan Koba, all of whom are longtime friends and professional colleagues. Their continuous support for this project has been invaluable.

Some of the original work upon which this publication is based was sponsored, wholly or in part, with funds from the U.S. Department of Education Office of Elementary and Secondary Education (OESE); Eisenhower Regional Mathematics and Science Education Consortia, under grant R319A000004; and the Institute of Education Sciences (IES), under Contract No. ED-01-CO-0006. The content does not necessarily reflect the position or policy of OESE, IES, the Department of Education, or any other agency of the federal government.

About the Author

Anne Tweed, a principal consultant with the Mid-continent Research for Education and Learning (McREL) in Denver, Colorado, also serves as the director of the North Central Comprehensive Center. Her work at McREL supports professional development in the areas of effective science instruction, inquiry-based instruction, formative assessment, high-quality instructional practices, teaching reading in content areas, analyzing instructional materials, and audits of science curricula and programs. The work is research based and includes ongoing professional development workshops. In her role as director of the North Central Comprehensive Center, she leads project activities that build the capacity of state education agencies through resource dissemination, group facilitation, building infrastructure and networking, planning and needs assessment, developing solutions that are part of statewide systems of support, and revising tools and templates that support schools in need of improvement. She is currently a co–principal investigator on an NSF DRK-12 project that supports implementation of nanoscale science and technology in secondary classrooms.

Tweed is a past president of the National Science Teachers Association (2004–2005). A veteran high school science educator and department coordinator, she spent the majority of her 30-year teaching career with the Cherry Creek School District in Colorado. Tweed earned an M.S. in botany from the University of Minnesota, a B.A. in biology from Colorado College, and a teaching certificate from the University of Colorado. Tweed has held several leadership positions with NSTA, the Colorado Association of Science Teachers, and the Colorado Alliance for Science. She was on the review committee for the National Science Education Standards and a contributor to the original Colorado Model Content Standards for Science. In addition, Tweed served on the program planning team revising the 2009 NAEP Framework for Science. Tweed has been recognized for her work in education and has received the Distinguished Service Award and the Distinguished High School Science Teaching Award from NSTA, the Outstanding Biology Teacher Award for Colorado, and is a state Presidential Award honoree. She has published many articles, coauthored several books, given more than 150 presentations and workshops at state and national conferences, and continues to be active with state and national science associations.

Introduction

Why This? Why Now?

Science teachers, like all teachers, start each school year with high hopes and expectations for students to succeed. They plan their lessons, scramble to get the necessary equipment, and work hard to engage their students. However, despite good intentions and best-laid plans, not all students do well in science classes, and even fewer achieve mastery. We see the effects of this all around us. Student performance on national and international assessments, including science assessments, is poor. More and more adults are unable to understand the scientific issues that affect their lives and society. The media reports that national economic competitiveness is at stake. It's clear that something must be done now to help science teachers put power behind their hopes and expectations for student achievement.

Designing Effective Science Instruction: What Works in Science Classrooms is meant to help teachers focus on what can and must be done. It draws upon recent research in science education, most notably a well-designed study of science classrooms which sheds light on possible reasons for poor student performance in science (Weiss et al. 2003; Banilower et al. 2008). This research study and subsequent report on effective science instruction revealed that in a national sample of science classrooms, about two-thirds of science lessons observed were of low quality. In other words, too many science students sit passively, never being asked to make sense of the content that teachers deliver. Too many science activities masquerade as science lessons and fail to develop students' understanding of science concepts. Too many teachers lower their expectations and avoid teaching a rigorous science curriculum. The pressure teachers feel to meet student achievement goals is immense. With emerging research findings about how students learn and how to teach effectively, guidance for teachers is available.

The Weiss et al. study also tells us that teachers often are unaware that research has identified teacher knowledge and skills that support the development and delivery of science lessons that foster student learning. This and other research on teaching and learning lead us to believe that designing high-quality science lessons that include research-based instructional practices is a logical first step to improving *all* students' science learning. As a result, *Designing Effective Science Instruction* focuses on strategies that science teachers at all levels can use to make their science lessons better.

Educational research on learning and effective science instruction has much to offer us in meeting the challenges of educating students to high standards. What is missing in previous books on effective science lessons and instruction is a synthesis of the research that focuses on the essential findings and the implications for instructional practice. *Designing Effective Science Instruction* provides that bridge between research and practice, and does so in a format that is easy to learn, use, and continue to apply.

This book will describe the characteristics of high-quality science lessons, help you reflect on what is working well with your current approach to designing lessons, and provide recommendations for improving existing lessons or creating effective new ones. Whether you are a novice or veteran teacher, the self assessments and recommendations in this book will provide guidance that supports and encourages you to refine what you do to become a more effective science teacher. You can use this book to decide what practices will work for you and your students, but you are encouraged to work with others as you plan for and revise instruction, interpret student work, and determine what changes you will make to your teacher practices. Planning for your own professional development is one way to use the information contained in this book. Many resources are available to help you plan for meaningful professional development that is ongoing and uses a model that features reflective practice in the real world of teachers. The National Science Education Standards (NRC 1996) for teaching and professional development provide a starting point and helped to inform this book.

No matter what grade level you teach, you will benefit from learning the Content-Understanding-Environment (C-U-E) instructional framework described in this book. We believe that if you understand and apply this framework, you will be able to approach lesson planning with confidence and develop well-planned, effective science lessons. In addition, you will be able to pinpoint aspects of your instructional practice that need improvement and seek out the content knowledge and experiences that will be most helpful in making you a more effective teacher. Together these will lead to positive teacher and student attitudes toward science learning and positive science achievement results for all students.

Organization of *Designing Effective Science Instruction* book

Designing Effective Science Instruction: What Works in Science Classrooms (DESI) is organized into five chapters. The next four chapters introduce the C-U-E instructional framework and provide details about each of its three elements (Content, Understanding, Environment). The contents of chapters 2 through 5 are described briefly below.

Chapter 1. Building the Framework. This chapter focuses readers on the following questions as the three components of the C-U-E framework are introduced:

- Effective science teaching: What does it mean and how does it look?

- What are the barriers to effective instruction?

- What does research say about effective science instruction?

- Why the Content-Understanding-Environment framework?

This chapter emphasizes that all three elements must be addressed during lesson design and implemented effectively when delivering science instruction.

Chapter 2. Identifying Important Content. This chapter focuses on identifying important content, clarifying student learning goals, sequencing learning activities to achieve those goals, and aligning assessments with content. This necessitates thinking about ways to prune the curriculum and determine student prior knowledge and preconceptions.

Chapter 3. Developing Student Understanding. Using the research on how students learn science, this chapter will help readers learn how to make lessons learner-centered, help students make meaning and build connections among science concepts, and develop each student's ability to learn. To support sense-making, we include strategies that address misconceptions, that make student thinking visible with classroom discourse and that encourage formative assessment processes to identify student learning and provide feedback.

Chapter 4. Creating a Learning Environment. Interactions, routines, and informal feedback that occur every day in the classroom can undermine or enhance learning. This chapter presents strategies related to teaching students to take responsibility for their thinking and learning and to developing positive working relationships with others. Student engagement and motivation are critical components of collaborative classroom environments, and strategies that address these components are included in this chapter also.

Chapter 5. Teacher Learning: A Beginning Teachers continue to learn throughout their lifetimes. All teachers can learn just as all students can learn. To move from "surviving to thriving" we need to look at how the instructional framework applies to us. The key to this work is establishing an environment for ourselves that promotes learning—learning and thinking about the content we teach, learning about content-specific strategies that move students' thinking forward, and learning how to keep a balance but still move forward.

The Audience for *Designing Effective Science Instruction*

First and foremost, this book is valuable for science teachers, both veteran and novice, at all grade levels. It is also of value to anyone concerned with improving science education and nurturing effective science teaching. This latter group includes principals and department heads, curriculum specialists, science mentors, professional development providers, and professors in schools of education. Different science professionals will use the information in this book differently, depending on their goals for improving science instruction.

Teachers at different grade levels and with different levels of experience will focus on different aspects of the book. This is not meant to be a prescriptive, one-size-fits-all book. All teachers will take away lessons that meet their individual needs and promote self-examination of their current instructional practices. For example, if you're a veteran high school teacher, you probably have significant content knowledge; thus, you will benefit most by focusing on lesson design and developing student understanding. In doing so, the biggest change for you may be shifting from a teacher-centered classroom to a student-centered environment. All teachers, though, whether novices or veterans, will want to learn more about how to promote effective science instruction that focuses on important content, engages students in science inquiry, promotes student sense-making using science discourse, and involves students in formative assessments and student self-assessments so that both students and teachers will know if learning is taking place.

Principals and department coordinators, who are responsible for ensuring that science lessons are of high quality, can use the recommendations in this book when analyzing curriculum, providing professional development for staff, and helping teachers create a community of support for instructional change. Without such support from principals and department coordinators, even well-intentioned and highly qualified teachers may become discouraged and some may choose to leave the profession altogether.

Other professional development providers, too, can use the information in *Designing Effective Science Instruction: What Works in Science Classrooms* to create professional development experiences that directly address the strategies in the framework or to help teachers develop a deeper understanding in each area of the framework. All professional development providers who use the research base and proposed strategies in this book, whether principals, department coordinators, or teacher leaders, are responsible for creating the conditions for teachers' success—making the appropriate connections between professional development experiences, helping them understand how all the pieces fit together, and providing them with opportunities to implement, then reflect on, new strategies as they develop a new repertoire of instructional practices.

Last but not least, *Designing Effective Science Lessons* contains valuable information for prospective science teachers. This book could be used as part of a course for preservice teachers, laying the foundation for effective science instruction and high-quality lessons as they learn how to teach. The instructional framework and recommended strategies could help preservice teachers set appropriate goals, envision effective science instruction, and learn how best to approach planning their lessons.

How to Get Started With the Book

The first step to getting started with this book is to get familiar with the C-U-E framework in Chapter 2. Because the C-U-E instructional framework represents a coherent whole, make sure to pay attention to all of its parts. Incorporating any one of the strategies in lesson design will increase lesson effectiveness, but this approach will not be as effective as using the entire framework to design your lessons. At the same time, selecting one or two strategies to practice at a time to see how they work can be a good approach initially. The strategies you choose as a focus will most likely relate to your biggest challenges. Your unique classroom and community context will determine how you will get started. The key to remember is that you will want to be able to answer the following three questions:

1. What essential learning are you including in your lessons and unit of study? (Content—C)

2. What learning experiences will you provide to develop student conceptual understanding? (Understanding—U)

3. How will you and your students support a positive classroom environment that supports learning by all students? (Environment—E)

Depending upon your prior teaching and learning experiences, some of the strategies may not be new to you. So, how do you know what you don't know? The first step is to take the self-assessment found in *Chapter 1: Building the Framework.* The results of this assessment, along with your knowledge of your students' needs, will help you select and prioritize the areas on which you will work first. After working on your highest priority, you can revisit your self-assessment results and pick up the next-highest priority area to reinforce the initial progress you will make.

As with anything new, the first time you try something in class, you may not achieve an instant solution to the instructional problem you were trying to solve. To avoid disappointment, we recommend that you take the approach of a learner when trying to improve your use of these strategies. That is, learn about the strategy, try it, reflect on it, practice and reinforce what is working well. You can also engage your students in a discussion of strategies that you are trying and ask for their feedback and suggestions. This will help students understand what is going on in class and alert them to the possibility of instructional experiences that might be different from what they are used to. And if you have the capacity to work with other teachers, engage in peer discussions and reflection as part of a continuous process of improvement.

Bear in mind that the areas in which educators most need to improve will be those with which they are least comfortable. Tackling areas that are difficult for you can lead to significant changes in instructional practice, but it will take time and practice to use new instructional strategies effectively. Engaging in action research—trying lesson revision strategies, gathering data about their effectiveness, reflecting on implementation, and perhaps involving students in evaluating what's working—is one way to help you persevere. Though the process of change is difficult, relying on the research and experiences behind the recommendations will also help keep you going.

A Personal Note

I believe that if you use the C-U-E framework, you will improve your teaching and your students' learning. I believe this because the C-U-E framework addresses essential aspects of effective science instruction and high-quality science lessons. If the lessons you use every day in your classroom are designed around this framework, positive results are highly likely. Although some of the strategies in this book are ones that you have already mastered, you may find that the way those strategies are organized represents a new approach to instruction for you. All the parts are put together into one complete framework that is easy to follow, practical, and empowering. And it is tried and tested; it reflects what I have learned over three decades of teaching and professional development combined with—and confirmed by—the practices of the best teachers that I know and the most recent research findings available.

Whether you are in a classroom teaching students, working with other science teachers, or learning on your own, I trust that you will find this book informative, relevant, credible, and enjoyable to read. My goal is not to provide an educational "silver bullet" for science teachers but, rather, to help build a community of science teachers willing to try new things and dedicated to helping all students learn.

References

Banilower, E., K. Cohen, J. Pasley, and I. Weiss. 2008. *Effective science instruction: What does research tell us?* Portsmouth, NH: RMC Research Corporation, Center on Instruction.

National Research Council. 1996. *National science education standards.* Washington, DC: National Academy Press.

Weiss, I., J. Pasley, S. Smith, E. Banilower, and D. Heck. 2003. *Looking inside the classroom: A study of K–12 mathematics and science education in the United States.* Chapel Hill, NC: Horizon Research, Inc.

Building the Framework

Chapter 1

Effective Science Teaching: What Does It Mean? How Does It Look?

A friend asked me these questions several months ago and it got me thinking. Should we use student achievement as the measure of teacher effectiveness? If improved student achievement is one indicator of effectiveness, we can look at the question of teacher effectiveness with this lens and consider inputs to teachers and outputs as determined by student measures that include engagement, conceptual understanding, and even increased achievement. If we consider science teacher capabilities as part of the inputs, then we need to include teachers' understanding of science concepts and their understanding of when and how to teach the concepts—their pedagogical content knowledge (Shulman 1987). To be more effective as teachers, we need to participate in professional development that increases our content understanding and our ability to decide when and how to present the content to students. But having content knowledge and pedagogical content knowledge is only part of what it means to be an effective teacher.

If we consider teacher effectiveness from the perspective of supporting student learning, then to be effective, teachers need to know instructional strategies that help students learn. In other words, we need pedagogical knowledge. Pedagogical knowledge also includes knowing how to provide learning opportunities that meet the individual needs of students, place the learner at the center of instruction, and facilitate learning opportunities that develop students' conceptual understanding. Since *learner-centered* means different things to different teachers, we use the term to refer to classroom environments that include the existing knowledge, skills, attitudes, and beliefs that our students bring with them. Learner-centered instruction occurs in classrooms that emphasize opportunities for students to construct their own meanings. Instruction begins with what students think and know and bridges their ideas to the subject matter we present (Bransford, Brown, and Cocking 2000).

What Does Research Say About Effective Science Instruction?

If you were to ask science teachers or teachers of elementary school science what effective teaching looks like, the answers would clearly depend upon a variety of factors such as how long they have been teaching, their understanding of learning theory, their ability to understand and apply recent brain research, their content and pedagogical content knowledge, the coaching and mentoring that they received during and after their teacher preparation work, the professional development that they receive, and the professional collaboration and conversations that are part of their day-to-day teaching. This is not a comprehensive list by any means, but it speaks to some of the different influences on teachers' conceptions of effective science teaching and their levels of preparation to design and provide effective teaching and subsequent learning for their students.

When reviewing the research base around effective science teaching there are several resources that provide guidance and insights that can be used to answer the questions "What does effective teaching mean?" and "How does it look?" As mentioned previously, the National Science Education Standards (NRC 1996) provide a framework for what effective science teachers know and do. *Looking Inside the Classroom* (Weiss et al. 2003), a National Science Foundation study, provides additional insights about effective science teaching. According to the study, the goal of all instruction should be to develop students' conceptual understanding. As a result, teachers need to provide students with opportunities to learn the content and be clear about the learning goals for each lesson (specific concepts being addressed). In addition, researchers conducting this study found that lessons judged to be of low quality often lacked meaningful opportunities for discussions or student sense-making and instead consisted of activities for activities' sake, with no clear learning target. As a result of their findings, the observers in the study concluded that "teachers need a vision of effective instruction to guide the design and implementation of their lessons" (p. xiii). It also was clear from the study that teacher content knowledge alone is not sufficient to prepare teachers to provide high quality instruction. A clear understanding of effective instructional practices (pedagogical knowledge) and pedagogical-content knowledge are also needed.

In other words, to adequately develop student understanding of science concepts, we have to go beyond a general understanding of effective instructional strategies and have an in-depth knowledge of the content and common research-based student misconceptions. With that understanding, we need to know when and how to introduce and develop the concepts in class to address students' prior conceptions. We must plan our instruction to engage students beyond a superficial level by using a variety of representations and instructional strategies which make sense to the learner and take into account individual learner needs (Shulman 1986, 1987). We must understand students' scientific thinking and be able to generate effective representations that result in student learning. This cannot happen unless we are prepared with both content and pedagogy and take the time to assess for student thinking.

Figure 1.1 (p. 4) provides lists of the characteristics of effective science lessons that the researchers looked for in the classrooms involved in the *Looking Inside the Classroom* study. The characteristics of effective lessons, along with the research findings, add to our understanding of what it means to offer effective science instruction.

Effective teaching also means assessing what students know as instruction occurs and taking that information into account to adjust instruction. This focus on formative assessment processes in science classrooms is consistent with the research on how students learn science (Minstrell 1989; Donovan and Bransford 2005). Findings from the meta-analysis on how students learn science emphasized the following important principles of learning:

- Assess for prior student understanding of the science concepts.

- Actively involve students in the learning process.

- Help students be more metacognitive so that they can acknowledge the science concepts they understand, the goals for their learning, and the criteria for determining achievement of the learning goals.

- ensure that learning is interactive and include effective classroom discussions.

In a recent publication titled, "Effective Science Instruction," Banilower and colleagues (2008) provide a summary of studies on science learning and suggest an instructional model based on that research. They identify five features of effective science instruction. The first feature is motivating students since students are unlikely to learn without some level of motivation. Second, it is important to elicit students' prior knowledge to find out what their ideas are about the topics or concepts being studied. We know that students have ideas of their own about how the natural world works and some of their ideas will make it difficult for them to learn new ideas. Third, to engage students intellectually with the content, we need to link learning activities to the learning targets. Fourth, effective science instruction helps students think scientifically. This means students are able to critique claims using evidence. Finally, effective science instruction includes opportunities

Figure 1.1
Characteristics of Effective Science Lessons

Quality of Lesson Design	Quality of Noninteractive/Dialogic (NI/D)
❏ Resources available contribute to accomplishing the purpose of the instruction.	❏ Teacher appears confident in ability to teach science.
❏ Reflects careful planning and organization.	❏ Teacher's classroom management enhances quality of lesson.
❏ Strategies and activities reflect attention to students' preparedness and prior experience.	❏ Pace is appropriate for developmental levels/needs of students.
❏ Strategies and activities reflect attention to issues of access, equity, and diversity.	❏ Teacher is able to adjust instruction according to level of students' understanding.
❏ Incorporates tasks, roles, and interactions consistent with investigative science.	❏ Instructional strategies are consistent with investigative science.
❏ Encourages collaboration among students.	❏ Teacher's questioning enhances development of students' understanding/problem solving.
❏ Provides adequate time and structure for sense-making.	
❏ Provides adequate time and structure for wrap-up.	

Quality of Science Content	Quality of Classroom Culture
❏ Content is significant and worthwhile.	❏ Climate of respect for students' ideas, questions, and contributions is evident.
❏ Content information is accurate.	❏ Active participation of all is encouraged and valued.
❏ Content is appropriate for developmental levels of students.	❏ Interactions reflect working relationship between teacher and students.
❏ Teacher displays understanding of concepts.	❏ Interactions reflect working relationships among students.
❏ Elements of abstraction are included when important.	❏ Climate encourages students to generate ideas and questions.
❏ Students are intellectually engaged with important ideas.	❏ Intellectual rigor, constructive criticism, and challenging of ideas are evident.
❏ Appropriate connections are made to other areas.	
❏ Subject is portrayed as dynamic body of knowledge.	
❏ Degree of sense-making is appropriate for this lesson.	

Adapted from Weiss, I. R., J. D. Pasley, P. S. Smith, E. Banilower, D. Heck. 2003. *Looking inside the classroom: A study of K–12 mathematics and science education in the United States.* Chapel Hill, NC: Horizon Research Inc.

for students to make sense of what they are learning by comparing their ideas to those presented by the teacher.

Another significant element of effective teaching comes from the research on formative assessment. Formative assessment provides ways for teachers to focus instruction on student learning. Incorporating formative assessments as part of teacher practices results in teaching and learning that supports an environment focused on learning for all, as Black and colleagues note,

> formative assessment is a process, one in which information about learning is evoked and then used to modify the teaching and learning activities in which teachers and students are engaged.... Feedback can only serve learning if it involves both the evoking of evidence and a response to that evidence by using it in some way to improve the learning. (2003, p.122)

The recent work on learning progressions as part of a formative assessment process provides additional guidance for effective teaching (Heritage 2007). Learning progressions can be created by districts to address coherence across the K–12 curriculum. For our purposes, we are referring to the sequencing of learning targets within a unit of study that leads to student mastery of the big ideas and key concepts. When teachers identify the learning goals (learning targets) in a learning progression and identify criteria for successfully meeting the goals, they can determine student achievement gaps. If students perceive the learning gap as too large, they also perceive the goal as unattainable. If students perceive the gap as too small, they might believe that closing it is not worth their effort (Sadler 1989). Clearly, effective teaching means identifying the "just right" gap for students.

Building a classroom environment that is conducive to learning is essential. Even when teachers clearly understand their content, and design and implement high-quality lessons, teaching will not be effective if the classroom environment does not provide a safe place for students to learn (Marzano 1997). Marzano's work, and that of others (Haertel, Walberg, and Haertel 1981; Bransford, Brown, and Cocking 2000), underscores the idea that effective teaching includes building an environment that is conducive to learning. Teachers' belief systems (how to teach and student accountability) greatly impact their abilities to create an environment where they can work collaboratively with students. That's why it is important to address teacher beliefs, even though it is challenging to do so. Fortunately, research-based strategies are available to help with this task.

As noted previously, effective science teaching develops students' understanding. A recent research-based publication from the National Research Council (NRC), titled *Taking Science to School* (2007), reminds us that in general, students have the capacity to develop understanding of science concepts, but they lack opportunities to do so. This report is not talking about special needs students but the majority of our students who are not achieving in science because they are not provided with sufficient learning experiences. To be effective, science teaching must, first and foremost, provide students with opportunities to learn important concepts. A next logical step is to use research-based instructional strategies to engage students with learning in ways that support development of conceptual understanding (Marzano 2003).

What Do We Know About the Barriers to Effective Instruction?

As science teachers, we have our own ideas about what constitutes effective science teaching. We use a variety of strategies to meet our students' needs and from experience select those that work best for us and our students. It doesn't take very many years of teaching to realize that, even with a clear idea of what effective science teaching is, you will face a variety of challenges that will keep you from being effective with each of your students. Some of these barriers to effective teaching are difficult to address, even when we know what is needed. We may be at a loss for ways to deal with some of the other challenges because we never imagined having to face them.

At a recent teacher workshop, I asked a group of science teachers to identify their current challenges and issues. Their concerns ranged from a lack of resources to a change in students' preparation (e.g., little instruction in science at the elementary levels and a lack of time to teach all of the standards and prepare students for large-scale state assessments). Figure 1.2 provides a visual representation of some of their concerns.

With the No Child Left Behind legislation, there has been a shift in education to a strong system of accountability for schools and districts. This is now a focus area for individual teachers as well. We are now being asked by administrators to be accountable for the learning of all of our students. This shift poses a huge challenge—teachers must find effective ways to differentiate instruction to meet the needs of each student and address gaps in learning. Obviously, many factors influence student achievement. Research, such as that reported in *What Works in Schools* (Marzano 2003), provides guidance about the factors over which schools and teachers have some control, and suggests actions that schools and teachers can take to make a positive difference in student achievement.

Figure 1.2
Challenges Concept Map

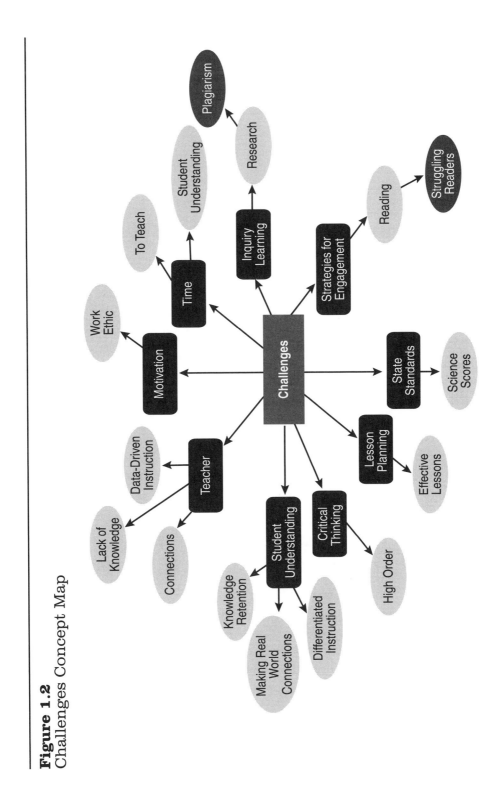

Table 1.1
Influences on Student Learning

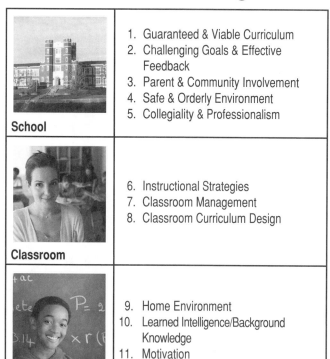

School	1. Guaranteed & Viable Curriculum 2. Challenging Goals & Effective Feedback 3. Parent & Community Involvement 4. Safe & Orderly Environment 5. Collegiality & Professionalism
Classroom	6. Instructional Strategies 7. Classroom Management 8. Classroom Curriculum Design
Student	9. Home Environment 10. Learned Intelligence/Background Knowledge 11. Motivation

Adapted from *What Works in Schools: Translating Research into Action*, by R. J. Marzano. Alexandria: VA, ASCD.

Table 1.1 summaries the 11 influences that need to be addressed in effective schools at the school level, classroom level, and student level. Although schools and teachers do not control a student's home life, this research emphasizes that there are actions schools and teachers can take to leverage parents' influence on their children's education. Also on the plus side, we can do something in classrooms to increase students' background knowledge and to motivate them.

Why Did We Develop the Content-Understanding-Environment Framework?

For the past five years, more and more research-based information has been published with clear implications for science teachers. We recognize that it is difficult for teachers to keep up with all of the research reports and revise their teaching to reflect the recommendations from research. To assist teachers with this task, we developed the Content-Understanding-Environment (C-U-E) framework. This framework incorporates key findings from research and is easy to use and remember. Further, current professional development for science teachers usually focuses on only one aspect of teaching and learning, which makes it difficult for teachers to formulate a "big picture" of effective science teaching. The C-U-E framework presents the research in a coherent format that creates a vision of effective science instruction. We acknowledge that the framework does not reflect an exhaustive review of research, but it does include a variety of research from science education and general education and is organized in a way that allows you to readily add new research findings to the ones featured in the book. As a result, the framework is a tool that can serve you well for years to come.

Our goal was to use research findings—those summarized previously in this chapter and other selected research—to create an instructional framework that would be easy for teachers to remember and include recommendations that could be implemented by any teacher. These recommendations are not restricted to K–12 teachers; they can be used by teachers in higher education and, specifically, in teacher preparation programs.

The Content-Understanding-Environment framework is designed to improve science teachers' abilities to deliver effective instruction to diverse student learners. Its effectiveness is due in large part to two qualities. First, all recommended strategies are founded upon a research base with positive links to improved student achievement. Second, the three-part framework helps teachers discern where improvements to their instructional practice are needed and how to take actions that are within their control. This book is based on the premises that delivering 100% effective science lessons is a lifetime professional quest, and immediate and steady improvements can be made by teachers at all stages of their careers.

Before we explain the framework further, we encourage you to reflect on your own teaching practices. To help you do that, we include a self-assessment tool that will prompt you to think about the strategies you currently use to support students' acquisition of significant content, develop student understanding, and create a climate conducive to learning. Figure 1.3, Figure 1.4, and Figure 1.5 encourage you to capture where you are at this moment. There are also places on the documents for you to identify areas you would like to work on or learn more about.

Figure 1.3
Content

Unit of Study/Course/Grade Level

Self-Assessment
Rate the following statements using this scale:

Not at all   To a high degree

To what degree do the lessons in my units

1	2	3	4	5

- __ contain science content that is significant and worthwhile
- __ contain science content appropriate for the developmental levels of the students
- __ engage students intellectually with important ideas relevant to the unit's essential understandings
- __ portray science as a dynamic body of knowledge continually enriched by conjecture, investigation, analysis, and/or proof/justification
- __ allow for developmentally appropriate sense-making of the science content
- __ align assessments with the targeted benchmarks
- __ allow students a variety of ways to demonstrate their knowledge
- __ promote a context for formative assessments with the purpose of adjusting instruction
- __ utilize rubrics that help students understand the criteria for quality work
- __ allow for teacher feedback with the purpose of providing students guidance for improving their performance and clarifying their understanding

My Goals for Improving Instruction Related to Content and Assessment

My Focus During the Book Related to Content and Assessment

Figure 1.4
Understanding

Unit of Study/Course/Grade Level				

Self-Assessment
Rate the following statements using this scale:

Not at all   To a high degree

1	2	3	4	5

To what degree do I feel comfortable

___ adjusting my own questioning and pacing given the outline of lessons in my unit of study

To what degree do the lessons in my unit of study

___ indicate opportunity for quality questioning

___ provide adequate time and structure for wrap-up

___ provide strategies and activities that reflect attention to students' preparedness and prior experience

___ provide opportunity for students to question, reflect, and challenge ideas

___ provide adequate time and structure for "sense-making"

___ portray a dynamic body of knowledge continually enriched by conjecture, investigation analysis, and/or proof/justification

___ provide opportunities for interactions among students that reflect collegial working relationships

My Goals for Improving Instruction Related to Student Understanding

My Focus During the Book Related to Student Understanding

Figure 1.5
Environment

Unit of Study/Course/Grade Level

Self-Assessment
Rate the following statements using this scale:

	Not at all				To a high degree
	1	2	3	4	5

To what degree do the lessons in my unit of study develop and value

__ active participation of all

__ a climate of respect for students' ideas, questions, and contributions

__ a collaborative approach to learning among the students

__ _____

To what degree do I actively plan instruction to

__ encourage and allow for critical, creative, and self-regulated thinking

__ help students develop positive attitudes and perceptions about classroom tasks and climate

__ provide timely feedback

__ provide appropriate recognition

__ reinforce effort

__ _____

To what degree do I actively plan instruction to

__ intellectual rigor

__ constructive criticism and the challenging of ideas

__ _____

My Goals for Improving Instruction Related to Environment

My Focus During the Convention related to Environment

The C-U-E Framework

The three elements of content, understanding, and environment are equally essential to improving student learning. A weakness in any one will undermine the effectiveness of the other two. We designate **Content** as the first element of the framework to underscore the idea that designing effective science lessons can only occur when we are clear about the big conceptual understandings and key concepts that will be included in the unit. Identifying the significant, worthwhile content also helps us begin thinking about how to sequence lessons as part of a coherent science unit and a coherent science program. We should think first about content at the course of study or grade level and then at the individual unit of study level. Creating that big picture and identifying the big ideas within a course or grade level are necessary steps before going to the smaller grain size of individual lessons.

Teachers have expressed two primary concerns with regard to content: insufficient time for students to develop conceptual understanding and too much content to cover to prepare students for statewide assessments. Aligning the science curriculum, instruction, and assessments to state and district standards is yet another challenge teachers face. To address time and coverage issues, we need tools and clear procedures to identify all of the content embedded in standards and benchmarks. This "unpacking" of standards and benchmarks helps us ensure that we focus instruction on the important learning objectives. Using lesson and unit templates helps us address alignment issues.

Since our focus is clearly on designing effective science lessons with effective science instruction to deliver those lessons, we also talk about some of the features of ineffective practices at the same time we are recommending effective strategies. Some of these ineffective practices are obvious, such as teaching lessons as if students were empty containers to be filled with science knowledge that we tell them, sometimes over and over again. We also want to guard against treating students as passive learners—learning is something students have to *do* themselves. In the remaining sections of this chapter, we introduce the recommended strategies for each component of the framework. Chapters 2, 3, and 4 provide details and tools related to the recommended strategies.

Identifying Important Content

When we talk about identifying important content, we mean starting unit planning and then lesson planning with clarity about the knowledge students should acquire—the information and ideas they should understand and the skills and processes they should be able to perform. Planning also includes identifying the criteria for successful demonstration of learning and deciding how students will demonstrate the required content knowledge. Once the big ideas and key concepts are clearly identified, we can identify specific learning targets as we plan activities that are sharply focused on helping students achieve conceptual understanding and procedural fluency. Intellectually engaging students with the content means that we need to include relevant, emerging content (e.g., plasma state of matter, genetic engineering, nanoscale science and technology) that captures the interests of our students and motivates them to learn. The specific strategies recommended for addressing the content element of the framework are included in Table 1.2 on identifying the important content. The focusing question "Why am I doing this?" asks teachers to reflect on the lesson they are about to teach and to think about the important learning target for that lesson. If a clear learning goal can't be articulated and the answer is "I don't know," then it is time to revise the unit or lesson and work on getting the learning target identified! We do not have time to waste in class, and doing an activity for activity's sake will not support student achievement.

Table 1.2
Identifying Important Content

Strategy 1: Identifying Big Ideas and Key Concepts Identify "big ideas," key concepts, knowledge, and skills that describe what the students will understand.	
Strategy 2: Unburdening the Curriculum Prune extraneous subtopics, technical vocabulary, and wasteful repetition.	
Strategy 3: Engaging Students With Content Create essential questions that engage students with the content.	**Why am I doing this?**
Strategy 4: Identifying Preconceptions and Prior Knowledge Identify common preconceptions and prior student knowledge.	
Strategy 5: Developing Assessments: How Do You Know That They Learned? Develop assessments that correlate to the conceptual understanding and related knowledge and skills.	**What are the important concepts and scientific ideas included in the lesson?**
Strategy 6: Sequencing the Learning Targets Into a Progression Clarify and sequence the learning targets into progressions to focus instruction on building conceptual understanding. Align learning activities with learning targets.	

14

Developing Student Understanding

Student learning is much better understood today as a result of important research findings over the past 15 years. We know from this research that making lessons more engaging, helping students make meaning and connections among science concepts, and developing each student's ability to learn are all part of developing student understanding.

One significant finding from research is that students come to us with prior knowledge and have ideas of their own to explain the natural world around them. If we do not elicit those ideas and confront the conceptions that are contrary to science knowledge, our students will continue to believe their own misconceptions. Classroom discussion that gets students to think about their thinking is an important strategy for helping them make sense of science concepts. Classroom discussions that promote sense-making are fueled by higher-order questions. Such questions also help students engage intellectually with ideas—a necessary ingredient for students to truly understand science concepts. Intellectual engagement is supported in classrooms that are inquiry-based. In these classrooms, students learn how to develop explanations based on evidence that has been critiqued and

Table 1.3
Developing Student Understanding

Strategy 1: Engaging Students in Science Inquiry Engage students in science inquiry to develop understanding of science concepts and the nature of science.	
Strategy 2: Implementing Formative Assessments Make use of formative assessments to gather feedback on student progress toward understanding.	
Strategy 3: Addressing Preconceptions and Prior Knowledge Build on prior knowledge and address preconceptions.	Who's working harder? A learner-centered classroom is necessary to develop conceptual student understanding.
Strategy 4: Providing Wrap-Up and Sense-Making Opportunities Provide daily opportunities for wrap-up that support student sense-making.	
Strategy 5: Planning for Collaborative Science Discourse Develop student understanding through collaborative science discourse.	
Strategy 6: Providing Opportunities for Practice, Review, and Revision Teach concepts in depth by allowing students to continually refine their understanding through practice, review, and revision.	

discussed in the classroom. The specific strategies recommended for developing student understanding are provided in Table 1.3 (p. 15).

Creating a Positive Learning Environment

Interactions, routines, and informal feedback that occur every day in the classroom can undermine or enhance learning. Research on learning environments and reflection on decades of my own and other teachers' experiences have yielded very specific advice on practices that support learning. The strategies included in this part of the framework address how to motivate students, support students in taking responsibility for their learning, and develop positive working relationships with and among students.

Elementary teachers often are expert at creating positive classroom climates. They know what kinds of reinforcement and feedback students need. In elementary school, students usually want to please their parents and teachers and are intrinsically motivated to learn science. When students reach middle school and high school, they often are more interested in listening to and pleasing their friends. As a result, secondary teachers often find it challenging to motivate their students. Fortunately, there are some clear recommendations about how to engage these students collaboratively to create a positive classroom climate.

Table 1.4
Creating a Positive Learning Environment

Strategy 1: Believing All Students Can Learn Show through your actions that you believe all students have the ability to learn.	
Strategy 2: Thinking Scientifically Teach students to think scientifically.	**What's really important?**
Strategy 3: Developing Positive Attitudes and Motivation Develop positive student attitudes and motivation to learn science.	
Strategy 4: Providing Feedback Give timely and criterion-referenced feedback.	**How do I create a positive learning environment?**
Strategy 5: Reinforcing Progress and Effort Keep students focused on learning by reinforcing progress and effort.	
Strategy 6: Teaching Students to be Metacognitive Involve students in thinking about their ideas and assessing their own progress.	

From a science perspective, we need to help students think scientifically, which includes taking risks in class by sharing their explanations and ideas about scientific concepts and phenomena. They must be able to share their ideas without fear of being ridiculed by their peers. Helping them act and think like scientists provides the structure for classroom discussions where it is safe for them to take such risks. The specific strategies recommended for creating a positive learning environment are included in Table 1.4. Remember, if we do not have a positive classroom environment, all of our efforts to provide instruction that addresses important content and to develop student understanding will likely not be effective.

Tools for Using the Framework to Design Lessons

To support your work with lesson revision and improvement, this chapter includes two "tools." The first tool is a lesson design template that includes abbreviated versions of the strategies included in the framework. This tool can be used as a "guiding document" for designing lessons. In addition to the tool for designing new lessons, we provide another template that can be used for revising existing lessons. This second lesson design template can also be used with existing activities, such as those provided in textbook-based materials; it asks you to be explicit about how you will address the C-U-E components. Some of the components of the lesson design framework are featured in Figure 1.6. This provides a quick reflection tool to help you determine what revisions are needed to improve the existing activity.

Figure 1.7 (p. 18) is a second tool to evaluate an existing lesson or activity that once again asks you to focus on the key characteristics of content, understanding, and positive classroom environment. This tool could be used by teachers who teach the same course or grade level to prompt discussions about the important learning targets, strategies that could be used to support student understanding, and ways to provide a supportive learning environment for all students.

Figure 1.6
Lesson Design Framework

1. **Content—Identifying Important Content**
   a. Identify key concepts and lesson objectives.
   b. Identify common preconceptions (misconceptions) and prior knowledge.
   c. Identify knowledge (facts and vocabulary) and skills.

2. **Understanding—Developing Student Understanding**
   a. Use inquiry-based activities that engage students.
   b. Implement formative/summative assessments to determine if students are learning (application).
   c. Provide sense-making and wrap-up activities (open-ended questions).
   d. Provide time for collaborative science discourse (discussion of multiple points of view and sharing of ideas).

3. **Environment—Creating a Positive Learning Environment**
   a. Include opportunities for students to work and think like scientists—reasoning, gathering data, using evidence-based thinking, communicating results.
   b. Reinforce progress and effort.
   c. Plan for criterion-referenced feedback.
   d. Provide multiple opportunities to learn.
   e. Ask students to assess their own progress.

Figure 1.7
Key Characteristics of Content, Understanding,
and Positive Classroom Environment

Lesson: _____

Evaluator: _____ **Date:** _____

1. Make notes of the strengths and weaknesses of this lesson.
2. Use your notes to prepare a summary and specific recommendations for improvement of the lesson design.
3. Keep in mind that our goal is to improve student understanding of important content.

---

1. **Big idea, key concepts, knowledge and skills** are described in terms of student understanding
   → are accurate
   → don't reinforce misconceptions

---

2. **Summative assessment** provides evidence of learning
   → has to relate back to key concept
   → students can demonstrate high cognitive ability when demonstrating conceptual understanding

---

3. **Essential questions or activities** engage students in the content and motivate them to learn
   → may be a discrepant event
   → should be age appropriate

---

4. **Students' prior knowledge** is acknowledged and built upon
   → background info on the concept for teachers
   → what are the prerequisite student learning's
   → how do we know what the students know (drawing, prediction, response to essential question...)
   → what are the common preconceptions

---

5. **Formative assessments** measure progress toward student understanding and inform instruction
   → include a variety of opportunities
   → give example and invite teachers to create their own

Figure 1.7 (cont.)
Lesson Design Framework

Lesson: _____

Evaluator: _____ Date: _____

6. Activities provide students with opportunities to **make sense of key concepts** → wrap-up supports student sense-making → summary, oral or written → quality questioning by teacher or re-engaging with essential question → probing questions or problems → analogies, visual representations
7. Students are involved in **collaborative science discourse** → is a community of learners being developed? → are there questions that encourage collaborative discourse? → are student ideas encouraged?
8. Students engage in **thinking scientifically** → hypothesizing/inferring → reasoning based on evidence → critique and defend answers → gives priority to evidence

Mid-continent Research for Education and Learning. 2005. *Classroom instruction that works: Facilitator's manual.* Aurora, CO: McREL.

Many districts are currently adopting and implementing kit-based instruction for elementary science. It is not always clear what key concepts are being taught during the kit-based lessons and students often get focused on facts and vocabulary rather than on understanding the science ideas. This tool will help you move beyond a focus on the activities of the science kit to a focus on the important ideas that students should learn as a result of the activities.

In Summary

Becoming a good science teacher doesn't just happen; it develops as a result of a variety of experiences over time. It is a result of continuous reflection about our practice that incorporates lessons learned. In the beginning, our college preparation provides theory, practice, and role-modeling by our professors. Student teaching provides some of our first mentoring and hands-on experiences. As novice teachers we observe and mimic the practices of our more experienced colleagues, and benefit from the advice and mentoring of the principal, fellow teachers, and—for the lucky few—professional development designed specifically for us as new science teachers. We then begin to collect resources—books on recommended topics, textbooks and materials, professional development experiences, and a mental checklist or a journal of what works and what doesn't work. We also learn from feedback about the quality of our practice. This feedback comes from supervisor evaluations, the students' test performance, and student and parent comments. All of these experiences contribute to our instructional skill, but as you'll learn throughout this book, there are specific actions we can take to further enhance the quality of our instruction and the effectiveness of our lessons.

During this journey from new teacher to professional science educator, how do we know if we are doing a quality job? What is the standard for effective science teaching and how good is good enough? How well are we meeting the NSES Teaching Standards (NRC 1996)? Is there a "state of the art" level of teaching that can be achieved? How do we know what we don't know—but should? And if research tells us what we should do to improve teaching and learning, how can we incorporate those findings into our teaching practices? All are good questions without simple answers.

Partial answers can be found in standards documents. For example, the National Science Education Standards describe professional teaching standards. These standards provide descriptions of what a professional science teacher should know and be able to do. The NSES document provides information that teachers can use to determine a level of science literacy that teachers must have, not just to prepare an informed citizenry, but as the baseline for teacher content knowledge.

Research provides additional guidance about effective science teaching, although that guidance is limited with regard to some aspects of teaching. The information and tools provided in this book reflect the standards for science teaching and the results of research on effective science instruction. Thus, this book can help you add to your understanding of effective science teaching so that you can reflect on your own practice and determine areas where you can use the information presented to increase your effectiveness.

References

Banilower, E., K. Cohen, J. Pasley, and I. Weiss. 2008. *Effective science instruction: What does research tell us?* Portsmouth, NH: RMC Research Corporation, Center on Instruction.

Black, P., C. Harrison, C. Lee, B. Marshall, and D. Wiliam. 2003. *Assessment for learning: Putting it into practice.* New York: Open University Press.

Bransford, J., A. Brown, and R. Cocking, eds. 2000. *How people learn, Expanded Version.* Washington, DC: National Academies Press.

Donovan, S., and J. Bransford, eds. 2005. *How students learn: Science in the classroom.* Washington, DC: National Academies Press.

Haertel, G. D., H. J. Walberg, and E. H. Haertel. 1981. Socio-psychological environments and learning: A quantitative synthesis. *British Educational Research Journal* 7: 27–36.

Heritage, M. 2007. Formative assessment: What do teachers need to know and do? *Kappan* 89 (2): 140–145.

Marzano, R. 1997. *Dimensions of learning*, 2nd ed. Alexandria, VA: Association for Supervision and Curriculum Development.

Marzano, R. 2003. *What works in schools: Translating research into action.* Alexandria, VA: Association for Supervision and Curriculum Development.

Minstrell, J. 1989. Teaching Science for Understanding. In *Toward the thinking curriculum: Current cognitive research*, eds. L. B. Resnick and L. E. Klopfer, 129–149. Alexandria, VA: Association for Supervision and Curriculum Development.

National Research Council (NRC). 1996. *National science education standards.* Washington, DC: National Academy Press.

National Research Council (NRC). 2007. *Taking science to school: Learning and teaching science in grades K–8.* Committee on Science Learning, Kindergarten Through Eighth Grade, eds. R. A. Duschl, H. A. Schweingruber, and A. W. Shouse. Washington, DC: The National Academies Press.

Sadler, D. R. 1989. Formative assessment and the design of instructional systems. *Instructional Science* 18: 130.

Shulman, L. S. 1986. Those who understand: Knowledge growth in teaching. *Educational Researcher* 15: 4–14.

Shulman, L. S. 1987. Knowledge and teaching; Foundation of the new reform. *Harvard Educational Review* 57 (1): 1–22.

Weiss, I., J. Pasley, S. Smith, E. Banilower, and D. Heck. 2003. *Looking inside the classroom: A study of K–12 mathematics and science education in the United States.* Chapel Hill, NC: Horizon Research, Inc.

Content

Chapter 2

What science content should I teach? That is a question that
all science teachers must consider as they design their lessons.
And if we want our lessons to be of high quality, we must ensure
that the content is rigorous, appropriate, and worthwhile. Rigorous, meaning that it challenges students and moves them forward in
their learning; appropriate, it aligns with the standards and benchmarks
for their grade level; and worthwhile, the learning is essential for students and
worth the time to teach it. The strategies associated with the "Content" aspect
of our framework help keep us focused on the question "Why am I doing this?"
Clearly, we need to know and be able to articulate why we are addressing particular content in our lessons and how that content is related to the important learning
goals established for students.

In this section, you will

- learn how to clarify what students should understand about science
  concepts, as the first step in a new method for planning effective lessons;

- practice identifying rigorous, appropriate, worthwhile content; and

- participate in a reflective process to check your units and lessons to make
  sure they are focused on important learning goals

Table 2.1 (Identifying Important Content, p. 24) gives an overview of the six strategies recommended in this chapter to help us get the content right.

Table 2.1
Identifying Important Content

Strategy 1: Identifying Big Ideas and Key Concepts Identify "big ideas," key concepts, knowledge and skills that describe what the students will understand	
Strategy 2: Unburdening the Curriculum Prune extraneous subtopics, technical vocabulary, and wasteful repetition.	
Strategy 3: Engaging Students With Content Create essential questions that engage students with the content.	**Why am I doing this?**
Strategy 4: Identifying Preconceptions and Prior Knowledge Identify common preconceptions and prior student knowledge.	
Strategy 5: Assessment—How Do You Know That They Learned? Develop assessments that correlate to the conceptual understanding and related knowledge and skills.	**What are the important concepts and scientific ideas included in the lesson?**
Strategy 6: Sequencing the Learning Targets into a Progression Clarify and sequence the learning targets into progressions to focus instruction on building conceptual understanding; align learning activities with learning targets.	

Content Strategy 1: Identifying "Big Ideas" and Key Concepts

When planning instruction, effort on our part is needed to establish clear learning goals. Once established, we need to give students a chance to understand the goals in positive classroom settings. From the 1999 TIMSS video study of 8th grade science teaching (Druker et al. 2006) in the United States, observers discovered that in 27% of classrooms, students were doing activities with no content, in 44% of classrooms, students were learning content with weak or no conceptual links, and in only 30% of the classrooms did the content have strong conceptual links. Each higher-achieving country engaged students with core science concepts and ideas and, except in the Netherlands, linked concepts and activities.

This tells us that before we walk into our classrooms to teach, we must determine the important content that students will learn and be clear about the "big picture" and key concepts. Planning a unit of study is like creating a book. There is a clear beginning, then the content storyline develops, and at the end we want our students to understand the "moral of the story." Identifying the big ideas—the concepts, themes, or issues that give meaning and connection to discrete facts and skills (Wiggins and McTighe 2005)—in the early stages of unit planning helps us focus the students and ourselves on the learning we want to occur. An idea is "big" if it helps students make sense of lots of confusing ideas and experiences and seemingly isolated facts. It's like the picture that connects the dots and reveals the image (big idea) by connecting the component pieces (key concepts). And keeping the overall goals in mind is necessary when preparing individual lessons that connect the concepts into a logical progression and lead students to conceptually understand the big ideas.

At the elementary level, the idea that we are all part of a "food chain" of living and nonliving things is big because it links seemingly different (and isolated) animals and plant matter into a bigger, comprehensible "ecosystem" of energy exchange. We then see the role of predators, trash, and the relationship of humans to nature in a completely new and meaningful way than before. At the middle and high school levels, Newton's laws of motion are three of the biggest ideas ever posed: Suddenly, thousands of seemingly unrelated facts and phenomena—apples falling, the motion and cycle of tides, seasons, the Moon's orbit—have a meaningful explanation and can be seen as part of a huge coherent system (Wiggins 2008).

The Issue

Teachers rely on textbook activities, often aren't clear about their lesson goals, and, even if they are, do not share these learning goals with their students. As a result, students are unclear about what they are supposed to learn and focus their learning on details and memorization of facts rather than on in-depth understanding of science concepts. Much of what students learn in science classrooms is new to them—they are science novices. Without thinking explicitly about all of the concepts that underlie the big ideas of science, teachers, who are science experts, might forget to address and connect all of the concepts that science novices must experience to learn science.

The DESI Approach

This is really about reflecting on the big ideas and key concepts that form the content storyline in our units and clarifying the learning goals for ourselves and our students. This involves aligning the curriculum with the standards for our grade levels or grade bands (e.g., grades 6–8); identifying the "big ideas" and important concepts that organize the science knowledge our students are to learn; and "unpacking" the standards, benchmarks, and key concepts to identify the finer details of content to be addressed by the learning targets for individual lessons within units of study. "Unpacking" involves taking the big ideas and listing the key concepts that when taken together, connect into a big idea. Once we identify the big idea and key concepts, the learning targets for individual lessons can be written in student-friendly language. Doing so helps ensure that students are working toward clearly defined objectives that focus on essential, conceptual understandings.

Selected Research Related to the Strategy

1. According to *Classroom Instruction That Works* (Marzano, Pickering, and Pollack 2001), there are two types of knowledge: declarative and procedural. Declarative knowledge comprises what a learner knows and understands, and procedural knowledge is what a learner does with that knowledge, i.e., processes and skills. Declarative knowledge includes organizing ideas, details, and vocabulary terms and phrases related to ideas (see Figure 2.1). Big ideas and key concepts fall

Figure 2.1
Levels of Generality of Knowledge

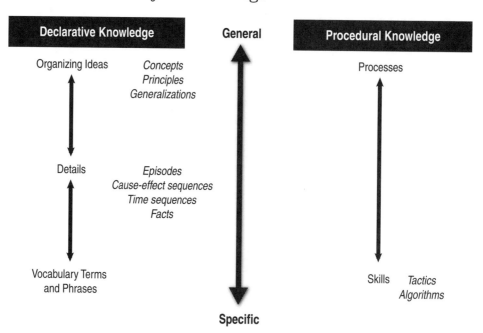

Marzano, R., D. Pickering, and J. Pollock. 2001. *Classroom instruction that works: Research-based strategies for increasing student achievement.* Alexandria, VA: Association for Supervision and Curriculum Development.

under the category of organizing ideas and are, therefore, an integral part of the declarative knowledge that students learn in science class.

Brain research reveals that students must have multiple experiences with declarative knowledge—big ideas, concepts, vocabulary—to learn it at an adequate level (Nuthall 1999; Rovee-Collier 1995). More than one experience is needed because declarative knowledge is stored in long-term memory through a complex process that involves the hippocampus and the cerebral cortex (Marzano et al. 2001).

2. Setting objectives is a strategy that is highly likely to improve student achievement (Marzano et al. 2001). Marzano and his colleagues indicated that use of this strategy resulted in an average gain of 23 percentile points in student achievement. These researchers also noted that when students know the instructional goals, they focus on the most important information. They cautioned that these goals should not be too specific, lest they focus student learning too narrowly. The research supported the idea that teachers should encourage students to personalize the academic goals identified by the teacher.

3. By taking the time to study a topic before planning a unit, teachers build a deeper understanding of the content, connections among concepts, and effective ways to help students achieve understanding of the most important ideas and skills (Keeley 2005).

What Is the Strategy?

The focus of this strategy is on designing lessons within a unit of study that present science as a coherent body of knowledge, organized around big ideas that connect and give meaning to other concepts, facts, and details. Though science textbooks are a central source of information in the classroom, we cannot rely on textbooks alone when identifying "big ideas" and key concepts around which to design lessons. In fact, in recent years, evaluations have revealed that, for the most part, textbooks are not organized coherently around important science concepts. Instead, they include many topics with little guidance about how students should think about science ideas (Kesidou and Roseman 2002). Similarly, science kits provide correlations to national standards, but they do not always include teacher notes which talk about the big ideas and important concepts around which to base the learning targets for each lesson.

For this strategy we want to identify big ideas and the concepts that compose them. As a first step, we must align curricular content with science standards to ensure that the focus is on the important content that students are to learn. This can be accomplished by reviewing national, state, and district standards and making a list of the standards and benchmarks that will be taught and assessed in the unit. Many states and districts are already working on curriculum alignment activities. As a result, you may have curriculum framework documents that identify the essential learning and big ideas related to standards and benchmarks for particular units. Once we have a clear idea about the content that we will include in the unit, we should think about how well we understand the content. If necessary, use science-related resources that you have available (including online information) to review the big ideas and key concepts. This will ensure that the content we teach will be worthwhile (relevant to understanding the science), significant (important for science literacy and subsequent learning), and accurate (based on recent science research findings).

Standards and benchmarks are often written in general terms or include multiple ideas in one statement. It might not be obvious which concepts, facts, vocabulary, or processes are included in the standards and benchmarks. As part of identifying the content of lessons, you can systematically analyze, or "unpack," the standards and benchmarks to pinpoint the specific knowledge and skills that should be the focus of lessons within each unit of study. When you are clear about the content, you can create a curriculum map that clearly shows how the content within the unit is connected. The map should include the big ideas, key concepts, facts, vocabulary, skills, and processes that the students are expected to learn. To finish the process, share the curriculum map with students (and parents) in a format that makes it easy for them to understand what students will be learning and how the various ideas within the unit are connected.

As a thought experience, consider the following big idea from a unit on climate change:

The unequal heating of the surface of the Earth between the equator and poles, Earth's rotation, and the distribution of land and ocean generate the global wind patterns that affect climate and climatic changes.

To unpack this into key concepts and ideas, try to answer this question: What would students need to experience to understand this big idea? The idea of unequal heating would be one idea that students wouldn't be able to grasp without opportunities to observe it, talk about it, and look at evidence. So when we unpack the big idea we would want to include lessons about unequal heating. Additional concepts that we would want to plan for include:

- Land and water retain heat differently.

- The temperature near the ground depends in part on the angle of the sunlight hitting the Earth.

- Higher elevations above sea level have cooler temperatures.

- The thickness and composition of the atmosphere of the planet affects heating and cooling at the surface.

- Sunlight is the primary source of heat for Earth.

What other important concepts can you think of to add to the list that would help students understand the big idea of the unit?

Exploring the Strategy

In this section, we will look at an example that takes you through a four-step approach. Because of the availability of research on children's ideas on matter and atomic and molecular theory, we will use the research findings to think about how to implement this strategy. Research has shown that this content provides a rich source of information for teachers at grades K–8 (Smith et al. 2004). The example below is explained in detail in the full study. To learn more about the study and the learning progressions identified for the atomic-molecular theory of matter, read chapter 8 in *Taking Science to School: Learning and Teaching Science in Grades K–8* (NRC 2007). We will revisit the idea of learning progressions that occur vertically across grade levels and learning progressions that exist within a course during our discussion of Content Strategy 6.

Step 1. Align the curricular content for the unit of study with science standards to focus on the important content.

This includes identifying the big ideas. Below is a list of big ideas that align with national standards and benchmarks that address matter and atomic and molecular theory.

1. Properties of Matter—Matter and the materials that they make can be studied through measurement, classification, and descriptions of the objects based on their properties.

2. Conservation of Matter—Matter can be changed and transformed but not created or destroyed either by chemical or physical means.

3. Atomic-Molecular Theory—All matter is made up of about 100 kinds of atoms, which bond together in different ways to form a wide variety of molecules.

4. Transformations of Matter—Changes in matter involve both changes in atoms and changes in their alignment and orientation in the molecules that are formed.

In this example, the big ideas were identified by the research team that wrote the report. AAAS has also been working on identifying big ideas that correlate to the Project 2061 Benchmarks for Science Literacy. It is not easy to come up with the big ideas yourself but it can be done. Think about the unit you will teach and summarize what you want the students to learn by the end of the unit. Take that summary and reduce it to the most important 2–3 sentences that contain the key concepts you included in the unit. Some standards and benchmarks are written as big ideas and represent the unifying concepts of the unit. No one said it would be easy but it is worth it. In fact, many of the resources mentioned in step 2 can also be used as you practice writing big ideas.

Step 2. Develop your content knowledge and understanding related to science topics.

Any or all of the following resources are likely to become indispensable in helping you increase your knowledge and understanding of science education and a range of science topics. You may not have these references in your library but many of them are available online. Don't forget to use your local resources such as mentor teachers and local experts. What we are trying to avoid is passing along misconceptions that we might have to our students. Setting a goal of developing our own understanding will help us relate the content to our students. Full citations for these resources, many of which are available online, are found in the references at the end of this book.

- *Atlas for Science Literacy, Volumes I and II* (AAAS 2001, 2007)—This is a two-volume collection of conceptual strand maps that show how students' understanding of the ideas and skills that lead to literacy in science, mathematics, and technology might develop from kindergarten through 12th grade.

- *Benchmarks for Science Literacy* (AAAS 1993)—This is a national standards document that discusses what students should know and be able to do in science, mathematics, and technology.

- *Designs for Science Literacy* (AAAS 2001)—This is a companion document to the Project 2061 Benchmarks and includes information about curriculum design, discusses ways to unburden the curriculum, and offers a variety of options for restructuring time, instructional strategies, and content.

- *Making Sense of Secondary Science* (Driver et al. 2005)—Research into children's science ideas are presented in this book. These ideas, right or wrong, form the basis of all that children subsequently learn. Research has shown that teaching is unlikely to be effective unless it takes into account the ideas with which children come to class.

- *National Science Education Standards* (NRC 1996)—This book contains the goals for achievement that are appropriate for all members of the science education community. Included are standards for content, professional development, teaching, systems, programs, and assessment.

- *Science Curriculum Topic Study* (Keeley 2005)—The Curriculum Topic Study (CTS) is a professional development resource developed to help K–12 educators deepen their understanding of the important science and mathematics topics they teach. CTS builds a bridge between state and national standards, explores research on students' ideas in science, and provides opportunities for teachers to improve their practice.

- *Science Matters: Achieving Scientific Literacy* (Hazen and Trefil 1991)—Organized as a compilation of basic facts and concepts that teachers need to understand the scientific concepts they teach, this book offers a quick read on scientific fundamentals.

- Textbooks and teacher's manuals

- Online resources by topic containing current and emerging science content

Deepening your knowledge about a topic will make it easier to determine the big ideas and key concepts. A good resource that helps with this process is the *Science Curriculum Topic Study* mentioned above. It takes the wonder out of where to find information about topics and the research into student's ideas about those topics. We can use this resource by ourselves, but it makes more sense when we work with collaborative groups of science teachers and with the support of administrators. For our example, attached is a list of the "big ideas" for matter and atomic and molecular theory broken into grade-level bands. This will also clarify the progression of learning from K–2, 3–5, and 6–8. This study did not include the high school level so it is not included (Smith et al. 2004).

Grades K–2 Learning Related to Big Ideas

Students' experiences at this age have prepared them to learn and think about what things are made of and some of the properties of matter. Therefore, grades K–2 students are able to understand the following big ideas:

- Objects are made of specific materials and have certain properties. The properties of objects can be carefully described, compared, and measured.

- Some properties change and some stay the same when objects are transformed in simple ways.

Grades 3–5 Learning Related to Big Ideas

When building on their earlier learning, older elementary students are able to go beyond knowledge of kinds of material and begin to use graphical representations and measurements to study the quantifiable properties of materials. They can also make predictions and design investigations to determine if objects contain the same materials. Therefore, grades 3–5 students can understand the following version of big ideas related to matter and atomic and molecular theory:

- There are some properties that characterize all matter; others characterize specific types of materials.

- Matter is conserved across certain transformations that radically change appearance.

Grades 6–8 Learning Related to Big Ideas

At this age, students are able to engage in abstract thinking so that they can understand the particulate nature of matter and represent that understanding using atomic-molecular models. Students can also use mathematical representations to understand the properties of matter such as density. They can design and conduct experiments to study the physical changes and chemical changes that occur when matter is transformed. Thus, grades 6–8 students can understand the following version of big ideas:

- There are properties that characterize all matter, specific materials, and phases of matter than can be quantified and related.

- Some transformations involve chemical change (e.g., burning, rusting) in which new substances are created. In other changes (e.g., changes of state, thermal expansion), materials may change appearance, but the substances in them remain the same.

- Matter and mass are conserved across both types of changes.

- All matter is made up of discretely spaced particles (called atoms) which are far too small to see directly through an optical microscope. There are empty spaces (vacuums) between atoms.

- Macroscopic properties can be explained in terms of atoms and molecules.

- Macroscopic transformations can be explained in terms of atoms and molecules.

- All properties of atoms and changes in atoms can be distinguished from the macroscopic properties and phenomena for which they account.

Step 3. Unpack the standards and benchmarks to identify the concepts, facts, vocabulary, and processes to include in the individual lessons that compose the unit of study.

In most instances, we have to unpack the big ideas to determine the key concepts, subconcepts, and factual knowledge that are embedded. Since a big idea pulls together a large number of ideas into a coherent explanation, a single scientific concept is a piece of a big idea that links at least two ideas together. We have already identified the big ideas; next, we must be clear about the concepts that underlie the big ideas and then design lessons that will help students learn those concepts. If our goal is that students understand an idea as a concept, then we must provide learning experiences that help them develop in-depth understanding rather than a surface understanding of the concept as represented by a word or phrase. When students understand a concept, they are able to talk about the key characteristics of the concept and generate a number of examples that illustrate each characteristic. For example, if students understand ecosystems as a concept, they understand that two characteristics of ecosystems are that (1) they provide a one-way flow of energy and (2) matter within an ecosystem is recycled. They are able to demonstrate their understanding by explaining, predicting, and analyzing what happens to the matter and energy in different ecosystems such as rainforests, temperate deserts, or midlatitude grasslands. If students understand *ecosystems* only as a vocabulary term, they have a general, but less accurate, understanding of what the concept means. In other words, they aren't as able to generate mental images of the word (as a concept) or connect it to experiences in which the word applies.

Unpacking the big ideas of matter and atomic and molecular theory makes it clear that there are many concepts and facts that students must learn in order to grasp the big ideas. Table 2.2 (p. 34) identifies the concepts, facts, and vocabulary—revealed by unpacking standards and benchmarks—that are related to the big ideas of matter and atomic and molecular theory at grade levels K–2, 3–5, and 6–8.

Table 2.2
Key Concepts, Facts, and Vocabulary Related to Matter and Atomic and Molecular Theory

Grades K–2	Vocabulary:
• Materials and objects can be classified based on appearance. • Matter is distinguished from nonmatter because matter is anything that has mass and takes up space. • Materials can either be made of matter that is made of the same substance or a mixture of different substances. • Different materials have different appearances and different properties which can be measured or observed using our senses. • Matter can change form and appearance when it undergoes transformations.	matter materials objects transformation
Grades 3–5	**Vocabulary:**
• Matter takes up space and has weight. Nonmatter does not. • Air is matter and takes up space and has weight. • There can be pieces of matter that are too small to see with the naked eye. • Materials have characteristic properties that are independent of the size of the sample (e.g., color, texture, hardness, heaviness for size, bendability). • Matter continues to exist across transformations in which it no longer is visible (e.g., dissolving). • Amount of matter and weight are conserved across melting, freezing, and dissolving. • Materials can be changed from solid to liquid form by heating, but are still the same kind of material.	solid liquid gas melt freeze dissolve air conservation
Grades 6–8	**Vocabulary:**
• Mass measures the amount of matter. Weight is proportional to mass and varies with the gravitational field. • Materials have quantifiable properties such as melting point, boiling point, and density. Density is quantified as mass/volume. • Conservation of mass is a fundamental law. • Heating changes the volume of materials but not the mass of the object. • Dissolving, phase change, and chemical change involve conservation of mass but not volume. • There are more than a hundred different kinds of atoms. Each kind has distinctive properties, including mass and the way it combines with other atoms or molecules. • Atoms can be joined to form molecules—a process that involves forming chemical bonds between atoms. Molecules have different characteristic properties from the atoms of which they are composed. • In solids, atoms or molecules move rapidly, but usually within spaces constrained by their neighbors. In liquids, atoms or molecules are also closely packed, but are more loosely associated, and constantly collide as they move past one another. In gases, atoms or molecules move freely in straight lines except when they collide with each other or their container. • Changes in matter include physical changes, in which molecules change arrangement and/or motion but remain intact, and chemical changes, in which atoms are rearranged (disconnected and reconnected) into new molecules, but the atoms remain intact.	physical change chemical change mixture compound phase change atoms molecules elements chemical bonds density

Adapted from Smith, C., M. Wiser, C. W. Anderson, J. Krajcik, and R. Coppola. 2004. *Implications of research on children's learning for assessment: Matter and atomic molecular theory.* Committee on Test Design for K–12 Science Assessment, Center for Education. Washington, DC: National Research Council.

These facts, concepts, and vocabulary were identified in the NRC report and if they are taken together as a whole, then they represent the big ideas identified earlier. When unpacking the big ideas into the separate concepts, these should always be statements of understanding, not just phrases or one or two words. This will help us focus the subsequent student lessons on important content.

Step 4. Create a curriculum map or planning template outline that shows how the content is connected.

"Strand maps" produced by the American Association for the Advancement of Science (AAAS) can be used to visualize what a curriculum map might look like. A portion of the strand map related to transformation of matter and energy is included in Figure 2.2 (p. 36). For the conceptual information provided in our example, you would create a separate curriculum map for each grade band to show the connections and guide instructional planning.

Planning for Classroom Implementation

As we think about using this strategy in our classrooms, keep in mind that big ideas represent the central principles of the science disciplines and are the underlying understandings embedded in science standards. Our first task is to identify the big ideas at the overall course or grade level. This helps us connect the goals for student learning into a coherent framework. Next, identify the big ideas and key concepts for each unit. (We'll focus on the unit of study level throughout this book.) To fully implement this strategy, we must complete another step: analyze the big ideas to identify the key concepts, facts, and vocabulary that are embedded in them. Although taking all of these steps might seem like a lot of work, there are good reasons for taking them. Organizing teaching around big ideas provides coherence to the curriculum. It also helps us align the curriculum with student learning so that what students should know and be able to do directly relates to the learning performances.

To uncover the big ideas, key concepts, and vocabulary for your own unit of study, go back to the four steps in the process. Use the resources mentioned as well as online resources to begin the process. A template is provided in the appendix for Content Strategy 1 for you to record the big ideas and key concepts for your unit of study. Also, an example of a completed planning template outline for a ninth-grade unit on evolution is included in Figure 2.3 (p. 37). This is an actual teacher example; keep in mind that different teachers focusing on the same big idea may create very different unit plans, depending upon the course and grade level in which the content will be taught.

Figure 2.2
Strand Map

Chemical Reactions

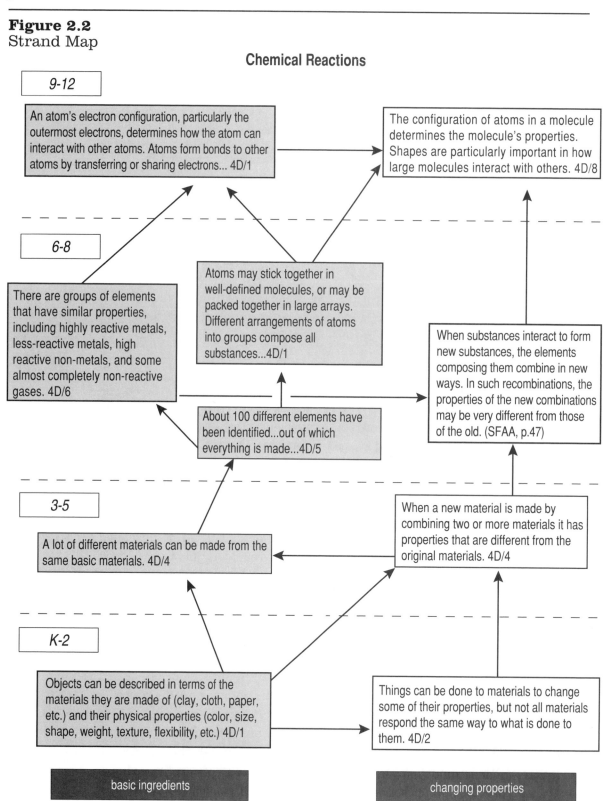

9-12

An atom's electron configuration, particularly the outermost electrons, determines how the atom can interact with other atoms. Atoms form bonds to other atoms by transferring or sharing electrons... 4D/1

The configuration of atoms in a molecule determines the molecule's properties. Shapes are particularly important in how large molecules interact with others. 4D/8

6-8

There are groups of elements that have similar properties, including highly reactive metals, less-reactive metals, high reactive non-metals, and some almost completely non-reactive gases. 4D/6

Atoms may stick together in well-defined molecules, or may be packed together in large arrays. Different arrangements of atoms into groups compose all substances...4D/1

When substances interact to form new substances, the elements composing them combine in new ways. In such recombinations, the properties of the new combinations may be very different from those of the old. (SFAA, p.47)

About 100 different elements have been identified...out of which everything is made...4D/5

3-5

A lot of different materials can be made from the same basic materials. 4D/4

When a new material is made by combining two or more materials it has properties that are different from the original materials. 4D/4

K-2

Objects can be described in terms of the materials they are made of (clay, cloth, paper, etc.) and their physical properties (color, size, shape, weight, texture, flexibility, etc.) 4D/1

Things can be done to materials to change some of their properties, but not all materials respond the same way to what is done to them. 4D/2

basic ingredients

changing properties

American Association for the Advancement of Science. 2001. *Atlas of Science Literacy* Vol. 1. Reprinted with permission.

Figure 2.3
Completed Planning Template Outline for Evolution Unit

Title: Evolution	Grade: 9	Length:

Step 1. Content

Big Idea
Natural selection provides a scientific explanation of the fossil record and the molecular similarities among the diverse species of living organisms.

Key Concepts
Modern ideas about evolution provide a scientific explanation for three main sets of scientific observations about life on Earth:

- There is an enormous number of different life forms that exist today, 99% of which did not exist in earlier times on earth.

- The systematic similarities in anatomy and molecular chemistry seen within that diversity are a result of common ancestry of organisms.

- The sequences of changes in fossils found in successive layers of rock that have been formed over more than a billion years show the changes that have occurred as organisms have descended from common ancestors.

The scientific explanation for the theory of evolution is based on a large body of evidence that explains the process of biological change over time that is occurring among living organisms.

Species acquire many of their unique characteristics through biological adaptation over many generations.

Fossilization is the process that turns a once living thing into a fossil.

Knowledge	Skills
• Fossils are the remains of animals and plants, or the record of their presence, preserved in the rocks of the Earth.	• Application of timelines to rock layers
	• Microscope skills
• Extinction is a naturally occurring process where all individuals in a species die out.	• Classification based on characteristics of fossils, or internal and external structures of animals and plants
• Variations exist within all populations.	
• Scientific theories are explanations of natural phenomena built up logically from testable observations and hypotheses.	• Preparation and participation in debate and discussion
	• Use of evidence in supporting conclusions

What Works in Science Classrooms: Implications for Teaching

Recommendation 1: Our challenge is to ensure that our lessons are designed to help students learn important content. When you ask yourself the guiding question for the content element of the framework ("Why am I doing this?"), you should be able to respond, "This content is important for students to learn because it addresses the big ideas of science." If the lesson doesn't help students make progress toward learning the big ideas and key concepts of the discipline, then redesign the lesson so that you make the most of instructional time. Remember, worksheets that do not help students understand concepts, important facts, or vocabulary related to the big ideas of science can be a waste of student time; they do not support student learning and achievement of essential science content.

Recommendation 2: Examine the learning goals (key concepts) you have defined from the perspective of a novice learner. Ask yourself, "Will these learning goals help novice learners focus their thinking and learning on the important science concepts in this unit?" Research studies have shown that novice learners don't know what is important to learn and tend to focus on memorizing facts and vocabulary. As a result, they develop only a superficial understanding of the content.

Recommendation 3: Ensure that each lesson focuses on an important science concept and provides appropriate opportunities for students to learn the concept. Remember, concepts connect several ideas. In order to learn concepts, students need multiple opportunities to think about the ideas and apply them in meaningful ways. If you decide to teach an idea as a vocabulary term or phrase as one of the opportunities for student learning, there are strategies you can use. *Teaching Reading in Science* (Barton and Jordan 2001) is one resource that provides many vocabulary strategies. Online resources are also readily available. Using a vocabulary strategy would be one opportunity, to which you would then want to add additional experiences, to help students retain and incorporate what they learned into their existing mental frameworks.

Content Strategy 2: Unburdening the Curriculum

The Issue

When science teachers are asked about the biggest issue that they face each year, time is always one of the top concerns. How will we find the time to teach everything included in the standards and have time to prepare students for state

Table 2.1
Identifying Important Content

Strategy 1: Identifying Big Ideas and Key Concepts Identify "big ideas," key concepts, knowledge and skills that describe what the students will understand.	
Strategy 2: Unburdening the Curriculum Prune extraneous subtopics, technical vocabulary, and wasteful repetition.	
Strategy 3: Engaging Students With Content Create essential questions that engage students with the content.	**Why am I doing this?**
Strategy 4: Identifying Preconceptions and Prior Knowledge Identify common preconceptions and prior student knowledge.	**What are the important concepts and scientific ideas included in the lesson?**
Strategy 5: Assessment—How Do You Know That They Learned? Develop assessments that correlate to the conceptual understanding and related knowledge and skills.	
Strategy 6: Sequencing the Learning Targets Into a Progression Clarify and sequence the learning targets into progressions to focus instruction on building conceptual understanding; align learning activities with learning targets.	

assessments? This drive for coverage stems from two fronts. First, because of new scientific discoveries, new content is being added all the time. Second, we are expected to prepare all students to perform at a proficient level on state assessments. To meet both of these goals, teachers struggle to provide enough opportunities for students to really learn.

The DESI Approach

The original TIMSS (Third International Math and Science Study) report released in 1997 found that teachers often try to teach too much and there isn't enough time for students to learn everything. U.S. schools teach so many science topics that the concepts are covered in superficial detail and employ technical language that exceeds most students' understanding. The consequence of superficial student learning is lack of retention of the learning in a durable way. Durability of learning is the degree to which students are able to transfer information or skills learned in one context to new contexts across time. The *How People Learn* report (Bransford et al. 1999) summarizes how we can promote durability of learning with our students. Key findings are

- More than one context is needed. Teachers need to help students understand abstract, general principles and provide multiple contexts for students to apply them.

- Learners need to know under what conditions, or when, to apply the knowledge or skill. It is necessary to explicitly teach students when, where, and why the skill or concept is to be applied—not just how.

In science classes, it is important that students experience and learn the science concepts through exploring, considering explanations, learning to think scientifically, and showing they understand through developing, presenting, revising, and defending their conclusions. Developing this level of scientific understanding takes time, and lack of time and opportunity to learn are well documented and well understood by teaching professionals. Unburdening or pruning the curriculum can help teachers fit it all in. In the pruning process we need to decide what is essential so that there is adequate time to teach the content.

Selected Research That Addresses This Issue

1. Developing durable student understanding happens only if units focus on a few, rather than too many, concepts and if each lesson focuses squarely on one concept (NRC 1999). This can be accomplished by pruning. Pruning helps focus instruction and improve understanding in classrooms where, too often, quantity takes precedence over quality and coverage wins out over student understanding. If we focus on essential learning, then supplemental learning needs to be eliminated.

2. According to *Why Schools Matter* (Schmidt 2001), there is powerful evidence that textbooks exert a strong influence on the content that teachers teach. Textbook coverage is important both for what topics (and concepts) are taught and for the levels of performance and understanding expected of students. However, we know that textbooks are not the curriculum and standards themselves are also not the curriculum. Standards and science frameworks from national, state, and local documents must be unpacked so that the appropriate concepts to be taught at each grade level can be identified. As we learned in Strategy 1, unpacking the big ideas means identifying the key concepts (organizing ideas from the standards), facts, and vocabulary that become part of a student's enduring knowledge.

3. Teachers are experts and students are novices when it comes to understanding science concepts. Science teachers know the structure of the knowledge in their disciplines; know the conceptual barriers that are

likely to hinder learning; and have a well-organized knowledge of concepts, inquiry procedures, and problem-solving strategies (Bransford et al. 1999). They notice features and patterns that students don't. An expert and a novice perceive the same content differently. In a sense, experts have learned what to look for. From a sea of data, they pinpoint the important, useful information. Novice learners, on the other hand, don't know what to look for and can lose focus trying to learn lots of facts and details without developing conceptual understanding. Novices need to learn the concepts; otherwise, they will never be able to make meaning out of the rest of the information that we teach (Donovan and Bransford 2005).

What Is the Strategy?

Pre-pruning. Before beginning the pruning process, let's look at some criteria we can use. *Designs for Science Literacy* (AAAS 2000) specifies that the two primary reasons for pruning content are (1) there was no compelling argument that it is essential for science literacy or (2) the amount of time and effort needed for all students to learn was out of proportion to its importance. In the appendix for Content Strategy 2 you will find one possible process to use if your school or district wants to practice a pruning process for their curriculum framework.

Pruning is important work that is best accomplished by teams of teachers with the support of schools and districts. However, if time and resources for pruning are not available, individual teachers can still do this on their own. It takes a significant amount of time to prune units and revise lessons, so we recommend working on one unit and the related lessons during the first semester and another one during the second semester. The next year, two more can be revised, and so on. Another strategy is to have a team of teachers divide up the units within a course of study and each teacher work on one unit; teachers then share their revised units with one another.

Using the two criteria already mentioned, we can also look at pruning topics and units that have already been taught and eliminate wasteful repetition. So what can and should we prune? Teachers and curriculum developers decide what science concepts and skills must be learned. If you are lucky enough to go through the pruning process as a school or district team, then reaching consensus on what to eliminate is itself an effective way for us to clarify in our own minds what is important. Some districts have already generated curriculum maps that include the key concepts. We can use those as a guide of what to keep.

As you decide what to keep, make sure to analyze conceptual strands by using the *Atlas of Science Literacy* (volumes 1 and 2 or the online resources). Conduct cross-grade surveys to determine what is being taught both before and after your course. Refer to district curriculum maps and guides if they are available. Districts often produce their own curriculum maps and guides, so refer to those if they are available to determine grade-level expectations. Remember, it is important to offer learning that is not too advanced or too easy, but appropriate for the developmental level of your students.

If you end up doing the pruning process by yourself, we suggest sharing your concept map or paragraph explaining the big idea(s) with a colleague to get feedback. This also allows you to reflect on your choices. There is no one set of objectives/concepts that works in every context, and variation is to be expected when teachers prune individually. What's more important is finding the time—for teacher and students—to focus on learning goals and providing students with multiple opportunities to learn the concepts and supporting knowledge they need to know.

Exploring the Strategy

For this example, we will use a standard statement from the *National Assessment of Education Progress* (National Assessment Governing Board 2005) as our big idea:

Energy can be converted from one form into another. Kinetic energy can be converted into potential energy, and potential energy can be converted into kinetic energy. Thermal energy is often one of the forms of energy that results during energy conversion. When energy is converted from one form to another, the quantity of energy before the conversion equals the quantity of energy after conversion. (Grade 8)

- This big idea is basically about energy transformations and conservation. Write a paragraph that elaborates and explains what this big idea means, or draw a concept map that details the relationship between the key concepts and knowledge embedded in the statements.

- Then, take each idea from your paragraph and match it to the concepts and objectives from the list below. Decide which statements you think are high priority and cross out those which should be pruned. In other words, if it doesn't clearly relate to the big idea above, then it is a candidate for pruning. This doesn't mean that the pruned ideas wouldn't be taught in other courses or at other grade levels, but it should clarify what to include in this unit on energy transformation and conservation.

List of Assessment Statements for Energy Concepts, Knowledge, and Skills:

1. **Recognizes that things that give off light often also give off heat**

2. Explains that energy is needed to do work

3. Identifies uses of energy

4. Understands that sound is a form of energy

5. **Relates kinetic energy to the speed of an object**

6. Recognizes that heat can move from object to object by conduction

7. Compares ability of materials to conduct heat

8. **Makes predictions about the transformation between kinetic and potential energy**

9. **Describes the transformations of energy that may occur in electrical systems**

10. Explains that a turbine is a machine that transforms mechanical energy to electrical energy

11. **Explains that energy cannot be created or destroyed, only changed from one form to another**

12. **Defines kinetic energy and gives examples**

13. Classifies examples of heat transfer as conduction

14. Understands that heat flows from warmer to cooler objects until both reach equilibrium

15. Gives examples of energy transfer through radiation

16. **Explains that when energy is converted from one form to another, heat is often produced as a by-product**

17. **Recognizes the major forms of energy**

18. **Defines potential energy and gives examples**

As you look at the statements that come directly from a state standards document, you'll notice that some of the statements relate directly to the four main ideas in our big idea. Those ideas are energy conversion, transforming kinetic to potential energy and the reverse, energy conversions resulting in heat energy, and conservation of energy. If we keep the bolded targets and plan instructional activities with these goals in mind, then we can prune away most of the other

Content

goals. With more time for learning the concepts, we can provide opportunities for inquiries into energy conversions and energy conservation.

Now, let's look at pruning the technical vocabulary in the following list from the same source. According to *Designs for Science Literacy* (AAAS 2001), if we include lots of technical vocabulary, then students focus on the terms rather than learning the science ideas (concepts). The key vocabulary that we do include has to be at the appropriate level for our students. Remember that some of the terms will already have been introduced in earlier classes or units so we are only talking about new vocabulary. The rule of thumb is no more that 3–5 new terms for elementary students per unit, 6–8 new terms for middle level students, and 8–10 for high school students. If we look at our state and national science standards documents and create vocabulary lists for the grade-level bands, the total number of vocabulary words will work out to the recommended number per unit. In the example below, there are lots of terms that can be pruned. Reflect on what this means for your current practice.

Vocabulary List from a State Science Standards Document:

direct sunlight	neutral	vocal cords
electrical conductor	neutron	chemical energy
electrical energy	Newton	circuit tester
conduct	parallel circuit	convection
conductor	positively charged	dimmer switch
conversion	prism	dry cell battery
electrical current	**potential energy**	electrical shock
electrical insulator	radiate	explosion
electron	radiator	heat transfer
filament	series circuit	infrared
flow of heat	sound energy	radiation
fluctuate	light energy	**energy transformations**
insulator	mechanical energy	visible spectrum
kilowatt hours	spectrum	wavelength
kinetic energy	stationary	alternating circuit
material	thermos jug	**law of conservation of energy**
minimize	transfer	
molecular motion	turbine	nuclear energy

Planning for Classroom Implementation

In summary, you just learned about a pruning process that you can use with your own units to help solve the issue of time. Recent research findings in *Taking Science to School: Learning and Teaching Science in Grades K–8* (NRC 2007) reveal that student understanding is more about opportunity to learn than it is about students' innate abilities. Not including students with cognitive deficiencies, students' brains are pretty much alike and are able to process science ideas in similar ways. What is different about each of our students is the learning experiences that they have in our classrooms. It is all about having the time to engage students in meaningful ways with important science concepts and ideas.

What Works in Science Classrooms: Implications for Teaching

Recommendation 1: Determine the essential learnings or key concepts students need to learn. Use the resources that you have (including those mentioned in Content Strategy 1) to figure out what constitutes essential learning. Supplemental learning, wasteful repetition, and technical vocabulary all need to be pruned. Only then will we have the time needed to engage students with important concepts.

Recommendation 2: Since students are novice learners when it comes to most science concepts, provide opportunities for them to engage in the content in ways that help them make sense of the ideas. This includes providing multiple opportunities to learn the key concepts and develop understanding of the big ideas.

Recommendation 3: Pruning is a process that we need to practice to develop proficiency. Ask yourself this question before the start of each lesson: "What is the important concept that students should be thinking about today?" To create that focus in the lesson, it makes good sense to eliminate others ideas and vocabulary that would distract students.

Content Strategy 3: Engaging Students With Content

The Issue

Students in secondary science classrooms complain that science is boring. Why? Probably because they either don't understand it or it seems irrelevant to their lives—or both. In any event, if students are not interested, they will not learn. So the key to successful science learning is "to be providing students an opportunity to engage with important science concepts and ensuring that they in fact make sense of these concepts" (Weiss et al. 2003).

Making science interesting must begin in elementary classrooms, where, thankfully, the amount of time given to learning science has increased recently, with the mandatory implementation of science assessments in each state. To engage students, think about what students like most about learning science. They like inquiry investigations and demonstrations, things that teach how things work. Most students love a mystery—and science is filled with puzzles and mysteries.

Table 2.1
Identifying Important Content

Strategy 1: Identifying Big Ideas and Key Concepts Identify "big ideas," key concepts, knowledge and skills that describe what the students will understand.	
Strategy 2: Unburdening the Curriculum Prune extraneous subtopics, technical vocabulary, and wasteful repetition.	
Strategy 3: Engaging Students With Content Create essential questions that engage students with the content.	**Why am I doing this?**
Strategy 4: Identifying Preconceptions and Prior Knowledge Identify common preconceptions and prior student knowledge.	**What are the important concepts and scientific ideas included in the lesson?**
Strategy 5: Assessment—How Do You Know That They Learned? Develop assessments that correlate to the conceptual understanding and related knowledge and skills.	
Strategy 6: Sequencing the Learning Targets Into a Progression Clarify and sequence the learning targets into progressions to focus instruction on building conceptual understanding; align learning activities with learning targets.	

How do we take advantage of students' natural curiosity and engage them intellectually? One approach is by using well-designed questions. The idea of engaging students is the first step in the BSCS 5E instructional model (Bybee 2002). In Bybee's instructional model he recommends engaging students with a new concept through the use of short activities that promote curiosity and elicit prior knowledge. The five features of inquiry (NRC 1999) also start with engagement—engaging students with scientific questions.

The DESI Approach

Using essential questions is a strategy that engages students in lively discussion, makes students think, and develops understanding as well as getting the students to ask even more questions. Essential questions directly relate to the key concepts and naturally recur every time the concepts are taught, but they are open-ended and have no obvious "right" answer. By carefully crafting questions ahead of time, we can make sure they are not too easy (and boring) and not too difficult (also boring) but challenge students to really think about what they understand and don't understand. For example, ask yourself the following questions: "Can you see an apple in a totally dark room?" and "Is there life on Mars?" Upon hearing the question, we immediately start to think about what we know already. Using "good" essential questions helps students access their ideas about how nature works and, just like us, students can't help but think about their thinking. Some of the science literature describes essential questions as conceptually rich problems or questions (Bell and Purdy 1985; Bransford et al. 1999). One example would be, "How does a tree get to be so big from a tiny seed?" These kinds of questions connect students to the content. Using probing or conceptually rich questions as a part of formative assessment will be discussed as part of Understanding Strategy 2.

Posing essential questions are easy for some teachers and challenge others. To generate essential questions, follow the advice provided by Wiggins and McTighe (2005) and others and practice writing some of your own.

Selected Research That Addresses This Issue

1. Essential questions are an innovative and effective element of the backward design model. Wiggins and McTighe propose that a question is essential if it meets a series of criteria. This information is contained in Table 2.3 (p. 48).

2. An important goal of using essential questions is student engagement with making sense of the science content. "Students' inclination,

Table 2.3
Criteria for
Essential Questions

 1. Cause genuine and relevant inquiry into the big ideas and core content

 2. Provoke deep thought, lively discussion, sustained inquiry, and new understanding as well as more questions

 3. Require students to consider alternatives, weigh evidence, support their ideas, and justify their answers

 4. Stimulate vital, ongoing rethinking of big ideas, assumptions, and prior lessons

 5. Spark meaningful connections with prior learning and personal experiences

 6. Naturally recur, creating opportunities for transfer to other situations and subjects

Wiggins, G., and J. McTighe. 2005. *Understanding by design.* 2nd ed. Alexandria, VA: Association for Supervision and Curriculum Development.

reinforced over the years of school, to substitute memorization for understanding is all the more reason for teachers to help students get better at learning content that has greater utility and durability" (AAAS 2001, pp. 227–8).

What Is the Strategy?

Drafting essential questions reminds us to ask ourselves, "What do we want students to understand?" One way to approach this strategy is to consider each concept that we will teach and come up with a question that really gets the students thinking. So to learn more about this strategy, in your own mind, which of the following questions are essential questions and why do you think so? Remember from the information in Table 2.3, they should not have an obvious right or wrong answer and they get at the heart of the conceptual ideas we want students to learn.

- Can a tree die of old age?

- How many legs does a spider have?

- What is "molecular bonding"?

- What makes a theory a "good" theory?

- What causes sound to echo?

If you look at the first question, it fits the criteria for an essential question. It engages students with the concept of aging and as a plant, how do trees age? Does it depend upon the conditions, kind of tree, climate? So this question prompts us to reflect on our knowledge and understanding of death and old age in plants and probably compare it to other organisms. The second question has an expected right answer of eight legs so does not meet our criteria for essential questions.

Exploring the Strategy

Remember that essential questions are not just lesson objectives written in question form. A question like "What are the steps in cell division?" clearly has a specific right answer associated with it. But if we ask the question, "What causes cells to divide?" then with this essential question we can get students to start thinking about different kinds of cells, the conditions that might trigger division, and what about aging, or cancer cells. And how are stem cells different? Is the answer different for a plant cell, animal cell, or other type of cell?

In an elementary classroom, teachers expect students to know the answer to the question "What do living things need to survive?" This has a right answer, which would include components such as food, water, and shelter. But what if we asked these essential questions: "Do living things have the same needs?" "How are living organisms adapted to different habitats?" Because there is not just one response depending on the living organism, students think more about their ideas and their previous experiences.

There are many examples of essential questions that teachers have created and others that come right from their students. The strategy here is to practice writing essential questions that engage students in the learning, are arguable, raise important questions, and focus the students on the key concepts.

Table 2.4 contains some examples that you can use to think about your own questions. Try to keep the number of essential questions to only a few for each unit and try to match them to your big ideas and key concepts.

Because this is tough for most of us to do, when you have some draft essential questions prepared, share your responses with others. Be sure you share the criteria for essential questions with the reviewers. Based on their feedback, should any of the essential questions be revised? This process is one that requires practice. Just like anything else that is worthwhile, it takes effort. Using electronic resources is a helpful way to get started since many teachers are working on this also.

Table 2.4
Sample Essential Questions

Why don't the oceans freeze?

If the oceans don't freeze, where do icebergs come from?

Can oceans be too salty or not salty enough?

How do organisms survive in harsh or changing environments?

What makes information "true"?

Is some information better than other information? How do we judge?

How do oceans affect climate change?

Planning for Classroom Implementation

Ultimately, essential questions are a way to get students to think about a topic and to connect to their ideas about how nature works. To craft essential questions that relate to each key concept, we need to engage in thinking about the concepts ourselves. What are some open-ended questions that invite multiple student ideas and relate to what you are teaching? Remember, these are not lesson objectives but questions designed to get students thinking "Hmm, that's interesting. I wonder..." The goal is to get our students to share their ideas and their thinking as they seek to answer the question and provide explanations. In this way, we get them to intellectually engage with the concepts. Since they will not have the scientific knowledge or understanding to accurately respond to the essential questions, the questions also invite opportunities for them to inquire and test their ideas. Try writing some essential questions that relate to your unit and compare them to criteria for essential questions. Get help! Some people are really good at "I wonder..." kinds of questions, so check out what others have created or get feedback on the ones you have written. You can even ask your students to create some "I wonder..." questions using the criteria provided. Remember that trying this for the first time is always the hardest but, with subsequent practices, it should get easier.

What Works in Science Classrooms: Implications for Teaching

Recommendation 1: Essential questions help engage students with the science concepts. There really aren't any right or wrong answers for whether a question is essential or not, but try to make them open-ended enough so that students think and engage intellectually with the content—beyond just a superficial level. Draft a few essential questions for your unit of study. Try to create an essential question for each of your key concepts. Check your questions against the criteria provided.

Recommendation 2: If you have trouble writing essential questions, use whatever resources you have available to you. Further thought and interactions with your students are sure to yield some new possibilities, so don't worry if this new element of planning high-quality science lessons doesn't go smoothly at first. Imagine questions that you have always wondered about and see if they can be revised into essential questions.

Content Strategy 4: Identifying Preconceptions and Prior Knowledge

The Issue

How do we know what students know? Each student has prior conceptions about the natural world and how it works, which come from a wide variety of learning opportunities both in and out of school. The challenge is to determine answers to the following questions:

- What do students know and think about a particular concept?

- Why do they think that?

- How do teachers uncover prior knowledge and preconceptions?

Table 2.1
Identifying Important Content

Strategy 1: Identifying Big Ideas and Key Concepts Identify "big ideas," key concepts, knowledge and skills that describe what the students will understand.	
Strategy 2: Unburdening the Curriculum Prune extraneous subtopics, technical vocabulary, and wasteful repetition.	
Strategy 3: Engaging Students With Content Create essential questions that engage students with the content.	**Why am I doing this?**
Strategy 4: Identifying Preconceptions and Prior Knowledge Identify common preconceptions and prior student knowledge.	**What are the important concepts and scientific ideas included in the lesson?**
Strategy 5: Assessment—How Do You Know That They Learned? Develop assessments that correlate to the conceptual understanding and related knowledge and skills.	
Strategy 6: Sequencing the Learning Targets Into a Progression Clarify and sequence the learning targets into progressions to focus instruction on building conceptual understanding; align learning activities with learning targets.	

The DESI Approach

Before teaching a new science concept in a unit of study, we must assess what our students already know and whether that knowledge is scientifically correct or incorrect. There is a wealth of information and research about student preconceptions that we need to review and use when planning lessons. But even before that, we must assess what we ourselves already know and whether our conceptual knowledge aligns with the scientific viewpoint. This was included in the Content Strategy 1. Once we have reviewed the concepts we are to teach and checked the research for information about common student misconceptions, then with this strategy the approach is to get students to reveal their ideas about the concepts that we will be teaching.

Selected Research That Addresses This Issue

1. "Knowledge-centered and learner-centered environments intersect when educators take seriously the idea that students must be supported to develop expertise over time; it is not sufficient to simply provide them with expert models and expect them to learn. For example, intentionally organizing subject matter to allow students to follow a path of 'progressive differentiation' (e.g., from qualitative understanding to more precise quantitative understanding of a particular phenomenon) involves a simultaneous focus on the structure of the knowledge to be mastered and the learning process of students." (Donovan and Bransford 2005, p. 14)

2. "[Teachers] also must be skilled in helping students develop an understanding of the content, meaning that they need to know how students typically think about particular concepts, how to determine what a particular student or group of students thinks about those ideas, and how to help students deepen their understanding." (Weiss et al. 2003, p. 28)

3. "The first thing to do is to consider the nature of any differences between children's prevalent thinking and the science viewpoint. Various possibilities exist and learning science might therefore involve

    i.   Developing existing ideas

    ii. Differentiating existing ideas

    iii. Integrating existing ideas

    iv. Changing existing ideas

    v.   Introducing new ideas

Once the teacher has identified the nature of any differences between pupils' thinking and the science viewpoint, then it becomes easier to plan activities which will support intended learning." (Driver et al. 2005, p. 10)

4. "An assessment probe is a type of diagnostic assessment that provides information to the teacher about student thinking related to a concept in science.... Probes are concerned less with the correct answer or quality of the student response and focus more on what students are thinking about a concept or phenomenon and where their ideas may have originated." (Keeley and Eberle 2008, p 203–204)

What Is the Strategy?

"Preconception" is the term used in the meta-analysis *How People Learn: Bridging Research and Practice* (Donovan et al. 1999) to describe the initial understanding that students have about how the world works. Student preconceptions are sometimes accurate, but frequently they are not (Carey and Gelman 1991). In the appendix for Content Strategy 4 is a tool to remind you of the steps that should be part of the process for identifying student preconceptions.

One key finding in the study *Looking Inside the Classroom* (Weiss et al. 2003) was that 35% of lessons observed elicited student prior knowledge in some way, but the ideas students were asked to share were not well aligned with the learning goal of the teacher. Without the connection to the learning, students weren't focused on the important ideas and as teachers, we therefore may not really know what students think. Once we know what ideas our students bring with them, then we can use our pedagogical content knowledge to know how to best present concepts, identify where students may go wrong in their thinking or have gaps in understanding, and determine effective methods to help our students engage meaningfully with their preconceptions and the science concepts.

Exploring the Strategy

To determine the prior knowledge of students, most teachers have used prewrites, KWL (What I *Know*, What I *Want to Know*, What I *Learned*) charts, brainstorming, and other strategies. You may want to think about what you have done in the past to gather evidence of student learning. As with any instructional strategy, students like variety and will become resistant if teachers use the same strategy for every unit. What follows is a sample brainstorming activity to determine what students know about photosynthesis. In this activity, we would provide the following instructions to the students.

Prompt: How do plants make their own food? And what factors affect the process?

- In teams, use the piece of chart paper provided to record what you know and understand conceptually about the process of photosynthesis by answering the two questions listed in the prompt.

- Each member of the group should use a different color of marker to record his or her ideas.

- Take turns writing and proceed around the group in a clockwise fashion until all of the ideas you can think of have been recorded. The information can be scattered around the page in any way that the group decides.

- At the end of your group work, sign your name on the poster using the same colored marker that you used to record your statements of understanding.

- Be prepared to share with the whole group.

At the conclusion of the brainstorming activity, we would engage the class in a debriefing activity where each group shares their ideas one at a time without repeating any idea already shared by another group. We would record all of the ideas on another piece of chart paper, chalk board, white board, Smart Board, or other surface. We can ask clarifying questions of the teams and, at the end of the reporting out time, summarize the ideas that centered on the process of photosynthesis and the two questions for the class. This information then can be used to determine existing preconceptions that need to be addressed and allow us to set instructional goals for upcoming lessons. Because student ideas were recorded in different colors, we can use this information to group students into appropriate cooperative learning groups. A student example of this activity is provided in Figure 2.4.

A variation of this idea is included in an article on effective science instruction published by the Center on Instruction (Banilower et al. 2008). In the article, second grade students were provided with a blank sheet of paper and asked to write everything they knew about weather. The students could draw pictures that they labeled, create diagrams, or use words. The teacher asked each student to share one of their ideas with the class. As before, the teacher asked for clarification from the students and ended by summarizing for the class. The prior knowledge gathered from the student ideas then formed the launching point for a lesson on water.

You may want to investigate the use of student webs that can be created using Inspiration software. The computer program includes organizational formatting,

Figure 2.4
Sample Student Work

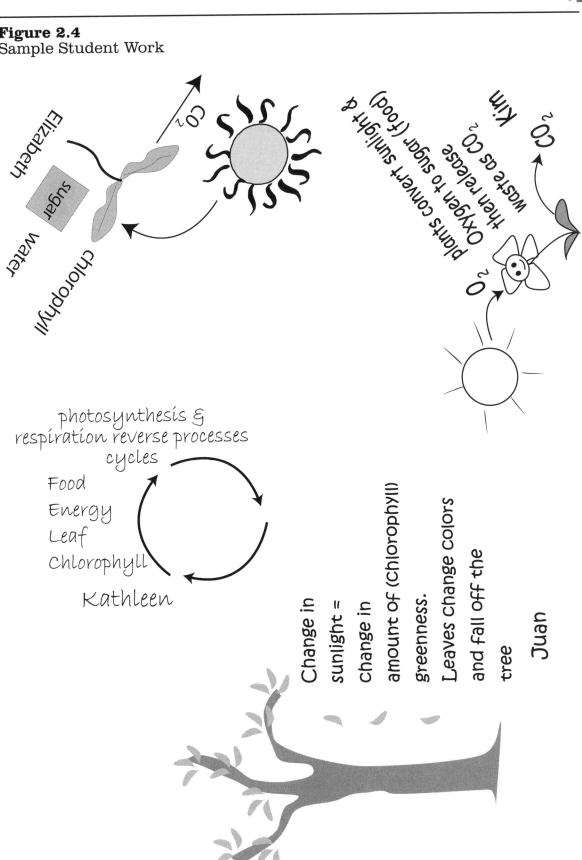

a basic flow chart, and a drawing palette. The students can create their own or group thinking-process maps. Additional ideas for mind-mapping are possible using visual tools that help students create visual representations of their conceptual ideas. Since the brain creates patterns, in essence, our students can draw their thinking (Hyerle 1996).

Another valuable strategy is to create a probing question or to create a formative assessment "probe." A process has been created "that links commonly held ideas identified through cognitive research to key concepts in state and national learning goals" (Keeley and Eberle 2008, p. 204). We can either create our own probes or use the resources already published. The probes themselves can be used to determine prior knowledge, used during the unit to provide formative assessment information, or used at the end of a unit to determine student conceptual understanding. If a probe is used to find out prior student knowledge, then the same probe should not be used as a formative or summative assessment later in the unit. The key goal is still to be able to uncover students thinking about a science concept. This is different from pre-assessment tests, which sample for student factual knowledge in addition to testing their comprehension of science concepts. (Note: There are currently four books that include dozens of examples of probes that can be used to find out what students think about key concepts in life sciences, Earth and space science, and physical sciences. These resources are available from NSTA Press under the titles of *Uncovering Student Ideas in Science* (Keeley et al. 2005–2009).

Planning for Classroom Implementation

Teaching for understanding requires that teachers have more than just science content knowledge. The many aspects of the art and science of helping students access and develop an accurate understanding of the science concepts has been labeled *pedagogical content knowledge*, or PCK. Simply put, PCK means knowing your subject, your audience, and how to introduce one to the other in ways that result in conceptual understanding that addresses students ideas.

To be able to understand student thinking we need to gather and examine the evidence that students use to explain their points of view. One way to accomplish this is through formative assessments called probes that were discussed in the "Exploring the Strategy" section. Remember that these are not tasks to find out if students are meeting learning goals but rather a way for us to go deeper into students' thinking to determine where students are before we begin instruction. We must identify the gap that exists between student thinking and the science viewpoint to set instructional goals for each of our students. This process will reveal differences in individual student understanding. By encouraging students to ask questions as they think about their thinking, we can interpret responses from students and use this information when planning classroom teaching and learning experiences.

Depending on the grade level you teach, you may feel like an expert in science content or you may be a little uncomfortable yourself when it comes to understanding science ideas. But whether you are a master teacher of science content or a novice, you should always reflect on what you know yourselves as you go about the task of discovering the prior knowledge of your students. With scientific advances there is often emerging content that will inform our teaching. It is hard to be an expert in all areas of science and there is no reason to pretend that we know it all. To review this strategy, return to Content Strategy 1. There will always be questions from students that we, as learners, can't answer or concepts that we don't completely understand. To address students' ideas about science phenomenon, it is logical that we start with our own ideas. Remember that there is a tool that includes the steps to follow included in the appendix Content Strategy 4 document.

As we go about the process of eliciting students ideas, it is always helpful to have our resources close at hand that describe what students should know and be able to do. Some of the resources that we recommended during the first content strategy include national, state, and local standards documents and curriculum frameworks. There are books (e.g., the *Stop Faking It!* series from NSTA Press), online professional development courses, internet resources, and virtual manipulatives that can be accessed electronically. *Science Curriculum Topic Study—Bridging the Gap Between Standards and Practice* (Keeley 2005) is an additional resource that aligns major topics in science with resources that identifies the key concepts and research on students' ideas related to the topics.

A second planning template is included in the Chapter 2 Appendix for strategy 4. The blank template can be used to gather background information and to plan for student preconceptions and prior knowledge.

What Works in Science Classrooms: Implications for Teaching

Recommendation 1: It is important to assess students' prior knowledge. Finding out what students ideas are is valuable, even if their thinking is consistent with scientific ideas. To learn science concepts, students must connect new ideas with preexisting ideas so getting students to explain their ideas is always a good plan. The key is to probe their explanations to reveal the experiences that they are using to make sense of the concepts.

Recommendation 2: Experience is one way that students learn, but it is not always the best way depending on how they make sense of their experiences. Without our help, many students use evidence from everyday experiences to come to incorrect conclusions about how the world works. Since learning is a social activity, opportunities that encourage kids to talk about their ideas and justify their explanations using evidence must be provided. When students discuss their ideas with one another and with our guidance, they have the opportunities that they need to make sense of the science concepts.

Recommendation 3: Students' ideas are not always consistent with the new ideas that they are learning. Research into how students learn indicates that to bring about conceptual change in students ideas, we must first confront students with evidence that helps them formulate new ideas and become dissatisfied with their former thinking. If this doesn't happen, students will persist in retaining their old preconceptions. More about this will be discussed in Chapter 3, which focuses on developing student understanding.

Content Strategy 5: Assessment—How Do You Know That They Learned?

The Issue

If improved student learning is our primary goal, then summative assessments that align with important learning goals are logical and necessary. Unfortunately, most of us are not trained psychometricians (testing and assessment specialists). We rely on test banks of questions. Summative assessments in science are often based upon how much time has passed in a unit, not whether students are prepared to provide evidence of their conceptual understanding. With the role of science teachers moving away from the giver of grades to the facilitator of learning, summative assessments must match the learning goals and the criteria for success.

A second issue is depth of understanding. We often accept student responses that show apparent signs of understanding, such as students being able to provide the right word, definition, or formula. Changing the question or terms and probing further may cause our students to reveal that they really do not understand

Table 2.1
Identifying Important Content

Strategy 1: Identifying Big Ideas and Key Concepts Identify "big ideas," key concepts, knowledge and skills that describe what the students will understand.	
Strategy 2: Unburdening the Curriculum Prune extraneous subtopics, technical vocabulary, and wasteful repetition.	
Strategy 3; Engaging Students with Content Create essential questions that engage students with the content.	**Why am I doing this?**
Strategy 4; Identifying Preconceptions and Prior Knowledge Identify common preconceptions and prior student knowledge.	**What are the important concepts and scientific ideas included in the lesson?**
Strategy 5: Assessment—How Do You Know That They Learned? Develop assessments that correlate to the conceptual understanding and related knowledge and skills.	
Strategy 6: Sequencing the Learning Targets Into a Progression Clarify and sequence the learning targets into progressions to focus instruction on building conceptual understanding; align learning activities with learning targets.	

the concepts at all. They may even show a variety of misconceptions. If "correct" answers can result in insufficient evidence of understanding, then how can we assess students so that we are really able to know if students can transfer their learning to new contexts?

The DESI Approach

Summative science assessments help teachers, students, and parents determine how well students are learning. Assessments *for* learning (formative assessments), as compared to assessments *of* learning (summative assessments), must also be planned and implemented to find out if students are learning. This feedback to and from teachers and students can be used to revise instruction. Designing formative assessment experiences as part of a formative assessment process is covered in more detail in the Understanding section. For our purposes here we are only talking about summative classroom assessments that would be integral to a unit of study. Different assessments have different purposes, so we will not try to tackle a complete assessment system that includes benchmark assessments (common assessments). End-of-course or end-of-year assessments recommend creating a summative assessment blueprint that clearly matches the learning goals and learning targets with the types of assessment questions.

To show understanding, students must be able to show how well they have learned. They need to be able to explain, to interpret, to apply and adapt knowledge, to have perspective, to ask relevant questions, to problem solve new situations, and to have self-knowledge about their understanding. So understanding is really a group of related abilities (Wiggins and McTighe 2005). The approach in this strategy then must be to design summative assessments that include questions or tasks that require higher cognitive demand where students analyze, synthesize, and apply their understanding of concepts to new situations.

Selected Research That Addresses This Issue

1. "Learning with understanding is often harder to accomplish than simply memorizing, and it takes more time. Many curricula fail to support learning with understanding because they present too many disconnected facts in too short a time—the 'mile wide, inch deep' problem. Tests often reinforce memorizing rather than understanding. The knowledge-centered environment provides the necessary depth of study, assessing student understanding rather than factual memory. It incorporates the teaching of meta-cognitive strategies that further facilitate future learning." (Donovan et al. 1999, p. 21)

2. "First, every assessment is grounded in a conception or theory about how people learn, what they know, and how knowledge and understanding progress over time. Second, each assessment embodies certain assumptions about which kinds of observations or tasks are most likely to elicit demonstrations of important knowledge and skills from students. Third, every assessment is premised on certain assumptions about how best to interpret the evidence from observations to draw meaningful inferences about what students know and can do." (Pellegrino et al. 2001, p. 20)

3. "Just as classroom science instruction should focus on core science concepts, so should classroom assessment. This principle represents a knowledge-based approach to instruction which always requires...an explicit linkage of all instructional and assessment activities to the core-concept curricular framework representing that knowledge....All classroom assessment should focus on student mastery or non-mastery of core science concepts or of subconcepts and examples related to the core concepts." (Vitale, Romance, and Dolan 2006, p. 3)

What Is the Strategy?

So where do we get well-designed summative assessment questions? And are grades based on evidence of student understanding? Summative assessments may not even be aligned with the big ideas and key concepts when we rely on test banks. So the question really isn't "Where do we go to get good questions?" but "Once learning concepts are clear, how do we design assessments that align with the learning goals and key concepts?" This has to be the next major step in our planning process after getting the content right—identifying big ideas and key concepts, pruning nonessential vocabulary and concepts, identifying possible student misconceptions and knowing where to start with students based on their prior knowledge. Continuing with a backwards design strategy we can now plan for summative assessments. In our own minds we must establish the criteria for success and what our students would need to provide as evidence of understanding. Only then can the instructional activity sequences be developed. First, we have to decide what is important to assess and what the best strategies to assess are.

Let's look at the first part of that statement: "Decide what is important to assess." There is a key distinction between science knowledge and conceptual science understanding. What is it? If we think about the hierarchy of declarative knowledge, what we know about a topic usually includes the facts and vocabulary and the concepts related to the topic. From the selected research, we know that asking students to demonstrate conceptual science understanding goes beyond mere recall. We will want to look at examples of current summative assessments (tests) we are providing for students that either come from test generators or that we constructed ourselves. Tally the number of questions that measure recall; the number that ask students to analyze, compare and contrast, critique evidence, and apply information; and the number of questions that go beyond and ask students to problemsolve, investigate, engage in decision making, or design and conduct experimental inquiries (Marzano, Pickering, and Pollack 2001). If we do this test review with a colleague, we can reflect aloud about what the tests are measuring and what we will know about our students as a result of their performance. Part of the discussion should be about what constitutes proficiency. What evidence do students need to provide to show a credible level of mastery of the concepts?

Exploring the Strategy

As we know from our previous strategy discussions, it is important to plan for assessment at the same time that big ideas and key concepts are determined. What is equally important is to match the type of assessment to the type of knowledge and understanding that the students are gaining. To start this process, we have to figure out what students should be able to do to provide the evidence we need that they have learned. A sample is provided for you in Table 2.5 related to grade level concepts about matter and energy transformations.

In our minds, when we think about the learning targets (conceptual targets), we automatically start to talk about how they would demonstrate science knowledge and conceptual science understanding. We say things like "The learner will…" and then insert a variety of verbs such as "list," "define," and "explain." These all require lower levels of cognitive demand as compared to statements such as "The learner will critique using evidence" or "The learner will inquiry, problem-solve, investigate, or design a way to test predictions about…"

A template is provided in the appendix (Content Strategy 5a) to help you reflect on what is the important learning and how we will know that students are demonstrating understanding that goes beyond providing recall information. Are they applying their learning to a new situation? Are we asking them questions that get them to think about what they know so that we can ask, "What would happen if…?"

These kinds of higher-order thinking questions provide students with multiple possible responses and help us reveal student thinking. One example that will help bring this idea home is a question about ecosystems. A typical assessment

Table 2.5
Sample Assessment Performance

Grade 4: Fourth-Grade Assessment Performances for Matter and Energy Transformations			
	Application	**Inquiry**	**Knowledge of Benchmark Ideas**
Food is the source of energy and materials.	Classify things that people eat as food or not food. Identify uses that people make of food.	Use tables to compare the calorie content and nutritional value of various foods and defend claims based on the data.	Identify food as the source of animal growth (e.g., the weight of a log, weight gain of an infant).
Animals need to take in air, water, and food.	Describe what happens to food that people and animals eat (some is used for repair and growth and some is eliminated).	Based on collected data, compare weight gains of individual organisms with various diets.	Identify materials that animals need to take in.
Plants need air, water, nutrients, and light.	Identify conditions for plant growth in different environments such as rainforests, deserts, or grasslands.	Based on collected data, compare dry mass of plants grown in various conditions.	Identify light, water, and air as essential to plant growth.

(continued on pp. 64–65)

question would be as follows: In the food chain shown below what would happen if all the mice disappeared?

Grasses ➔ Mice ➔ Snakes ➔ Hawks

a. Snake population would increase

b. Grass population would increase

c. Hawk population would increase

d. None of the above

What has happened in the question is that the scientific concept of interdependency, which is a key concept in our understanding about how ecosystems work, has been so simplified that we don't really know what their answer to this question tells us about their understanding. Instead we may want to ask the students,

Table 2.5 (cont.)
Sample Assessment Performance

Grade 8: Eighth-Grade Assessment Performances for Matter and Energy Transformations			
	Application	**Inquiry**	**Knowledge of Benchmark Ideas**
Food provides the molecules that serve as fuel and building material for all organisms.	Explain how specific food substances are used for energy and/or growth by animal cells. Design a snack food that meets specified nutrition requirements.	Use simple tests to identify food substances.	Identify food as the source of both building material and fuel for both plants and animals.
Plants use the energy from light to make sugars from carbon dioxide and water. This food can be used immediately or stored for later use.	Account for a plant's increase in mass from the molecular building blocks it makes. Explain why plants need light. Describe two possible fates of the sugars that plants make.	Criticize reasoning in arguments about claims that do not follow logically from data about plant growth under various conditions.	Identify the inputs and the outputs of photosynthesis.
Organisms that eat plants break down the plant structures to produce the materials and energy they need to survive.	Explain what happens to food substances when animals gain and lose weight. Explain how animals digest and use food. Predict results of experiments involving animal nutrition or the effects of diet and exercise.	Criticize conclusions about likely consequences of consuming various diets based on flawed premises or flaws in logic of reasoning.	Given a food web, predict the effects of a change in one population on another.
Then they are consumed by other organisms.	Trace food substances and energy through food webs.		Given a diagram of a food web, predict the effects of a change in one population on another.

"What happens when an ecosystem becomes unbalanced?" We may also want to provide a more robust food web for a grassland that represents a wide variety of interrelationships. It is all about asking the right questions and using the right type of assessment.

Table 2.5 (cont.)
Sample Assessment Performance

Grade 12: High School Assessment Performances for Matter and Energy Transformations			
	Application	Inquiry	Knowledge of Benchmark Ideas
The chemical elements that make up the molecules of living things pass through food webs and are combined and recombined in different ways.	Trace chemical elements through food webs. Describe the individual matter transformations that occur from one organism to the next in food webs. Explain how the law of mass conservation applies to ecosystems.	Compare alternative explanations about matter transformation and conservation in food webs in light of their consistency or lack of consistency with data.	Distinguish between organic and inorganic compounds based on chemical formulas.
At each link in a food web, some energy is stored in newly made structures, but much is released into the environment as heat.	Trace the path of energy in an ecosystem. Explain how the law of energy conservation applies to ecosystems.	Criticize conclusions about likely consequences of consuming various diets based on premises or logic of reasoning about heat loss data.	Identify forms of energy found in living systems.
Continual input of energy from sunlight keeps the process going.	Explain why ecosystems need a continual input of sunlight in terms of the heat loss at each step in a food web.	Use data about populations in ecosystems to construct possible food chains.	Identify sunlight as the ultimate source of energy for all living organisms.

Planning for Classroom Implementation

Remember that after we determine what to assess it is important to choose the right type of assessment. What are the different kinds of assessment? Look at the chart in Table 2.6 (p. 66) and think about these questions:

- When is it appropriate to use multiple-choice assessments?

- When is using a performance-based assessment worthwhile?

- What is the best way to assess conceptual understanding?

Table 2.6
Assessment Methods

Target to be Assessed	Assessment Method			
	Selected Response	**Essay**	**Performance Assessment**	**Personal Communication**
Vocabulary	Multiple choice, true/false, matching, and fill-in can sample mastery of vocabulary.	Essay exercises can tap vocabulary knowledge.	Not a good choice for this target	Can ask questions, evaluate answers, and infer mastery, but may be a time-consuming option
Fact/Details	Multiple choice, true/false, matching, and fill-in can sample mastery of facts and details.	Essay exercises can tap knowledge of facts and details.	Not a good choice for this target	Can ask questions, evaluate answers, and infer mastery, but a time-consuming option
Organizing Ideas *Concepts* *Principles* *Generalizations*	Higher-order multiple choice questions can tap organizing ideas to some degree but are not the best choice.	Essay exercises can tap understanding of relationships among elements of knowledge.	Performance tasks that require the use of thinking and reasoning skills can tap understanding of organizing ideas.	Journals, learning logs, interviews, and discussions can provide information about students' understanding of organizing ideas.
Skills	Can assess mastery of the knowledge prerequisite to skillful performance, but cannot rely on these to tap the skill itself	Can observe and evaluate skills as they are being performed (e.g., proficiency in carrying out steps in product development)		Strong match when skill is oral communication proficiency; also can assess mastery of knowledge prerequisite to skillful performance
Reasoning Processes	Can assess application of some patterns of reasoning	Written descriptions of complex problem solutions can provide a window into reasoning proficiency.	Can watch students solve some problems or examine some products and infer about reasoning proficiency	Can ask student to "think aloud" or can ask follow-up questions to probe reasoning
Dispositions	Selected response questionnaire items can tap student feelings.	Open-ended questionnaire items can probe dispositions.	Can infer dispositions from behavior and products	Can talk with students about their feelings

Adapted from Stiggins, R. 1997. *Student-centered classroom assessment.* 2nd ed. Upper Saddle River, NJ: Prentice-Hall.

The key is to match the assessment type to the knowledge, skills, and conceptual understanding that should be assessed. To create a blueprint for a unit, use the template in Appendix Content Strategy 5b that provides spaces to make a list of the key concepts (learning targets), knowledge, and skills. Then determine which assessment tool maps to that learning target. In the template you can jot notes about how many questions to include on the summative assessment, what kind of performance assessment to use, or the actual essay question to ask. Include as much detail as possible.

Performance assessment prompts can be recorded on a separate sheet or on the back of the template. That completed, we need to make sure to include a certain percentage of questions that target

- simpler ideas, facts, and skills presented during instruction;

- more complex conceptual understandings based upon what was taught in class; and

- in-depth inferences and applications that go beyond what was taught in class.

Now is the time to go to assessment resource sites to find some conceptually rich questions. One source of assessment items would be the released NAEP assessment questions, which can be accessed online. Most state departments of education also have a place on their sites for released items and expected student responses. Finally, the National Center for Research on Evaluation, Standards, and Student Testing (CRESST) is another good source for information.

When we are designing our own summative assessment tasks or problems, there are a few important questions teachers should ask:

1. Does this assessment map to important, rigorous content?

2. Is the assessment task cognitively complex?

3. Is this assessment developmentally appropriate?

4. Is the assessment fair for all of my students?

5. Is this assessment meaningful and does it provide sufficient evidence of student understanding?

6. What are the consequences of the assessment?

7. What will I do with the data?

In summary, summative assessments must be designed to reveal what students understand and the student responses must provide evidence of that understanding. To determine if learning with understanding has occurred, summative assessment must measure more than memorization of facts and vocabulary. Most widely used assessments don't effectively assess the complex understanding and skills that cognitive science research indicates are important to determine levels of student understanding.

What Works in Science Classrooms: Implications for Teaching

Recommendation 1: As teachers we tend to design our tests (summative assessments) based upon the summative assessments provided with teachers resources or based on previous tests we have given. The important first step is to determine the key learning targets we want to assess from the broader learning goals and then determine the criteria for success. We have to be clear about what we are looking for and the students also need to know the criteria for success so they will know what they should be learning.

Recommendation 2: Assessment questions should be mapped to the learning goals and learning targets. Once we determine learning goals and targets for a unit of study step two is to create an assessment that assesses for each learning target. This is not something we hope happens but something that needs to be planned for by creating a blueprint for the assessment.

Recommendation 3: Assessment types must be matched to the learning targets. Think about it. Can multiple-choice questions reveal student understanding of concepts? The answer is sometimes yes and frequently no. Being thoughtful about the types of assessments we use is a strategy that should yield higher-quality student evidence of knowledge and conceptual understanding. We can only expect the data from the summative assessment to be as good as the questions, problems and tasks that we design.

Content Strategy 6: Sequencing the Learning Targets Into a Progression

The Issue

Ideas in science are not taught in a coherent way. Evidence from science teacher interviews suggests that teachers rely extensively on textbooks and emphasize "coverage" as the way to decide which learning activities to include in lesson design (Stigler and Heibert 1998). Concepts are stated rather than developed. We feel pressure to prepare students for state assessments, which means trying to cover more information than our students can reasonably learn in a year. This affects the quality of science lessons because the learning experiences often become super-ficial in order to address time constraints. Practical experience shows that direct teaching of concepts that results from too little time does not result in student learning beyond the definition level. Students do not always process this learning into their durable memory, so we are confronted with students who do not retain the learning. Many science ideas appear and disappear from science classes and

Table 2.1
Identifying Important Content

Strategy 1: Identifying Big Ideas and Key Concepts Identify "big ideas," key concepts, knowledge, and skills that describe what the students will understand.	
Strategy 2: Unburdening the Curriculum Prune extraneous subtopics, technical vocabulary, and wasteful repetition.	
Strategy 3: Engaging Students With Content Create essential questions that engage students with the content.	**Why am I doing this?**
Strategy 4: Identifying Preconceptions and Prior Knowledge Identify common preconceptions and prior student knowledge.	**What are the important concepts and scientific ideas included in the lesson?**
Strategy 5: Assessment—How Do You Know That They Learned? Develop assessments that correlate to the conceptual understanding and related knowledge and skills.	
Strategy 6: Sequencing the Learning Targets Into a Progression Clarify and sequence the learning targets into progressions to focus instruction on building conceptual understanding; align learning activities with learning targets.	

the learning experiences do not progress in a coherent fashion. Water, for example, is introduced in a weather unit in an elementary class, then may appear again in a middle school physical science unit, and finally may be found in a high school biology unit. Or students may encounter an idea in second grade and then visit it again in fifth grade and finally in a tenth grade science course. As a result, students feel that they are learning the concepts for the first time each time it is presented and frequently answer our question, "Haven't you studied this before?" with the response, "No, I've never heard about this from my other science teachers." From their perspective, they are giving us accurate feedback. They really did not learn the concepts before and the knowledge and facts that they knew long enough to pass a quiz or test were never stored in their long-term memory.

The DESI Approach

Rather than jumping from topic to topic, teachers must first prune the curriculum (See Content Strategy 2) and then sequence the learning activities to allow enough time to support development of conceptual understanding. To build the conceptual understanding we have to take the learning goals and break them down into learning targets that we can sequence to form unit-based learning progressions. When the literature talks about learning progressions, they usually are referring to the development of student learning across grade bands from K–12 as they progress from novice learners to masters of the concepts. There are also horizontal learning progressions that exist in each of our units of study. Let's dig a little deeper into what learning progressions are, what is to be gained by sequencing learning targets (why we need them), and finally how we build them.

Selected Research That Addresses This Issue

1. Learning progressions are based on research into student learning, and they develop a student's conceptual framework by deepening their understanding in increasingly more sophisticated ways that move students from novice learners to more expert learners about to progress in their demonstrations of understanding. Learning progressions can track student learning across grade levels or it can map out the growth of students' knowledge and understanding within a single unit (Roberts et al. 1997; Wilson and Sloane 2001; Wilson 2005).

2. "A well-constructed learning progression presents a number of opportunities to teachers for instructional planning. It enables teachers to focus on important learning goals in the domain, centering their attention on

what the student will learn rather than what the student will do (i.e., the learning activity). In planning instruction the learning goal is identified first, and the sequence of activities or experiences that teachers will use to enable students to meet the goal is connected to the goal. Consequently, the all too common practice of learning being activity driven rather than driven by the learning goal is avoided." (Heritage 2008, p. 4)

What Is the Strategy?

For this strategy, there are some clear steps that need to be followed before we can sequence learning activities to develop conceptual understanding. Various parts of this process have already been addressed in the earlier content strategy explanations so this is not a completely new process. The steps are listed below in Table 2.7.

Remember that our goal here is to develop learning progressions that help plan useful and effective instruction. Work to build learning progressions for the big ideas in all of the disciplines of science is currently underway. While that work is taking place with the help of science education researchers, we can still use the AAAS Project 2061 strand maps contained in the two volumes of *Atlas of Science Literacy* as a starting point. Sequencing the learning targets can help close the learning gaps for students by providing a pathway for them to progress. The most important part of the process is aligning the learning activities with the learning targets. As a teacher who taught for almost three decades, I, like many other teachers, had files full of activities to choose from. For newer science teachers, review the activities that have been provided as part of the district curriculum and those activities provided in the kit-based materials and textbook-based materials and through online resources. As explained in the research from Gooding (1990) and Goodwin (2000), scientific concepts are never developed without participation in specialized forms of practice, such as creating instruments, inventing representational systems, or developing models. What they discovered is that the kinds of activities we provide can greatly enhance students' scientific knowledge. Engaging students

Table 2.7
Steps for Sequencing Learning Targets Into Learning Progressions

1. Unpack the key concepts to identify the individual learning targets included in the key concepts for your unit of study (see Content Strategy 1).

2. Identify the criteria for success for each learning target by determining the student learning performances.

3. Sequence the learning targets to develop student comprehension of the learning goals (key concepts) in ways that build sophistication of student understanding.

4. Match learning activities to learning targets and their related learning performances.

with nonlinguistic representations, asking them to compare and contrast, asking students to predict and hypothesize (Marzano, Pickering, and Pollack 2001), creating models, and critiquing the results gathered from data collection all increase the likelihood that learning will be improved. So to improve instruction you must align quality learning activities with the learning targets. If the activities are not just activities for activities' sake, then we stand a greater chance of intellectually engaging students with the important ideas.

Exploring the Strategy

Let's look at an example using a portion of the Diversity of Life strand map (AAAS 2007). Referring to the steps in the process listed in Table 2.7, we will start with the unit big ideas and the key concepts (learning goals) that are part of the topic of diversity of life. Remember that these are not the big ideas that are central to the science domains but rather these big ideas represent the conceptual understanding that we want for our students. For our example, the key concepts come from the *Atlas* strand map document shown in Figure 2.5, and the learning targets and learning activities criteria are adapted from the work of Catley, Lehrer, and Reiser (2005), who proposed a learning progression for developing student understanding of evolution. The concepts related to diversity and survival are represented in Figure 2.6 (p. 74). Key to this document is the alignment of the learning activities that map to the sequenced learning targets.

Why do we need progressions? Within this sample progression, the learning targets are sequenced to develop students' conceptual understanding of the broader key concepts (learning goals). First, lessons that are coherent and build from one lesson to the next help students learn. Second, creating the learning target progressions focuses the instruction in our own minds so that we can make the learning goals clear to both our students and their parents. Third, this allows us to prune away unnecessary learning targets and unnecessary or repetitious learning activities. Finally, when we find out what students already know by assessing their prior knowledge, then we know where to begin instruction with our students.

Planning for Classroom Implementation

We did a little bit of this work using Content Strategy 4, where we referenced resources to find out what students' prior understandings should be. The reason this is important now is to remind us that we are not just developing basic student understanding of an individual science concept. The larger goal is to link ideas from year to year to develop a deeper and more sophisticated conceptual under-

Figure 2.5
Strand Map Example

Diversity of Life

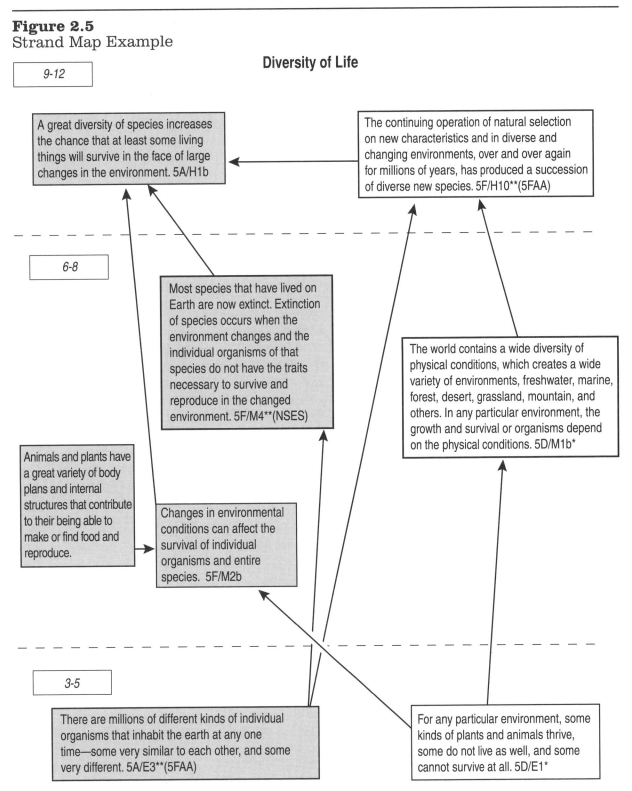

9-12

A great diversity of species increases the chance that at least some living things will survive in the face of large changes in the environment. 5A/H1b

The continuing operation of natural selection on new characteristics and in diverse and changing environments, over and over again for millions of years, has produced a succession of diverse new species. 5F/H10**(5FAA)

6-8

Most species that have lived on Earth are now extinct. Extinction of species occurs when the environment changes and the individual organisms of that species do not have the traits necessary to survive and reproduce in the changed environment. 5F/M4**(NSES)

The world contains a wide diversity of physical conditions, which creates a wide variety of environments, freshwater, marine, forest, desert, grassland, mountain, and others. In any particular environment, the growth and survival or organisms depend on the physical conditions. 5D/M1b*

Animals and plants have a great variety of body plans and internal structures that contribute to their being able to make or find food and reproduce.

Changes in environmental conditions can affect the survival of individual organisms and entire species. 5F/M2b

3-5

There are millions of different kinds of individual organisms that inhabit the earth at any one time—some very similar to each other, and some very different. 5A/E3**(5FAA)

For any particular environment, some kinds of plants and animals thrive, some do not live as well, and some cannot survive at all. 5D/E1*

American Association for the Advancement of Science (AAAS). 2007. *Atlas of Science Literacy,* volume 2. Reprinted with permission.

Figure 2.6
Concepts Related to Diversity and Survival

Big Ideas	Key Concepts	Learning Targets	Learning Activities
Diversity: Diversity of species, diversity within species and diversity of habitats **Survival**: Populations of organisms are likely to affect other populations that live in that habitat. Changes in habitats affect the ecology and thus the chance that organisms will survive and replicate.	The world contains a wide diversity of physical conditions, which creates a variety of environments: freshwater, marine, forest, desert, grassland, mountain, and others. In any particular environment the growth and survival of organisms depend on the physical conditions. Changes in environmental conditions can affect the survival of individual organisms and entire species. Most species that have lived on Earth are now extinct. Extinction of species occurs when the environment changes and the individual organisms of that species do not have the traits necessary to survive and reproduce in the changed environment.	1. Different environments occur due to the physical conditions that exist (i.e., precipitation, temperature, elevation). 2. Organisms are adapted to living in particular environments based on their structures and the conditions. 3. Competition for limited resources (food, water, or space) can occur between organisms with similar needs. 4. Competition occurs between kinds of organisms and within a population. 5. Such competition for resources remains stable in a healthy environment; however changes in the environment can disrupt this stability. 6. The variation between members of a population result in some organisms having an advantage over others and so survive to mature and reproduce. 7. Changes in environmental conditions can introduce environmental stress or pressure on organisms, affecting survival of individuals or species.	Students *compare* and *contrast* environmental conditions that exist in different ecosystems. Students *predict* how variations of a trait might affect an organism's chances of surviving in an environment. Students *identify* competitors and *analyze* data that measures population levels to identify which species are competitors and for what resources. Students *analyze* population level data and *explain* the changes over time due to the introduction of a new competitor in the environment. Students *analyze* data to discover changes in the distribution of the variations of a trait within a population, as the result of an environmental stress. Students *construct* and *present/defend* an explanation about how an environmental stress will affect the variations of a trait in future generations of a population. Students *construct, revise, present/defend,* and *critique* explanations about how the variations in traits of a single species give some individuals advantages over others in surviving an environmental stress and in reproduction.

standing. If we do not know the learning progressions that surround the big ideas in science, we won't know what to look for when asking students about their ideas and prior knowledge and we won't know what is appropriate for students at the grade levels that we teach.

For our purposes, we want to make sure that we are creating clear learning progressions for each of our units of study. To do that, we need to know the starting point of the learning progression and when the students will have had sufficient opportunities to learn so that we can assess their understanding of the big ideas and key concepts. Once the progression has been created, we can then match the learning activities to the progression of learning targets.

This takes practice and requires us to think about our own thinking to prioritize the learning targets. A blank template is provided in the Appendix for Content Strategy 6 to try this yourself. Don't get discouraged. Determining a clear sequence is not easy. We have to keep in mind the findings from the cognitive research into students' ideas. We have to check for prior student understanding and possible preconceptions. We need to refer to state and district standards to guide our choices. And finally, we need to rely on our own expertise as science teachers to know what is appropriate for our students in the context in which we work. Developing learning trajectories (progressions) that make connections for students moves us from trying to cover everything to trying to cover what is really important.

What Works in Science Classrooms: Implications for Teaching

Recommendation 1: The big ideas and key concepts for our unit need to be unpacked in ways that reveal the learning targets. Key concepts are actually several ideas that, together, make a larger understanding. So, we need to identify the individual learning targets embedded in the key concepts before they can be organized into a sequence.

Recommendation 2: The learning targets themselves are best learned instructionally in ways that ask students to think and reason. This includes opportunities for students to compare, predict, analyze and critique evidence. The criteria for success—how we know that the students understand the learning target—and also the goal itself should be identified both for our use and for our students. We need to be explicit with this information so that it is not a mystery. Students should know what to work on and how to progress.

Recommendation 3: The learning targets should be sequenced to build the conceptual framework of a unit of study. Sequencing the learning targets is a critical step to support all of our students on the learning continuum. Some students will struggle with the first learning target in the sequence while others will be at learning target four. Identifying smaller steps that lead from one to the next breaks the learning goal down in ways that make the overall big ideas attainable. If we only share the big ideas and key concepts with students, many of them think that the science concepts are too hard and they give up. Knowing where they are heading and the steps they will take makes the learning more attainable for students and moves them along the trajectory (progression).

Recommendation 4: All activities are not created equally. Some merely ask students to fill in data charts and others ask them to identify facts and vocabulary without applying their work to learning about the important concepts. Every learning activity we select must be aligned to the learning targets and the conceptual understanding in the activity should help them think about the science ideas. So once again, the learning activities need to be more than activities for activities' sake. Look at the lesson activities that you have available and think about how to change them so that the conceptual learning is the focus.

Understanding

This chapter focuses on strategies you can use as you work with your students to develop their understanding of science concepts. In Chapter 2 we learned about identifying the right content and in Chapter 4 you will learn about creating a collaborative learning environment in the classroom. After reviewing the research on effective science instruction, we are recommending six instructional strategies that help develop student understanding. Table 3.1 provides an overview of all of the strategies. Remember, the strategies help you focus on the question "Who is working harder?" Your lessons should be structured such that the answer is "The students!" As a result of this chapter, we hope you will understand the suggested strategies for developing student understanding and be able to apply them to your classroom. In thinking about what you do already to support a learner-centered classroom, we hope the ideas presented will be useful as you strive to improve students' conceptual understanding.

Understanding Strategy 1:
Engaging Students in Science Inquiry

The Issue

Learning science is often confusing for our students. Much of what we teach must be modeled for students because direct observations of the science phenomena are not possible. For example, studying the chemical and physical changes in matter can require sophisticated technology to provide direct observations, so we use models and diagrams to illustrate the science concepts. Studying populations of organisms and changes in the environment that happen over long periods of time often exceeds the time we have with students so we provide sets of data for stu-

Table 3.1
Developing Student Understanding

Strategy 1: Engaging Students in Science Inquiry Engage students in science inquiry to develop understanding of science concepts and the nature of science.	
Strategy 2: Implementing Formative Assessments Make use of formative assessments to gather feedback on student progress toward understanding.	
Strategy 3: Addressing Preconceptions and Prior Knowledge Build on prior knowledge and address preconceptions.	**Who's working harder?**
Strategy 4: Providing Wrap-Up and Sense-Making Opportunities Provide daily opportunities for wrap-up that support student sense-making.	**A learner-centered classroom is necessary to develop conceptual student understanding.**
Strategy 5: Planning for Collaborative Science Discourse Develop student understanding through collaborative science discourse.	
Strategy 6: Providing Opportunities for Practice, Review, and Revision Teach concepts in depth by allowing students to continually refine their understanding through practice, review, and revision.	

dents to analyze. As novice learners, students can get bogged down in the details of information and develop a superficial knowledge of the science ideas.

The DESI Approach

Using an inquiry approach engages students with the content in meaningful ways. Students learn how scientists develop explanations using evidence, teachers uncover students' existing science conceptions, and students recognize what they understand and what they don't understand. Inquiry-based instruction provides an approach to student learning that goes beyond following a scientific "method" for investigation. Using inquiry instruction rather than telling students about science discoveries allows students to think about, reason, discuss, and make sense of science concepts. One myth about inquiry instruction is that it takes lots of time, specialized equipment, and student-designed experiments. While inquiries may last one class period or stretch across a week, a semester, or even across several years, inquiry instruction as a strategy will engage students with the concepts and will develop student understanding. As you learn more about providing inquiry science instruction and implement it in class, your students will build on their earlier knowledge and progress toward conceptual understanding.

Selected Research Related to the Issue

1. Understanding science is more than just knowing facts. Through scientific inquiry, students can gain new data to change their ideas, deepen their understanding of important scientific principles, and develop important abilities such as reasoning, careful observing, and logical analysis (Minstrell 1989).

2. Inquiry helps students develop an understanding of science concepts; an appreciation of "how we know" what we know in science; an understanding of the nature of science; skills necessary to become independent inquirers about the natural world; the disposition to use the skills, abilities, and attitudes associated with science (NRC 1996).

3. The process of generating and testing hypotheses is a cognitive skill that has the potential of raising student achievement as much as 30 percentiles for a student functioning at the 50th percentile level (Marzano, Pickering, and Pollack 2001).

4. The new [research-based] guidelines [on how students learn] emphasize helping students develop

    *   familiarity with a discipline's concepts, theories, and models;

    *   an understanding of how knowledge is generated and justified; and

    *   an ability to use these understandings to engage in a new inquiry (Donovan and Bransford 2005).

5. "The inquiry mode is a productive way to cultivate understanding of science concepts. Inquiry-based learning

    *   engages students in the lesson and arouses their interest.

    *   promotes teamwork and makes sense out of what seems mystifying.

    *   prepares students to successfully defend findings before an audience of critics" (Layman et al. 1996, p. 21).

6. "Teachers who regularly use guided-inquiry science materials in their classrooms report that students understand science concepts more deeply and thoroughly than students who learn through more traditional methods" (Thier 2002, p. 27).

What Is the Strategy?

We recommend that you implement inquiry teaching methods that focus on the five features of inquiry, as shown in Figure 3.1. Students must learn about scientific inquiries conducted by scientists and learn how to design and implement inquiries that are either teacher-guided, open-ended student inquiries, or something in-between.

To accomplish this, there is not a definite set of steps that you should follow. Some teachers provide the questions for students to investigate and then let them determine the procedure they will use. Others provide the question to study and the data set to analyze. Both of these contain features of inquiries. What some teachers don't realize is that they already provide many of the features of inquiry teaching in their classrooms. Open-ended, inquiry-oriented teaching takes the form of long-term investigations in which students revise their approaches; defend their lines of argument (usually in groups) over a period of days, week, and months; then make collective decisions about how to present their results. This is possible in kindergarten to senior level high school classrooms. What is critical, however, is that you have an understanding of what inquiry is and is not and figure out ways to appropriately include inquiry-based methods into your lessons. Figure 3.1 includes the five features of inquiry. If you implement the variations on the left, the inquiry will be more open-ended. If you use the variations on the right, the inquiry will be more guided. When we start to include inquiry-based teaching and learning, we can start by teaching students how to ask scientific questions. We can begin by providing a question and helping students recognize why it is a "scientific" question. (Remember, not all questions can be studied scientifically. For example, "Are all people basically good?" is not a scientific question.) Students also need experience writing questions and converting some into scientific questions.

Many teachers have different beliefs about what it means to have a classroom that is inquiry-based. As a result, several myths about inquiry-based learning and teaching have developed. More about these myths can be found in the *Inquiry and the National Science Education Standards* (NRC 2000) publication. The five common myths discussed are summarized below.

Myth 1: All science subject matter should be taught through inquiry.

This myth stems from the thought that if inquiry helps develop student understanding then we should teach all science using inquiry. From research into effective science instruction, we know that using a variety of methods is the best approach, and balancing hands-on inquiry instruction with direct instruction helps

Figure 3.1
Five Essential Features of Inquiry

Essential Features	More Self-Direction and Less Teacher Direction	Variations		Less Self-Direction and More Teacher Direction
1. Learner engages in scientifically oriented questions.	Learner poses a question.	Learner selects among questions, poses new questions.	Learner sharpens or clarifies question provided by teacher, materials, or other source.	Learner engages in question provided by teacher, materials, or other source.
2. Learner gives priority to evidence in responding to questions.	Learner determines what constitutes evidence and collects it.	Learner directed to collect certain data.	Learner given data and asked to analyze.	Learner given data and told how to analyze.
3. Learner formulates explanations from evidence.	Learner formulates explanation after summarizing evidence.	Learner guided in process of formulating explanations from evidence.	Learner given possible ways to use evidence to formulate explanation.	Learner provided with evidence.
4. Learner connects explanations to scientific knowledge.	Learner independently examines other resources and forms the links to explanations.	Learner directed toward areas and sources of scientific knowledge.	Learner given possible connections.	Learner given connections.
5. Learner communicates and justifies explanations.	Learner forms reasonable and logical argument to communicate explanations.	Learner coached in development of communication.	Learner provided broad guidelines to use to sharpen communication.	Learner given steps and procedures for communication.

Adapted from National Research Council (NRC). 2000. *Inquiry and the National Science Education Standards.* Washington, DC: National Academy Press.

students learn (Banilower et al. 2008). We also have time and practical constraints that would not make it feasible to use only inquiry.

Myth 2: True inquiry occurs only when students generate and pursue their own questions.

When we review the five features of inquiry, the first feature is that the "learner engages in scientifically oriented questions." The questions can come from the teacher, the class, or individual students. All inquiries begin with a question that can be studied by gathering and interpreting evidence but students do not need to come up with their own question unless they are designing their own investigation.

Myth 3: Inquiry teaching occurs easily with hands-on or kit-based instructional materials.

As teachers we need to go beyond the kits and activities to determine if the learning goals are clear both to us and to our students. Once the goals are clear, do the hands-on activities adequately address the goals? Additionally, we need to review the hands-on materials to see if the five features of inquiry are addressed. Hands-on does not equal inquiry-based.

Myth 4: Student engagement in hands-on activities guarantees that inquiry teaching and learning are occurring.

Hands-on activities tend to engage students but inquiry engages students with the materials and intellectually with the science ideas. Hands-on sometimes results in playing with the equipment but does not always focus students with the question being studied.

Myth 5: Inquiry can be taught without attention to subject matter.

Since students start with what they know and their ideas, inquiries should be designed to get students to inquire into questions about content that they do not know. This can only happen by linking content to the learning about inquiry (NRC 2000).

Exploring the Strategy

There is an increasing number of research studies on the effectiveness of inquiry as an instructional strategy. *How Students Learn: Science in the Classroom* (Donovan and Bransford 2005) provides detailed information about the current research findings on scientific inquiry and how people learn. Before you plan for how to make your lessons more inquiry-based, review the essential features of classroom inquiry included in Figure 3.1 (p. 81). Think about why is it essential for us to vary classroom inquiry to support student understanding.

As we mentioned earlier, inquiry instruction is not the same as teaching students a scientific method where students follow a prescribed set of steps. To more accurately capture the work of scientists into a visual representation, look at the inquiry wheel included in Figure 3.2 (p. 84).

The inquiry wheel features questions at the center of the wheel. This shows the inquiry process to be more of an iterative activity as compared to a "scientific method," which usually identifies a series of steps. In the inquiry wheel, student scientists may identify their scientific questions and then move to gathering background information to determine what is known. With this information they may need to go back and revise their scientific questions. At each point on the wheel, with more information, they may need to return to another part of the inquiry and revise it. To learn more about the role of inquiry in the development of conceptual understanding, let's look at an example of an inquiry physical science investigation using toy cars. This lesson would be used in a unit on force and motion, and the intended student population would be middle school students. If you teach at the elementary level, students can look at the position and motion of objects and you can use toy cars. At the high school level, the laws of motion can be used to calculate precisely the effects of forces on the motion of objects. Continuing with our middle school model, we suggest that before looking at the inquiry lesson, we must review the science standards and learning goals related to this investigation. Table 3.2 (p. 85) includes the Sample Unit Plan on Force and Motion.

To begin the inquiry, we want to give students a chance to explore and make some initial observations. We also want them to think about what they know and understand about velocity. From there we can get them to ask questions and determine a problem that they want to investigate. (For example, does the velocity of the toy car remain constant? Does the velocity change if the surface upon which it travels changes? Does the velocity change if the car travels up an incline or down a decline path?)

In this inquiry investigation students get to determine their own question to investigate. (Refer to Figure 3.3, p.86, for a copy of the inquiry.) They also make predictions based on their prior knowledge and initial observations. The students then determine what data to collect and they record the data when they conduct the experiment. With the discussion and group presentations using white boards, students develop explanations from the evidence, then communicate and justify

Figure 3.2
The Inquiry Wheel

Scientific investigations all begin with a question but do not necessarily test a hypothesis!

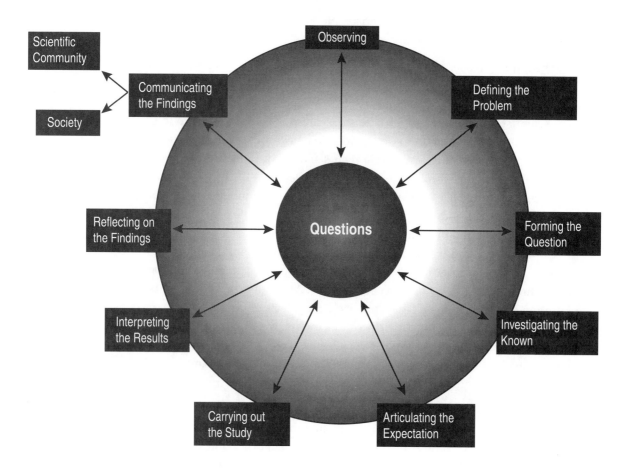

From Reiff, R., W. S. Harwoodk, and T. Phillipson. 2002. A Scientific method based upon research scientists' conceptions of scientific inquiry. In *Proceedings of the Annual International Conference of the Association for the Education of Teachers in Science (Charlotte, NC, January 10-13, 2002)*, eds. P. A. Rubba, J. A. Rye, W. J. DiBiase, and B. A. Crawford. Pittsburgh: AETS. Reprinted with permission of the authors.

Table 3.2
Sample Unit Plan on Force and Motion

Title: Force and Motion
Standards (Benchmarks): Grade 5–8 NSES on Motion and Forces The motion of an object can be described by its position, direction of motion, and speed. That motion can be measured and represented on a graph.
Step 1. Content
Big Idea The motion of an object can be described by its position, direction of motion, and speed.
Key Concepts Motion is described by referring to the relative position of an object with respect to time. The rate of motion is described as a change in position per unit time and the direction that it is moving is known as an object's velocity not its speed. An object moving with a constant velocity has a uniform change in position with respect to time and, therefore, has a velocity that does not change.
Essential Questions Does a car with the cruise control set move with a constant velocity?

Prior Knowledge	**Preconceptions**
• The position of an object can be described by determining its location in relationship to another object. • The motion of an object can be described by tracing and measuring its position over time.	• Time interval and instant of time are not the same thing. • Velocity and speed are not the same. • Concepts of distance, velocity, and acceleration are often confused with one another.
Facts/Knowledge	**Skills**
• Position is where an object is at that moment in time. • Speed is how fast something is moving and can be measured by dividing the distance it moved by the time it took to move that distance.	• Designing an open-ended inquiry • Measuring distance and time • Graphing • Interpreting position v. time, and velocity v. time graphs • Preparing nonlinguistic representations of observations • Develop explanations based on evidence

Step 2. Assessment and Evidence of Learning
Student is able to analyze and discuss multiple representations of the constant velocity model including graphical and diagrammatic representations. Given a toy car that moves at a constant velocity, the student will be able to predict at what position the car will be at a given time and then demonstrate success by running the car in the lab. Written post-unit assessment.
Step 3. High-Quality Instructional Activities—These should be matched to the key concepts, knowledge, and skills and sequenced to develop conceptual understanding.

Figure 3.3
Sample Inquiry Activity

Background Information: The toy cars are battery powered and there is a switch at the front of the car to turn it on or off.

Observations: Turn on the car and let it move across the table and record your observations.

Variables: Identify variables that you could test in an inquiry designed to investigate the motion of the toy car.

Materials: Stopwatches, masking tape, toy car, measuring tape or metersticks

Procedure: In groups no larger than three people, prepare an experimental design diagram (EDD) and provide it to the instructor for approval before conducting the experiment. Once approved, begin the experiment and collect data.

Note: Adapted from *Students and Research* by J. Cothron, R. Giese, and R. Rezba, 1989. Copyright 1989 by Kendall/Hunt Publishing CO. Adapted with permission.

Experimental Design Diagram			
Title:			
Hypothesis:			
Independent Variable:			
(levels of IV including the control)			
(number of trials)			
Dependent Variable:			
Constants:			

Discussion Questions:

- What were the findings of your group?
- Was your hypothesis supported?
- What possible explanation can you offer for the findings?
- What recommendations do you have for further investigations?

Post-lab Discussion: Prepare a whiteboard that includes a diagram of your group's experiment, a data table, and a graph. Be sure your group has answered the discussion questions. On the whiteboard, provide

- simple diagrams
- a data table with average values only
- a rough graph with minimum and maximum values only and a best fit line

Notes from the post-lab discussion: Summary of your understanding of constant velocity:

From Tuomi, J., A. Tweed, and H. Hein. 2005. *Designing effective science lessons: Developing student understanding, participant manual* 18. Denver, CO: Mid-continent Research for Education and Learning (McREL). Copyright 2005 by McREL. Reprinted with permission.

their explanations to the class. Finally, students are asked to summarize their thinking after a facilitated discussion to determine how their explanations now connect to the scientific viewpoint.

Throughout the inquiry, students are thinking like scientists would, they are intellectually engaged with the science concept, and they are practicing the essential features of classroom inquiry. Since learning is basically a social activity (meaning they need time to interact with one another). Posing questions, discussing ideas, and justifying and presenting logical arguments combine to help students develop understanding of the concept of constant velocity.

Planning for Classroom Implementation

Clarifying the characteristics of inquiry and the work of scientists provides a start for our students to think and act scientifically. Additionally, there are several specific things that we need to practice doing that support our inquiry-based learning and teaching strategy. These suggestions can be addressed at all grade levels. Students will not understand these ideas unless we teach them. We will expand on this in Chapter 4 when we review the strategy on thinking scientifically.

Inquiry Instruction and Scientific Thinking

- Scientific investigations all begin with a question but do not necessarily test a hypothesis.

- There is no single set and sequence of steps followed in all scientific investigations (i.e., there is no single scientific method).

- Inquiry procedures are guided by the question asked.

- All scientists performing the same procedures may not get the same results.

- Research conclusions must be consistent with the data collected.

- Inference and observation are not the same thing. Scientists use inferences and observations when developing explanations (Lederman and Lederman 2004).

Inquiry learning activities, whether they are guided inquiries or open-ended inquiries, give students a series of experiences that challenge their thinking. By exploring concepts, students are better able to think about their understanding so that they can analyze and interpret data, synthesize their ideas, build models, and clarify their conceptual understanding.

What Works in Science Classrooms: Implications for Teaching

Recommendation 1: Students learn concepts better when they experience something by engaging in an inquiry rather than reading about it or hearing a lecture. When students work like scientists, they use language to organize, recognize, and internalize the concepts and information they encounter. Because students ask questions and discuss their results, inquiry activities help students engage in explanatory talk that promotes understanding.

Recommendation 2: In a unit of study, you should choose those concepts that are difficult for students to understand and teach them using inquiry instruction. This way we can involve students in scientific questions, completing an investigation that connects to their existing ideas, answering the question, and presenting and discussing their results with others. Through observation, manipulation of variables and discussion of results, students will reveal their thinking, make sense of the learning, and develop conceptual understanding that can be applied to new learning experiences.

Understanding Strategy 2: Implementing Formative Assessments

The Issue

Students learn at different rates and bring different background understanding with them to class. As a result, the learning gaps between where students are and where we want them to be differ. The problem is our lessons don't usually take this into account and most lessons are taught assuming that students start with basically the same background. Sometimes teachers even teach concepts that the students already understand, but if we don't check for prior understanding, we won't know that and won't plan accordingly.

The DESI Approach

We recommend implementing formative assessment processes that provide the teacher with feedback about student understanding. Taking the feedback into account, we can plan for additional learning experiences that meet our students' needs. Formative assessment of student learning can be incorporated into any les-

Table 3.1
Developing Student Understanding

Strategy 1: Engaging Students in Science Inquiry Engage students in science inquiry to develop understanding of science concepts and the nature of science.	
Strategy 2: Implementing Formative Assessments Make use of formative assessments to gather feedback on student progress toward understanding.	
Strategy 3: Addressing Preconceptions and Prior Knowledge Build on prior knowledge and address preconceptions.	**Who's working harder?**
Strategy 4: Providing Wrap-Up and Sense-Making Opportunities Provide daily opportunities for wrap-up that support student sense-making.	**A learner-centered classroom is necessary to develop conceptual student understanding.**
Strategy 5: Planning for Collaborative Science Discourse Develop student understanding through collaborative science discourse.	
Strategy 6: Providing Opportunities for Practice, Review, and Revision Teach concepts in depth by allowing students to continually refine their understanding through practice, review, and revision.	

son but should be included after teaching a concept. The information generated can be used to inform teaching and learning. Formative assessments can be used before instruction (to determine prior knowledge), during instruction (to determine conceptual progress in thinking), and/or after instruction (to determine readiness for summative assessments.) Obviously we would not generally use the same formative assessment for all of these purposes. There are a variety of methods teachers can use depending upon what works for you and your students.

Selected Research Related to the Issue

1. "Formative assessment includes all those activities undertaken by teachers and students [that] provide information to be used as feedback to modify the teaching and learning activities in which they [teachers and students] are engaged" (Black and Wiliam 1998a, p. 7).

2. In their meta-analysis of formative assessment based research, Black and Wiliam examined 250 studies addressing current classroom practices; student motivation and student participation in assessment practices; learn-

ing theory; specific classroom strategies such as discourse and questioning; and the properties of effective feedback. They found that formative assessments produce significant learning gains with effect sizes ranging between .4 and .7. Effect size expresses the increase or decrease in achievement of the experimental group in standards deviation. A .4 indicates a medium achievement gain and .7 can be considered a large gain which statistically correlates to more than a 20 percentile gain. They found that this is also a strategy that helps low-achieving students more than other strategies and motivates them to learn (Black and Wiliam 1998b).

3. "Improvement by teachers of formative assessment practices will usually involve a significant change in the way they plan and carry out their teaching, so that attempts to force adoption of the same simple recipe by all teachers will not be effective. Success will depend on how each can work out his or her own way of implementing change" (Black and Wiliam 1998b, p. 146).

4. There are four core elements of formative assessment: 1) identifying the "gap," 2) feedback, 3) student involvement, and 4) learning progressions... (Heritage 2007). "[The] purpose of formative assessment is [to provide] the means to identify the gap between a student's current status in learning and some desired educational goal. If the gap is perceived as too large by a student, the goal may be unattainable, resulting in a sense of failure and discouragement on the part of the student. Similarly, if the gap is perceived as too 'small,' closing it might not be worth any individual effort. Hence, to borrow from Goldilocks, formative assessment is a process that needs to identify the 'just right gap'" (Sadler 1989). Educational psychologists call this "just right gap" the zone of proximal development (ZPD) from the principles formulated by Lev Vygotsky.

5. The process of planned formative assessment can be accomplished through the use of "probes" (simple-to-use scenarios) that allow teachers to elicit, interpret, and act on assessment information. This is usually used by teachers to obtain information from the whole class about prior knowledge or progress in learning science. This information is then used to inform interactions with the class as a whole while providing information about individual students (Keeley, Eberle, and Farrin 2005).

What Is the Strategy?

Formative assessment is a process that we can use to inform teaching and learning for us and our students. Formative assessments are not quizzes and tests (which are summative assessments); rather, formative assessment involves actions and probing questions designed to gather two kinds of feedback: the first from students to teachers (prior student knowledge, checking for understanding) and the second from the teacher to the student (using descriptive comments to help student improve). For our purposes, therefore, we are defining formative assessment in terms of a process that involves taking action to improve learning based on student responses (Black 1993; Cowie and Bell 1996; Crooks 2001). Formative assessment is only effective when we use the information for some purpose. Either we need to revise our teaching or we need to provide information to the individual learner that focuses on what they have achieved and what needs to be worked on next. Quizzes and tests can be used formatively if the information informs instruction and is not graded. Some teachers offer "practice" quizzes or pretests to gather formative information.

If we refer back to the selected research, we know that there are several ideas about a formative assessment process that we would like you to think about. When should you implement a formative assessment and how will you go about capturing student responses that you can then use instructionally? Planned formative assessments, like the probes provided in the *Uncovering Students Ideas in Science* (Keeley et al. 2005; 2007; 2008; 2009) allow you to connect student responses to the *National Science Education Standards* and *Benchmarks for Science Literacy* and also provide instructional approaches teachers can use with elementary, middle, and high school students. Most teachers have used formative assessments that they conduct on the fly, which can be characterized as teachers listening, noticing, questioning, and responding in an interactive way. These interactions are usually not planned and can occur at any time with individual students, small groups, or with the whole class. The situations usually arise when we realize that students need help making sense of what they are learning. One of the most important ways that we can use formative assessment is to elicit a student's prior knowledge and understanding (Donovan, Bransford, and Pellegrino 1999). Determining what students know already is a strategy that we described in Chapter 2 when we discussed eliciting student prior knowledge and formative assessment is one way to accomplish this. Think about how you find out about your students' ideas before initiating instruction into a new big idea or key concept. How do you deal with the student responses? Interpreting the evidence (student feedback to the teacher) and determining the learning gaps for each student—where the students are on the learning scale toward achieving the instructional goals (i.e., understanding the big ideas and key concepts or the individual learning goals) is a logical next step for teachers. Using that information, teachers can set the instructional goals that take into account the "just right gap" for each student. We are then able to select instructional strategies and activities to respond to our students and provide scaffolding to assist students as they progress with the learning goals. This is an iterative process and with new feedback from our students, we loop back to figuring out how they are progressing and determining what happens next instructionally.

Think about some formative assessment strategies that you have used effectively. Formative assessment cycles can be short (within a lesson), medium (at the end of a concept), or long (at the end of a unit). Consequently, we use different strategies for different purposes. What is most important is to select formative assessment methods that work for you. We need to use what is comfortable for us, so what works for me may not work for you in the same way.

When building a formative assessment system in the classroom, one of our goals must be to reverse our students' focus on points and grades (i.e., if it isn't going to be scored or given a grade, then students don't want to do it) and create a climate that redirects their interest and effort toward learning. The research on motivation and self-efficacy (students believing in their ability to succeed) suggest that formative assessment practices will build student confidence since they are receiving regular feedback about their learning. The research and our recommended strategy to support motivation is included in Chapter 4. As we help students to be more performance oriented they will develop intrinsic motivation and feel more competent as they master the learning goals and key concepts. Remember that we want to comment on the work that students produce and not comment on the students themselves to reinforce their belief in their capability to learn.

Exploring the Strategy

Formative assessment involves natural questioning and follow-up as teachers interact with students during the course of instruction. The interaction between us and our students is more targeted to specific student needs, in the context of purposeful lessons, and more time efficient because it occurs as a part of normal teaching (Shepard 2001). To develop student understanding in the context of our normal teaching, we have to time the formative assessments at important junctures in the learning. Focusing on significant concepts as students progress allows us to use their feedback to adjust teaching and learning. From years of experience, some teachers can predict student responses to the formative assessments.

There are many good resources available that provide sample methods you can use to identify student uncertainties when it comes to their learning. The process itself asks students to be more metacognitive so that they are aware of what they understand and what is still confusing. As with any strategy we use in class, we want to provide a variety of methods so that students are more positively engaged with the process. Listed below are several examples of methods that can be adapted to your classroom context.

1. **Index Cards.** Instruct students to do the following:

   - *On side 1:* Based on classroom learning experiences, summarize the understanding that you have about the science concepts. What was your "take away" message?

   - *On side 2:* Identify something about the unit (or learning that day) that you do not yet fully understand. Write it as a statement or question.

2. **Socratic Seminar.** Ask students to write down questions that they have about the science concepts at the end of a lesson or the end of a unit. Organize the students into small groups and designate one person as the facilitator to guide the group discussion. Each student can put forth one question to the group for discussion. The teacher can assist any group that needs support.

3. **Hand Signals.** Ask students to display a designated hand signal to indicate their understanding of a specific concept, process, or skill. (This could include thumbs up, side, or down or a show of one to five fingers on a scale.)

4. **Question Box or Board.** Establish a location where students may leave or post questions about concepts, skills, or processes that they do not understand. This can help students who have trouble saying that they don't understand.

5. **Visual Representation.** Ask students to create a (nonlinguistic) visual representation (e.g., web, concept map, flow chart, picture, or diagram) to show the elements or components of a concept or process and how they relate to one another.

6. **Inquiry Questioning.** Examples include the following:

   - Why do you think that?

   - How do you know?

- Could you give me an example?

- What do you mean when you say…

- What data do you have to support your position?
  Tell me more about…

- How might you find out or confirm…

7. **Misconception Check.** Present students with common or predictable misconceptions about a designated concept, process, or principal. Ask them whether they agree or disagree and have them explain why.

8. **White Board Group Presentations.** Allow for student presentation of ideas and conceptual understanding, which lead to classroom discussion that challenges student thinking and understanding. (Remember that white boards are just tools for students to share their ideas.)

9. **3-2-1 Assessment.** Ask students to prepare sticky notes that record

- 3 things that they learned

- 2 things that they don't understand

- 1 question that they still have

Have them post the sticky notes on poster paper as they leave the room. Teachers will then be able to respond to the questions and revise their plan for instruction.

10. **Designing Exam Questions.** Have students design two exam questions. They must provide both the question and the answer to the question AND their explanation of both the correct and incorrect responses.

11. **Scientist's Workshop.** Have students present their experimental design diagram to the class. The rest of the class then asks inquiry questions of the "scientist" as they would in their role as an experimental design detectives (Cothron, Giese, and Rezbe 1989)

12. **Traffic Light Icons.** Students label their work green, amber, or red according to whether they thought they had good, partial, or little understanding. Teachers can also make tents of flags that the students can put on their desk while working in groups to let the teacher know if they are "getting it" or need help.

13. **Posttest as Pretest.** Give the class the end-of-topic test in the first lesson to become informed about what the students already know.

14. **K-W-L.** Use this strategy to record class discussion at the beginning of a unit, record what is learned in the third column during wrap-up sessions, and cross out incorrect "know" statements as students' progress.

15. **"Clickers."** These are handheld computers that allow teachers to ask questions and then record the student responses on a computer. This gives real-time feedback to the teacher and students. Group discussion after the question is more effective. Teachers can do this in a low tech way using note cards with A, B, C, and D on different cards.

One formative assessment strategy that is very effective at determining student understanding is inquiry questioning. This process is mentioned in the previous examples but it is such a useful strategy that we are providing additional information about this model. Figure 3.4 (pp. 96–97) includes the open-ended question stems that can be used to probe for additional information from students. These questions automatically ask students to be metacognitive and to think about their ideas and explanations. This strategy works when asking students about their conceptual understanding.

Students can also use the question stems when they are discussing their ideas with other students in the class. These kinds of questions don't come to mind easily and you and your students will need to practice using them. Depending on the grade level you teach and the content that students are learning, draft some worthwhile questions that allow you to determine student conceptual understanding. Some sample questions are provided below. To implement this formative assessment strategy in class, ask students to pair up. Have one student ask, and the other student answer, open-ended inquiry questions. The answers to the questions lie in their understanding of basic science concepts. Here are some examples:

- Explain what happens when an ice cube falls on the floor and melts. (This reveals what students understand about energy transfer and phase changes of matter.)

- Explain how a lightbulb lights when you turn the wall switch on. (This reveals what students understand about circuits and the flow of electricity.)

- Explain what happens when a low pressure system moves into an area. (This reveals what students know about air currents and their relationship to weather events.)

- If every human being has a similar genetic code that makes them human, explain how each person can have their own "DNA

Figure 3.4
Developing Scientific Thinking With Effective Questions

To help students build confidence and rely on their own understanding, ask...
- Why is that true?
- How did you reach that conclusion?
- Does that make sense?
- Can you draw a model to show that?

To help students learn to reason scientifically, ask...
- Is that true for all cases? Explain.
- Can you think of a counterexample?
- How would you prove that?
- What assumptions are you making?

To check student progress, ask...
- Can you explain what you have done so far?
- Why did you decide to use this procedure?
- Can you think of another procedure that might have worked?
- Is there a more efficient strategy?
- What do you notice when...?
- Why did you decide to organize your results like that?
- How do you think this would work if you changed the variable being tested?
- Have you thought of all the possibilities? How can you be sure?

To help students collectively make sense of science, ask...
- What do you think about what _____ said?
- Do the rest of you agree? Why or why not?
- Does anyone have the same answer but a different way to explain it?
- Do you understand what _____ is saying?
- Can you explain why your answer makes sense?

To encourage hypothesizing, ask...
- What would happen if...? What if not?
- What are some other possibilities?
- Can you predict what happens if you change the variable?
- What decisions should be made to answer the question?

To promote problem solving, ask...
- What do you need to find out?
- What do you already know?
- What information do you have and what information do you need?
- What strategies are you going to use?
- How will you solve the problem?
- What tools or equipment will you need?
- What do you think the answer or result will be?

Figure 3.4 (cont.)
Developing Scientific Thinking With Effective Questions

To help when students get stuck, ask...
- How would you describe the problem in your own words?
- What data do you have?
- Would it help to create a diagram? Make a data table?
- Have you compared your work to anyone else's work?
- What have you tried? What did other members of your group try?
- What background information do you know that might help you?
- What about putting things in order?
- Could you try your experiment again?

To make connections among ideas and applications, ask...
- How does this relate to...?
- What previous concept understanding connects to this question?
- What science issues did you find in the paper last night?
- Can you give me an example of...?

To encourage reflection, ask...
- How did you get your answer?
- How does you work demonstrate conceptual understanding?
- Does your data seem reasonable? Why or why not?
- Can you describe your procedure to the rest of the class? Can you explain why you got the results that you observed?
- What if you had started with...rather than...?
- What if you could only make observations of...?
- What have you learned or discovered today?
- What are the key concepts or big ideas in this lesson?
- Can you summarize what you learned today?
- Can you create a diagram to show the relationship of the concepts?

Adapted from the PBS Teacherline document *Developing Mathematical Thinking With Effective Questions*, 2004.

fingerprint" that is unique to them. (This reveals what students understand about DNA and how this code determines the proteins that are produced that make up the structure and functioning elements in an organism.)

- What happens to an apple when it falls to the ground and disappears? (This reveals what students understand about decomposers and chemical/physical changes during decomposition.)

Planning for Classroom Implementation

The information generated by formative assessments can be used diagnostically to alter teaching and learning. In a broad sense, these assessments encompass our observations, classroom discussion, and analysis of student work. Because formative assessments require asking students about their ideas, students learn to be more willing to submit their ideas for discussion and be challenged by their peers as well as by teachers. Students have to listen to one another, respect opinions, and understand that learning occurs when thinking is challenged. This promotes a collaborative classroom environment. A further discussion of positive classroom environments is included in Chapter 4.

As you plan for formative assessments, consider the following focus questions:

1. *Are the learning target and the criteria for success clearly identified?* Without this information, the formative assessments will not provide useful feedback.

2. *Do I know what prior knowledge students possess?* It is critical to know where students are in their learning to determine the gap between what they understanding and the learning goal.

3. *Since formative assessments must relate to the learning in the classroom, won't different students be in different places on the learning?* It is unrealistic to expect all students to learn at the same pace. Therefore we need to use formative assessment data to individualize and differentiate instruction for students to address their specific needs.

There are several books available for science teachers that provide formative assessment probes and examples of formative assessment methods. There is the series of four books mentioned earlier that can be used in elementary, middle, or high schools classrooms titled, *Uncovering Student Ideas in Science* (Keeley et al. 2005; 2007; 2008; 2009). Another resource, *Weaving Science Inquiry and Continuous*

Assessment, provides examples that link inquiry and continuous assessment to promote changes in student thinking and learning (O'Brien Carlson, Humphrey, and Reinhardt 2003). A third resource, *Everyday Assessment in the Science Classroom*, provides a collection of ten essays on the value of formative assessment. It is written to build teachers' confidence in their abilities to implement formative assessments into daily class work (Atkin and Coffey 2003). A final resource, *Science Formative Assessments*, provides 75 different formative assessment classroom techniques that can be used with any science curriculum (Keeley 2008).

What Works in Science Classrooms: Implications for Teaching

Recommendation 1: According to the research by John Hattie, feedback should be given in "dollops" (1992, p. 9). This means that when a piece of instruction is completed and conceptual understanding should have occurred, then it is time to formatively assess and gather student feedback that you can respond to with descriptive comments. Some teachers use simple checks for understanding on a more regular basis (i.e., red light, green light or thumbs up, thumbs down) to get a feel for student thinking about their learning. Remember that this is a personal decision and you need to do what works for you.

Recommendation 2: Formative assessment feedback is not useful unless we do something with it. Sometimes the feedback will indicate that students need more opportunities to engage with the ideas and additional instruction is needed. Sometimes, students will need probing questions so that they know what to think about next. Written comments by students clarify the evidence of understanding that is clear in their work but also provides suggestions for what to work on next or where to go for additional resources. Depending upon the feedback that you asked for, your decisions will vary from providing flexible groups in the classrooms to individual discussions and coaching with students. There is no set strategy; our planning and approach will also need to be responsive to the needs of the students.

Table 3.1
Developing Student Understanding

Strategy 1: Engaging Students in Science Inquiry Engage students in science inquiry to develop understanding of science concepts and the nature of science.	
Strategy 2: Implementing Formative Assessments Make use of formative assessments to gather feedback on student progress toward understanding.	
Strategy 3: Addressing Preconceptions and Prior Knowledge Build on prior knowledge and address preconceptions.	**Who's working harder?** A learner-centered classroom is necessary to develop conceptual student understanding.
Strategy 4: Providing Wrap-Up and Sense-Making Opportunities Provide daily opportunities for wrap-up that support student sense-making.	
Strategy 5: Planning for Collaborative Science Discourse Develop student understanding through collaborative science discourse.	
Strategy 6: Providing Opportunities for Practice, Review, and Revision Teach concepts in depth by allowing students to continually refine their understanding through practice, review, and revision.	

Understanding Strategy 3: Addressing Preconceptions and Prior Knowledge

The Issue

Students hold on to science preconceptions (which may be misconceptions) that make sense to them, and these ideas can be difficult to change even in the face of scientific evidence. They get their ideas from a variety of sources and use the information to develop their own personal explanations of how the world works.

The DESI Approach

Student misconceptions (their existing incorrect ideas about science) that are revealed during instruction must be confronted. Using a conceptual change model (Strike and Posner 1985), students are presented with evidence and data that will cause them to reflect on their own ideas and make them dissatisfied with their existing explanations. This is necessary for change to occur. If the scientific explanation does not offer a more plausible explanation, students will hold on to their prior ideas, even when faced with observations and evidence to the contrary. First, we need to be aware of common student misconceptions and then elicit student ideas that are part of their prior knowledge. Next we can provide learning opportunities that cause students to evaluate their ideas and think more deeply about their thinking. Finally, we need to plan for and provide sense-making experiences to bring students to an understanding of the scientific concept.

Selected Research Related to the Issue

Following are highlights from selected research on prior knowledge and misconceptions and their implications for teachers.

1. Understanding means to know relationships, and the ability to know relationships depends on *prior knowledge*.

   - Learning manifests itself through the ability of children to make connections and construct patterns.

   - Children seek patterns as a means of explaining and understanding (Lowery 1990).

2. Students build new knowledge and understanding based on what they already know and believe. Many learners' preconceptions, however, are inconsistent with the accepted scientific explanations. These preconceptions are

   - ideas that seem reasonable and appropriate from the student perspective and may apply in a limited context, but

   - students inappropriately apply them to situations where they do not work (Driver et al. 1994).

3. Changing students' naive preconceptions can occur using a conceptual change strategy. In order for the change to occur, the following conditions are necessary:

   - The students must be dissatisfied with their existing views.

   - The new conception must appear somewhat plausible.

   - The new conception must be more attractive.

   - The new conception must have explanatory and predictive power (Strike and Posner 1985).

4. *How People Learn* emphasizes that instruction in any subject matter that does not explicitly address students' everyday conceptions typically fails to help them refine or replace these conceptions with others that are scientifically more accurate (Donovan, Bransford, and Pellegrino 2005).

5. The current perspective on the process of conceptual change finds that students add and restructure their ideas and do not just replace their prior understanding with a new understanding. The process itself is iterative and includes sometimes dramatic and sudden restructuring of student knowledge. The research also found that students will deal with information that does not match their existing models in different ways. And presenting the learner with the correct conceptual explanation doesn't result in conceptual change. Restructuring of student knowledge happens through adding, replacing, and revising relationships and shifting categories of ideas. So prior knowledge and misconceptions (preconceptions) must be acknowledged to build a student's understanding of scientific concepts (Zimmerman and Stage 2008).

What Is the Strategy?

The research basis for *How People Learn* is very clear about the need for us to address prior knowledge and preconceptions. When learning science, students' everyday experiences often reinforce conceptions of phenomena that contain faulty reasoning and are often contrary to scientific reasoning. For example, if you ask a person, "If air particles are widely spaced apart, what lies between air particles?" they often give the answer of "more air" since their common sense tells them that we would suffocate if there was just empty space.

It is important for us to uncover students' prior knowledge and preconceptions. If they are not addressed during the unit of study, the preconceptions that students have "may lead them to simply not notice, quickly dismiss, or not believe what they do not expect to see" (Magnusson and Palinscar 2005, p. 425). If you discuss this with other teachers, you would probably discover that this is a common occurrence. Students will stick to their own explanations, since their experiences support their ideas. Arguing with or debating students is not a particularly successful strategy and may even disrupt a positive classroom climate. What can we do to respond to the incorrect conceptions of our students?

We recommend the following four steps from the research to address student preconceptions (or research-based misconceptions) once the learning goals for the lesson are clear:

- **Step 1.** Determine common research-based student misconceptions.

- **Step 2.** Elicit students' ideas that are part of their prior knowledge.

- **Step 3.** Provide learning opportunities that cause students to evaluate their ideas and think about their thinking.

- **Step 4.** Plan for and provide sense-making experiences to bring students to an understanding of the scientific concept.

Even though we provide this information as steps for us to consider, the entire approach to teaching for understanding is not this straightforward. Knowing about the research into children's ideas helps us understand how our students think. Getting students to make their thinking visible reveals how their ideas match with the research into the ideas that children hold about the natural world. From this point, we need to use a variety of instructional activities to meet the challenge of addressing student preconceptions.

Exploring the Strategy

Once teachers identify common student preconceptions, they also have to plan for how to address them. To implement science teaching that develops conceptual understanding, we must help students go from everyday ways of talking to scientific talking. For example, if you ask students why a dropped ball falls to the earth, they may express their everyday view that the ball falls because it is heavy. The scientific view would be that the ball falls because of the gravitational pull of the Earth. So the concept that needs to be developed is gravity, not heaviness. It takes many more learning experiences to help students understand concepts that don't make common sense to them. For example, students have trouble with the three states of water. Their mental models of solids, liquids, and gases lead them to conclude that solids have particles that are more closely packed so solids must have greater densities than liquids and gases. In the case of water, ice (solid water) floats in water (liquid), so it must be less dense. Observations that are contrary to our general observations of the world around us often lead to misconceptions.

The video *A Private Universe*, produced by the Harvard-Smithsonian Center for Astrophysics (1987), is a good source of examples for us to study that both captures students' existing ideas and suggests ways to confront their thinking. The video clips investigate common preconceptions/misconceptions that seem to persist even though teachers taught the scientific viewpoints. In the companion video, *Minds of Our Own*, produced by the Harvard-Smithsonian Center for Astrophysics (1997), students defend their thinking and reveal how they came to their incorrect

Figure 3.5
"Can You See the Apple?"
Vignette

One clip from the video *A Private Universe* identifies the learning concepts of light, light transmission, and the absence of light. In the clip, a student is asked if she has had prior experiences in a totally dark space and the girl answers and explains her prior experiences. She then joined the interviewer in a room that is totally dark and in which no light can enter from the doors or windows. The student is asked: "Can you see the apple in the dark?" She replies, "Yes, when my eyes adjust." What are the steps that the interviewer followed?

- First the interviewer was clear about the learning goal and then elicited the student's ideas about vision and darkness.
- From her response, he identified her misconception that she could see objects in the dark. By definition, darkness means an absence of all light so there would be no light being reflected that can be seen by the eye.
- To confront her idea, the interviewer set up a room that was totally dark with an apple and conducted the experiment with the student.
- When confronted with the dark room the girl still suggested that if she waited long enough, her eyes would adjust.
- After a significant period of time she reflected that maybe her idea wasn't correct, but because it was based on years of experience with rooms that had low levels of light, she was resistant to change her thinking.

What would you do next to help this student understand how we see and the role of light to vision?

conceptions. One classic clip from the video identifies the learning concepts as light, light transmission, and the absence of light. In the clip, a student is asked if she has had prior experiences in a totally dark space, and the girl answers and explains her prior experiences. She is then asked to imagine that she is sitting in a dark room with a red apple on the table in front of her. The question posed is "Can you still see the apple in a dark room?" Refer to Figure 3.5 to learn what happens. In this example, as with others in the video, the steps listed earlier are modeled for us.

To review the steps, in this example we had the learning target identified for us. Students were then asked to share their understanding of the concepts and provide an explanation using their own evidence. Finally, the girl was asked to reflect on her thinking in light of new experiences that were designed to confront her misconceptions. Even with the new experience, some misconceptions persisted. She wasn't ready to give up her ideas with just the one experience. In those cases we need to include additional learning opportunities and sense-making discussions or activities. A physical science assessment probe on this same misconception is provided in *Uncovering Student Ideas in Science: 25 Formative Assessment Probes, Volume 1* (Keeley, Eberle, and Farrin 2005). Using formative assessment probes is another way to address student preconceptions (misconceptions). Even though student ideas can contain misconceptions, we usually refer to them as preconceptions. The word *misconception* denotes an error in thinking about the science concept, while *preconception* is often more accurate, since the ideas arose from their own experiences and without formal science instruction. There now exist many probing formative assessments designed to reveal student ideas. Remember that gathering this information is just one of the first steps. We can't ignore the fact that some students don't "get it." We then need to use the information to plan learning that helps students to be self-aware of their ideas in relation to scientific ideas.

In the Harvard study, the researchers interviewed hundreds of children and adults over years and discovered that regardless of age or training, people held misconceptions concerning fundamental science concepts. These concepts included the cause of the Moon phases and the seasons. In the interviews, the researchers noticed that some "private theories" were particularly common. None of us are immune to having misconceptions, either as adults or as teachers. The study found that even with coursework and experience, elementary, middle, and high school science teachers also hold misconceptions similar to those addressed in the video. This is because, like our students, we also have personal theories.

Simply telling a student the "right answer" is not enough. We have to show them, provide opportunities to confront their ideas so they can prove it to themselves. (To learn more about this research, the video [1987] survey questions and viewer's guide from Annenberg Media are available in the resources section.) Remember to refer to the content strategy on identifying prior knowledge and misconceptions for references that identify research into children's ideas.

We know that students learn from one another. They can also be motivated to learn the new concepts when we select examples and use techniques that are relevant to them. Making local connections and asking them to make predictions or choose a "side" of a debate contributes to their personal engagement with the learning. Using technology tools, including Web 2.0 resources provides the additional learning experiences that many students need and leads to sense-making discussions. More about sense-making will be provided later in this chapter.

Planning for Classroom Implementation

We must provide learning experiences that allow students to make connections to their prior learning experiences so that they can make sense of the new learning. When we use exploratory or inquiry lessons, learning experiences can be connected back to prior knowledge (student preconceptions) to help students construct mental models that help them make sense of the concepts. Students often hold onto their preconceptions so tightly that their understanding can be resistant to change, particularly in the face of conventional teaching strategies. We must provide opportunities for students to confront their own preconceptions and those of their classmates and then work toward resolution and conceptual change.

Making connections for students is one way that we can successfully address student preconceptions. Using computer animations provides visual information that students can use to compare and connect to their own ideas. Using virtual manipulatives allows students to conduct experiments and manipulate variables over and over again so that they can connect their ideas with their observations. Another powerful way to make connections is through analogies. Teachers can teach using analogies that connect the target learning idea to something that is known and familiar to them (Mason 2004). Biology teachers often help students understand enzymes using the analogy that they function like an old-fashioned bicycle lock and key where the enzyme would be represented by the key. In this example the principal function of the key (to open the lock and separate it into two parts) is like the function of an enzyme (to break apart a molecule or put it back together while the enzyme remains unchanged). A common middle school analogy is to teach that a cell's structures and functions are like a factory. Analogies have limitations and in this case, the analogy does not extend to cell division. Asking students to create a new analogy also connects and reorganizes their ideas to help them understand the targeted learning concept.

What Works in Science Classrooms: Implications for Teaching

Recommendation 1: To address common preconceptions, teachers must identify the key science concepts to be taught, consider the nature of students' existing thinking, analyze the differences between a scientific way of knowing and a student's existing thinking, and plan instruction. The key is to plan instruction that engages the students with the evidence needed to confront their existing "personal theories."

Recommendation 2: Teaching using discrepant events is one way to get students to confront their preconceptions. Discrepant events encourage students to reflect on what they observe and wonder why since the outcome is not what they expected. This tests their current conceptions and prompts discussion related to the new learning experiences. Students must be given the opportunity to resolve conflicts between their original ideas and their observations to develop new conceptual understanding. This can happen with a well-planned inquiry, demonstration, or visual tools that get students to ask why. Figuring out science mysteries that these experiences reveal connects to their previous assumptions and when they do figure out the scientific conception, the new conceptual understanding persists and is retained.

Table 3.1
Developing Student Understanding

Strategy 1: Engaging Students in Science Inquiry Engage students in science inquiry to develop understanding of science concepts and the nature of science.	
Strategy 2: Implementing Formative Assessments Make use of formative assessments to gather feedback on student progress toward understanding.	**Who's working harder?**
Strategy 3: Addressing Preconceptions and Prior Knowledge Build on prior knowledge and address preconceptions.	A learner-centered classroom is necessary to develop conceptual student understanding.
Strategy 4: Providing Wrap-Up and Sense-Making Opportunities Provide daily opportunities for wrap-up that support student sense-making.	
Strategy 5: Planning for Collaborative Science Discourse Develop student understanding through collaborative science discourse.	
Strategy 6: Providing Opportunities for Practice, Review, and Revision Teach concepts in depth by allowing students to continually refine their understanding through practice, review, and revision.	

Understanding Strategy 4: Providing Wrap-Up and Sense-Making Opportunities

The Issue

Too often teachers neglect the importance of sense-making and wrap-up opportunities in quality science instruction. As they try to cram a hands-on activity into a 45-minute class period, sense-making activities are abandoned in an effort to finish the activity and clean up the room. Given these realities, it is even more important for teachers to be intentional about planning and implementing explicit opportunities for student reflection.

The DESI Approach

To aid student learning, teachers need to include both sense-making activities for each new concept and wrap-up activities at the end of each lesson. These activities provide students with opportunities to ascertain the purpose of a given activity, to connect their new learning with their previous knowledge, to consider how their thinking has changed as a result of a lesson, and to apply their new understanding, (Banilower et al. 2008).

Selected Research Related to the Issue

1. Brain research tells us that you can either have your learners' attention or they can be *making meaning,* but never both at the same time. Therefore

   • teachers must allow time for small group discussion,

   • new material must be sorted out, and

   • students must be allowed to ask questions and propose what-if scenarios (Jensen 1998, p. 46).

2. "When children look at phenomena, the sense that is made will be influenced by their existing ideas. Children will focus their observations on what they perceive to be the important factors (which may or may not be those identified by the teacher).... Rather than seeing themselves as passive absorbers of information, pupils need to see themselves as actively engaged in constructing meaning by bringing their prior ideas to bear on new situations." (Driver et al. 1994, p. 7)

3. "Talk [is] central to the *meaning making* process and, thus, central to *learning*.... As the talk proceeds, each participant is able to make sense of what is being communicated, and the words used in the social exchanges provide the very tools needed for individual thinking....Meaning making can be seen to be a fundamentally *dialogic* process, where different ideas are brought together and worked upon. Ultimately the dialogue is always played out in the individuals' head, but this can be in the context of solitary musing over ideas, or face-to-face discussions with another person, or through individual reflection on the ideas presented in a book." (Mortimer and Scott 2003, p. 3)

4. Closure and wrap-up: Those actions or statements by a teacher that are designed to bring a lesson presentation to an appropriate conclusion. Used to help students bring things together in their own minds, to make sense out of what has just been taught. "Any questions? No. OK, let's move on," is not closure. Closure is used

   • to cue students to the fact that they have arrived at an important point in the lesson or the end of a lesson;

   • to help organize student learning;

- to help form a coherent picture, to consolidate, eliminate confusion and frustration; and

- to reinforce the major points to be learned... to help establish the network of thought relationships that provide a number of possibilities for cues for retrieval. Closure is the act of reviewing and clarifying the key points of a lesson, tying them together into a coherent whole, and ensuring their utility in application by securing them in the student's conceptual network (Hunter 1982).

What Is the Strategy?

Incorporating sense-making and wrap-up activities into lessons does not happen by accident. Teachers need to intentionally plan activities that will help students reflect on their learning, and they also need to provide adequate time for students to process what they're learning. Below are some strategies to ensure that students are having ample opportunity for reflection.

- *Articulate the understanding you want students to have.* Consider the old adage "If you don't know where you're going, how will you know when you've arrived?" Before providing opportunities for sense-making, you need to first determine those concepts you most want your students to understand. Focus your teaching here and eliminate extraneous information; students will then have an easier time of zeroing in on what it is you want them to examine.

- *Intentionally plan for sense-making and wrap-up activities.* Incorporating activities into lessons that allow for reflection requires advance planning. As a part of designing a lesson, teachers should plan at least one sense-making activity for each new concept and a wrap-up activity for each day's lesson. These experiences should be designed such that they help students reflect upon and process their learning.

- *Provide adequate time for sense-making and wrap-up activities.* Even teachers with the best of intentions for providing opportunities for reflection find those pieces of the lesson are the first thing to go when they are pressed for time. While omitting the sense-making and wrap-up activities may seem like a quick way to gain some time, in the long run, it costs much more time than it saves. If students don't have the opportunity to connect what they are learning to what they already know and to make sense of the new information, then the instructional time has been wasted. It is also important to keep in mind that sense-making and wrap-up activities do not necessarily require a lot of time. One simple technique is to set a timer that will alert you when there are ten minutes of class remaining; this will provide you with time to clean-up and engage in wrap-up.

- *Gather and reflect on the evidence of student learning.* The quote by Driver et al. (1994) bears repeating, "Children will focus their observations on what they perceive to be the important factors (which may or may not be those identified by the teacher)..." (p. 7). Thus it is crucial that teachers determine that students are in fact making sense of those things that are most important and that they are making the correct sense of those concepts. It is not enough to provide the opportunities for sense-making and wrap-up; you must also ascertain if students are learning what you want them to learn.

Exploring the Strategy

Sense-making and wrap-up activities can take many forms. Here we will explore three broad categories for sense-making and wrap-up: conversations, written reflections, and nonlinguistic representations.

Conversations

As noted earlier, Mortimer and Scott (2003, p. 3) explain that "talk [is] central to the *meaning making* process and, thus, central to *learning*." Presenting students with the occasion for discussing new ideas is one way to help deepen their understanding of the content. For example, the "Think-Pair-Share" strategy, where students think about an answer to a question, pair with a partner, and then share their ideas, is a simple way to provide a space for dialogue in your classroom. You can also use "triads," a conversation structure where groups of three engage in discussion. For example, you might provide various groups with different images, ask each group to discuss the image in terms of the new science content, and then share their ideas with the whole class.

Written Reflections

Students can also make sense of new ideas using written reflections. Many teachers ask their students to keep a Science Journal, where students can record their thoughts about what they are learning. Sometimes, students are provided with a sentence stem such as "One question I have from today is..." or "The most important thing I learned today was..." Another strategy that works particularly well for middle school and high school students is to allow them to pass notes. In other words, ask them to have a written conversation about a question they have regarding new material. For example, one student might write to another student about how she doesn't understand the phases of the Moon. Together, using writing, the two students can work to make meaning of the content.

Nonlinguistic Representations

In *Classroom Instruction That Works*, Marzano, Pickering, and Pollack (2001) identified the use of nonlinguistic representations as having a strong affect on student achievement. By nonlinguistic representations, he means graphic representations, physical models, mental pictures, drawings, pictographs, and kinesthetic activity. Asking students to create their own nonlinguistic representations after a new topic is presented or at the end of a lesson requires them to make meaning of what they are learning.

Planning for Classroom Implementation

Take a moment to consider your own practice. Do you provide your students with sufficient opportunities for sense-making and wrap-up? What are you already doing well? What could you improve on? By increasing the opportunity your students have to engage in reflection, you will be deepening their understanding of scientific concepts. Their learning of science will be about more than just being able to parrot information; it will be about confronting and correcting any preconceptions they have. This deep understanding will be demonstrated when they are able to apply what they have learned.

What Works in Science Classrooms: Implications for Teaching

Recommendation 1: Good science instruction doesn't happen without careful preparation. One important piece of that preparation is to explicitly plan for opportunities for students to reflect. This means both determining specific activities you will ask students to do to make sense of new topics and to conclude the day as well as carving out the time for those activities. Each lesson plan should include answers to these questions: (1) How and when am I providing time for students to make sense of what they are learning throughout the lesson? (2) How will I make sure to leave enough time to wrap-up and what strategy will I use?

Recommendation 2: Engage students in making their own meaning about science. Eleanor Duckworth (1996) writes, "Thoughts are our ways of connecting things up for ourselves. If others tell us about the connections they have made, we can only understand them to the extent that we do the work of making these connections ourselves" (p.26). In other words, for students to truly comprehend new concepts they need to have time to make their own connections.

Recommendation 3: Use a variety of strategies to help students deepen their thinking about science concepts. One size doesn't fit all. Different students will find some ways of reflecting more valuable than others. By using oral, written, and nonlinguistic representations, you will be more likely to help all students engage in productive sense-making and wrap-up.

Understanding Strategy 5: Planning for Collaborative Science Discourse

The Issue

In secondary science classes, 80% of the activity observed was communication, where the teacher engaged in question-and-answer sessions in which students were looking for and got the "right" scientific answers from the teacher. Similar questioning practices have been observed in elementary and middle school class-

Table 3.1
Developing Student Understanding

Strategy 1: Engaging Students in Science Inquiry Engage students in science inquiry to develop understanding of science concepts and the nature of science.	
Strategy 2: Implementing Formative Assessments Make use of formative assessments to gather feedback on student progress toward understanding.	
Strategy 3: Addressing Preconceptions and Prior Knowledge Build on prior knowledge and address preconceptions.	Who's working harder?
Strategy 4: Providing Wrap-Up and Sense-Making Opportunities Provide daily opportunities for wrap-up that support student sense-making.	A learner-centered classroom is necessary to develop conceptual student understanding.
Strategy 5: Planning for Collaborative Science Discourse Develop student understanding through collaborative science discourse.	
Strategy 6: Providing Opportunities for Practice, Review, and Revision Teach concepts in depth by allowing students to continually refine their understanding through practice, review, and revision.	

rooms. This kind of teaching often limits students' abilities to understand science concepts as they perceive learning as a search for right answers. If one student successfully provides the correct knowledge response, then the teacher moves on with the assumption that all of the students learned. The learning in this situation is often superficial, with students focusing on the details and vocabulary and not on conceptual understanding.

The DESI Approach

According to brain research and research into how people learn, learning is a social activity and is more effective when we are able to discuss our ideas and thinking with others. The research shows that student learning improves when cooperative learning methods are used and discussion is a key feature. Teachers must plan opportunities for students to work together toward common learning goals. To be effective, students need to participate in interactive dialogue with the teacher and one another. This supports a learner-centered classroom rather than one where the teacher is the science authority who provides all of the scientific knowledge and ideas.

Selected Research Related to the Issue

Following are highlights from selected research on collaborative science discourse.

1. Recent research into *science discourse* indicates two basic types of interaction with one or multiple points of view:

   • **Direct Instruction** involves noninteractive/authoritative communication: The teacher presents one specific point of view and there is a one directional interaction with students.

   • **Inquiry Instruction** involves interactive/dialogic communication: The teacher and students explore ideas, generate new meanings, pose genuine questions and offerings, and listen to and work on different points of view using a back-and-forth interaction (Mortimer and Scott 2003, p. 39).

2. There are a wide variety of different cooperative learning methods. According to a survey of all of the research projects on 20 different methods, cooperative learning methods had a significant positive impact on student achievement. When the impact of cooperative lessons was compared with individualistic learning, Learning Together (LT) promotes the greatest effect, followed by the other cooperative learning strategies (Johnson, Johnson, and Stanne 2000). "Learning Together" is defined as

students working *cooperatively* with a vested interest in one another's learning, as well as their own (Johnson and Johnson 1997).

3. There is a difference between simply having students work in a group and structuring groups of students to work cooperatively. A group of students sitting at the same table doing their own work, but free to talk with one another as they work, is not structured to be a cooperative group, as there is no positive interdependence. This would be called individualistic learning with talking. For this to be cooperative learning there needs to be an accepted common goal for the group (Johnson and Johnson 1994).

In first- and second-grade classrooms, a study showed that paying attention to students' ideas and questions that arose from classroom discourse and using them to teach science created a classroom of inquirers. This was a break from past instruction and focused learning on students' interests, questions, and ideas (Gallas 1995). In this and a subsequent study with a third- and fourth-grade teacher (Kelley, Brown, and Crawford 2000), the teacher functioned as a coinvestigator and the learning community became one that valued listening and following student suggestions in science investigations. Students learned to pose science questions rather than just answer questions posed by the teacher.

What Is the Strategy?

There are different communication approaches that teachers use for different reasons. One productive strategy is direct instruction, which most teachers have experienced as learners and now use with their own students. Beyond lecture, there are many different communicative approaches and the key is to link them with the teaching purposes. Before we can learn about the steps included in this strategy, let's learn more about the four basic kinds of communication within a classroom. Refer to Figure 3.6 to learn about the kinds of classroom activities that would represent the communicative approaches. First, we need to clarify the terms *interactive, noninteractive, authoritative,* and *dialogic.*

1. **Dialogic:** There is more than one point of view in the conversation; more than one voice is heard as a variety of different ideas are explored (takes into account a student's ideas or multiple scientists' ideas).

2. **Authoritative:** Communication is focused on just one point of view, and there is no exploration of different ideas (focuses on the scientific point of view).

3. **Interactive:** The communication includes talk between the teacher and the students and between student flowing in both directions.

Figure 3.6
Classroom Communication—The Talk in Science Classrooms

Noninteractive/Authoritative (NI/A)	**Noninteractive/Dialogic (NI/D)**
• Lecture • Going over safety rules • Presenting only the scientific viewpoint • Reading textbook • Viewing science audiovisual	• Students presenting their experimental results • Teacher presenting multiple scientific viewpoints • Teacher presenting changes in theories as history has progressed • Students presenting results from science research
Interactive/Authoritative (I/A)	**Interactive/Dialogic (I/D)**
• Question and answer sessions focused on the "right" answer • Review sessions for tests and quizzes with students answering questions asked • Using "clicker" technology to determine if students know the correct science knowledge	• Investigations where students share and discuss their ideas • Demonstrations where students ask questions and discuss observations • Assessing for student prior knowledge • Formative assessments using probing questions

Based on Mortimer, E., and P. Scott. 2003. *Meaning making in secondary science classrooms*. London: Open University Press.

4. **Noninteractive:** The communication is one-directional from the teacher to the students or from a student to the other students (Mortimer and Scott 2003).

From the chart, you will recognize teaching activities that we see in all science classrooms. So why are we suggesting that there is something that we need to do differently? Remember, that from a Vygotskian perspective of learning, we learn best when we move from learning in social contexts and move to individual understanding. This means that when we present new science concepts we want students to talk, visualize, write, and interact socially to discuss their ideas. This collaborative learning approach lets students make individual sense of what is being communicated (Vygotsky 1978). Collaborative discussions need to be guided by the teacher as students move to individual thinking. Subsequently, students should be encouraged to talk out loud as they think about their thinking and ultimately move toward a scientific viewpoint. The fundamental idea here is that meaning making is essentially a dialogic process. So we need to find ways to promote classroom discussions.

When implementing a dialogic process in your classroom, you will want to vary your approaches based on the learning goals (Mortimer 1998; Mortimer and Scott 2003).

- *Get students to talk about their everyday ideas related to the concept you are teaching.* (Interactive/Dialogic, or I/D)

- *Provide experiences that engage them in learning about the concepts where they can make meaning of the science ideas.* (Interactive/Authoritative, or I/A)

- *Confirm the scientific viewpoints that relate to the science concepts.* (Noninteractive/Authoritative, or NI/A)

Each of these interactions can be accomplished with a variety of communicative approaches. For students to understand the concepts, however, collaborative learning that includes interactive dialog must be a part of our planned instruction.

Exploring the Strategy

The three approaches listed above can form a minicycle that will form a sequence. First the teacher and students explore the ideas that form the basis for the scientific story (big ideas and key concepts) being studied (I/D). Then the teacher intervenes to develop some aspect of the content that is important for an overall understanding of the story (I/A). Finally, the teacher reviews the student progress in the developing understanding of the scientific story, summarizes the key points, and moves the conversation toward the next steps in the learning (NI/A). Most of a unit's big ideas and key concepts contain smaller subconcepts, so this minicycle can be repeated many times.

Let's see how this would play out in a lesson. For our example, let's think about the concepts we reviewed in Chapter 2 related to the physical and chemical changes of matter. At the middle level we know that students learn that when matter changes both physically and chemically the molecules can be changed and rearranged even though the atoms remain unchanged. To teach this lesson a teacher might start out with a simple activity such as the following:

- Provide students with a shiny nail and ask them to put it in a place that will cause it to rust quickly. After two to three weeks, have them bring in their rusty nails and make observations. The nails can be arranged from most rusty to least rusty, and students should provide information about the conditions they provided. Have students talk about their ideas about what happened. (Interactive/Dialogic)

- Then the teacher can ask students about what the conditions were like that made the nails rust. The goal here is to gather and summarize the evidence to identify the conditions that are essential for rusting. Students can nominate the conditions and create data tables to summarize the results. (Interactive/Authoritative)

- Finally the teacher would summarize the progress thus far, provide information about setting up an investigation where variables are controlled, and move the students forward to the next step in the learning. (Noninteractive/Authoritative)

From this point, the teacher would have the students design their own experiments to test their combined ideas about what essential conditions for rusting would be. This starts the communicative cycle over with an interactive dialog. The more we include interactive discussions, the more the students will be prompted to think about and make sense of their ideas as they relate to scientific viewpoints.

Planning for Classroom Implementation

Research has shown that most classrooms promote learning by the individual and often rely on student competition to motivate students. This research shows that student learning improves when cooperative learning methods are used. Teachers must plan their lessons to include time for students to work together toward common learning goals.

Teachers and students need to understand what is meant by working cooperatively. It is not when students are grouped together with only some of the students engaged in the learning. Rather, teachers need to provide experiences where all students help one another and all are accountable for the learning and understanding. You will know that this is happening when students celebrate one another's successes, encourage one another to do homework, and learn to work together regardless of their backgrounds.

The research and resources on collaborative learning and flexible grouping are many. One suggestion is to ask students which class members they would like to be grouped with and which members they would not like to have in their group. When you create the groups, make sure you include at least one class member that they wanted to work with in their group, and you may include one member that they didn't mention they wanted to work with. Once you have put the teams together discuss this with students so that they understand your group choices. One of your goals is probably to help students work with others, and creating and changing groups is necessary to meet this goal. The work of Roger T. Johnson and

David W. Johnson spans decades and will provide useful information about cooperative learning and student grouping.

Flexible grouping of students and collaborative student interactions are part of the classroom learning environment. Dozens of studies with thousands of students have shown that there is a positive relationship between student achievement and the quality of the classroom environment. If we pay attention to the classroom interactions it should pay off when it comes to student learning. Developing a positive learning environment is discussed further in Chapter 4. Flexible grouping is one way to differentiate instruction and scaffold learning for students. Carol Ann Tomlinson has written many articles and books about differentiated instruction and would be a good resource for learning more about this strategy.

In science classes, as much as 80% of the discourse observed was interactive/authoritative communication. However, the type of communication that revealed the highest increase in student understanding and achievement was found in the classrooms where teachers had changed their method of communication to one that featured interactive/dialogic (Mortimer and Scott 2003). These teachers used inquiry questioning strategies and explored student ideas.

We should plan for instruction that includes interactive dialogue between the teacher and the students by asking them to clarify their thinking, explain their ideas, and discuss with others so that the ideas can be critically analyzed. This occurs in a learner-centered classroom rather than one where the teacher is the authority that provides all of the scientific information. Without this interactive discourse, students will miss the opportunity to inquire, discuss, and experience the concepts themselves so that they can think, problem-solve, and understand what they are learning.

To help plan for implementation in class, one suggestion would be to script your lesson. A template is provided in Figure 3.7 that asks you to think about the

Figure 3.7
Script Template

What I'll Do and Say	Type of Communication	What I Expect Students to Do

kind of communication approach you will use, the classroom activities that would be provided for that approach, and the expected student responses.

It isn't so much a script as it is a series of prompts to yourself to move you through the lesson. Where the scripting is important is drafting the open-ended questions you want to use to get students to think about the learning. And asking questions that require higher cognitive levels may be hard to come up with if not written out ahead of time. Some example questions follow:

- To get students to apply concepts to new situations: What will be the effect of this [change in variable]?

- To get students to analyze data: What is the connection between the height of an object and the rate at which it falls?

- To get students to synthesize their data: Based on the class data, what can you conclude?

This is also a time when you want to develop probing questions that will reveal understanding of the concepts.

To complete the template, select one lesson from your unit of study that is focused on developing student understanding of a key concept. Use the template to write out the communication that will happen in class during that lesson. Label each part of the script with the types of communication:

- NI/A = noninteractive/authoritative

- I/A = interactive/authoritative

- NI/D = noninteractive/dialogic

- I/D = interactive/dialogic

For those parts of the script that are interactive/dialogic, write the open-ended inquiry questions that you will use to guide the interactive dialogue. To find out if this strategy is working in your classroom, you may want to jot down the student responses. Use what you learned as you work on creating questions for the next lessons.

What Works in Science Classrooms: Implications for Teaching

Recommendation 1: Cooperative learning is essential when developing student understanding. Learning is basically an interactive activity and is best accomplished in a setting where students can discuss their ideas and their thinking with other students and with the guidance and facilitation of the teacher. Collaboration also supports learning by everyone in the group since the learning target is being investigated by the group. Working together allows the group to gather data and refer to the evidence when they try to come up with explanations of what is happening.

Recommendation 2: When students have the chance to consider multiple ideas in class, they can use their reasoning abilities to accept or reject the ideas by critiquing the idea based on the evidence. Whether the multiple ideas are student-generated or a variety of scientists' ideas, interactive dialogues are critical for students to make sense of observations and learning experiences. To foster high-quality discourse, we need to practice asking open-ended questions that probe for student thinking. One way to get students started even in early grades is to ask "What if…?" questions that ask them to make predictions based on what they have observed or understand about the science ideas. "What if…?" questions can also be used to get students comfortable discussing their own ideas.

Understanding Strategy 6: Providing Opportunities for Practice, Review, and Revision

The Issue

According to the TIMSS reports (Martin et al. 2004), science teachers are teaching a curriculum that is a mile wide and an inch deep. As a result, coverage takes precedence over comprehension, and students are exposed to concepts only briefly. The research of Marzano, Pickering, and Pollock (2001) has shown that even several interactions with new content are not sufficient to develop durable student understanding. If students are not provided with opportunities to deeply explore new ideas or with the occasion to refine their thinking about them, it is unlikely they will truly grasp them.

DESI Approach

To improve understanding of the content that is being learned, teachers must focus on the most important learning goals and choose effective strategies and contexts for student learning and sense-making. But all of that is for naught if students are only exposed to the content once or twice. Marzano and colleagues' (2001) research establishes that students need a minimum of four to six learning experi-

Table 3.1
Developing Student Understanding

Strategy 1: Engaging Students in Science Inquiry Engage students in science inquiry to develop understanding of science concepts and the nature of science.	
Strategy 2: Implementing Formative Assessments Make use of formative assessments to gather feedback on student progress toward understanding.	
Strategy 3: Addressing Preconceptions and Prior Knowledge Build on prior knowledge and address preconceptions.	**Who's working harder?**
Strategy 4: Providing Wrap-Up and Sense-Making Opportunities Provide daily opportunities for wrap-up that support student sense-making.	**A learner-centered classroom is necessary to develop conceptual student understanding.**
Strategy 5: Planning for Collaborative Science Discourse Develop student understanding through collaborative science discourse.	
Strategy 6: Providing Opportunities for Practice, Review, and Revision Teach concepts in depth by allowing students to continually refine their understanding through practice, review, and revision.	

ences, along with chances to practice, to develop understanding of new content. For each unit, teachers must carefully sequence the learning activities so that students have the opportunity to encounter concepts multiple times, practice applying their new ideas, and refine their thinking.

Selected Research Related to the Issue

1. "How will students master complex ideas and tasks if they encounter them only once?...Therefore, the flow of the unit and course must be iterative, students be made fully aware of the need to rethink and revise in light of current lessons, and the work must follow the trail back to the original ideas or techniques." (Wiggins and McTighe 2005, p. 213)

2. "[E]xpertise and expert performance are acquired by extensive engagement in relevant practice activities, and individual differences in performance are for a large part accounted for by differences in the amount of relevant practice. Deliberative practice activities...enable successive refinement by allowing for repetition." (van Gog et al. 2005, p.75)

3. "To support development of student understanding, teachers must plan opportunities for students to practice, review, and apply knowledge. Possible activities include:

    • Assign homework that requires students to practice, review, and apply what they have learned; however, be sure to give students explicit feedback on the accuracy of all homework.

    • Engage students in long-term projects that involve generating and testing hypotheses.

    • Ask students to revise the linguistic and nonlinguistic representations of knowledge in their notebooks as they refine their understanding of the knowledge." (Marzano, Pickering, and Pollock 2001, p. 152)

What Is the Strategy?

Teachers need to recognize that changes in understanding "involve gradual and time-consuming processes because the student must revise and restructure an entire network of beliefs and presuppositions" (Özdemir and Clark 2007, p. 354). One chance to learn the curriculum is not enough. Thus, teachers must be intentional about planning multiple opportunities to engage with new concepts so that students have this time to revise and restructure their understanding.

Scheduling time for student practice, review, and revision happens when we engage in personal reflection about the learning we currently offer our students. Think about the activities that we can do something about. Addressing time constraints that are a struggle for all of us is one of our biggest concerns. The better our advance planning, the greater the likelihood that we can budget time to provide the multiple learning opportunities that all students need. One dilemma that arises is that different students need different amounts of practice. We try to meet individual needs but still must balance time to practice with the overall time available. As you plan for your classroom, reflect on these three suggestions:

1. *Prune the curriculum.* Allowing for time to practice, review, and revise ideas depends heavily on a teacher's ability and willingness to unburden the curriculum (as discussed in Chapter 2). The most common reason teachers give for not spending more time on a topic is that there just isn't enough time. Effectively pruning the curriculum will create the time necessary for providing students with multiple opportunities to encounter new concepts, practice applying them, and revise their insights about them.

2. *Put instructional activities into a sequential order that supports ongoing, in-depth student understanding.* For each key concept, determine the logical sequence of learning activities to support conceptual understanding. This sequence includes many of the strategies already presented in this chapter. One sequence might be as follows:

- Activity 1: Introduce the concept being sure to plan for students' prior knowledge and preconceptions.

- Activity 2: Use inquiry to learn about the concept.

- Activity 3: Employ sense-making and collaborative science discourse activities.

- Activity 4: Provide formative assessments to check for student understanding.

- Activity 5: Include opportunities for students to practice and apply new ideas, review the new content, and revise their understanding.

- Activity 6: Afford students the opportunity to demonstrate their understanding through a summative assessment.

- Continue the process with the other key concepts.

3. *Provide opportunities for students to reflect on their work and then revise it based on teacher, peer, or self-assessment comments.*

Exploring the Strategy

In this section we will provide three examples that you can use when planning for student learning opportunities. We do not include a discussion of homework here but leave it to you and your school and district policies to determine homework policies and practices that address the strategy of practice, review, and revision for students.

K-W-Ls

K-W-Ls (What I Know, What I Want to Know, and What I Learned) are a popular strategy for helping elicit students' background knowledge, personalize their learning objectives, and reflect on their learning (Grall Reichel 1994). Individual students or whole classes fill in a chart similar to the one on page 124 and refer to it throughout a unit.

What I Know	What I Want to Know	What I Learned

McLaughlin (1994) suggests these additional columns as possibilities:

- What do we think we know, but aren't sure about?

- What's our evidence for what we know?

- How might we find out what we want to know?

- What could we find out by interacting with or observing the materials/phenomena, rather than by reading or asking experts?

For example, a fourth-grade teacher might use this strategy with her students while studying electricity. To begin the unit and elicit her students' background knowledge, prior experiences, and preconceptions, she asks the class to work in small groups to brainstorm what they already know about electricity. She then invites the groups to share their ideas with the whole class while she records them on a large piece of paper for all to see. She next provides students with individual think time to make a list of all the questions they have about electricity. Again, she gathers their ideas onto the class K-W-L chart. Throughout the unit, the teacher and students refer back to the chart to determine if what they thought they knew was correct, to verify if they have answered their questions, and to reflect on what they have learned throughout the unit. See also the Chapter 3 appendix for a K-W-L student handout template.

Long-Term Projects

Another way to provide students with multiple opportunities to interact with content is to engage them in long-term projects. Instead of presenting information once and moving on to the next topic, long-term projects allow students to incorporate each new piece of the pie into their understanding; thus they have the chance to review, revise, and refine their thinking.

For example, a high school or middle school physical science teacher may engage his students in preparing for a schoolwide science fair. In the months before the science fair, the teacher introduces the concept of motion and force. Two weeks into the unit, he asks his students to decide on a question they would like to investigate for the science fair; he provides a variety of sample questions.

124

As the students deepen their understanding of motion and force, they begin to make connections between their new learning and their science fair question. On a weekly basis, he asks students to write one paragraph about how the week's lessons helped inform their project. He reads these and provides each student with written feedback the following day. Thus, over time, students have the opportunity to revise and refine their understanding.

Journals or Science Notebooks

Many teachers ask their students to keep science journals or notebooks. These notebooks provide a place for students to document and later reflect on their learning; the students may record their thoughts using writing or nonlinguistic representations (e.g., graphic representations, physical models, mental pictures, drawings, pictographs, and kinesthetic activities). Within these journals, teachers can also ask students to complete activities that engage the students in practicing new skills and mastering content. Journals also fit nicely with formative assessments. We can designate a place in the journal to provide descriptive comments for the students. The students can then reply to those comments and a continuous dialogue results.

For example, a middle school science teacher asks her students to use their journals as places to practice graphing. For each investigation the students complete that involves data that can be graphed, she asks them to create graphs in their journals. She provides her class with a checklist of things to include on a graph, which they paste into their journals. After students have completed their graphs, the teacher asks them to both self- and peer-assess their graphs. In this way, she can determine if her students require more instruction and practice on making graphs.

Planning for Classroom Implementation

Overcoming the pressure to cover everything isn't easy. We glance at the three-inch thick textbook or district curriculum guide and wonder how we will possibly plow through it in one year. Moving from covering the curriculum an inch deep to a mile wide happens one inch at a time. Start by examining one unit. Consider the following questions:

- What is one thing that students could live without knowing?

- What is one concept that students find particularly difficult and might need additional time to grasp?

- What is one strategy I could use that will provide students time to practice and review new content and skills?

- What is one strategy I could use to provide students with the opportunity to refine and reflect on their insights?

By starting small, you are less likely to become discouraged and more likely to be successful.

It is also important to keep in mind that the majority of students are not used to having these types of opportunities. It is likely that helping them learn how to engage in meaningful practice, review, and revision will require that you explicitly teach them what you want them to do and the skills required to do it. Many students do not realize that scientists work by formulating and revising explanations, that is, that scientists don't have the right answer before they investigate. The National Science Education Standards (1996) states that students should engage in discussions and arguments that result in the revision of explanations. This prospect can be frightening for students who have previously been rebuked for not having the correct answer. Thus it is important to be explicit about this aspect of the nature of science with students.

What Works in Science Classrooms: Implications for Teaching

Recommendation 1: The only way to know if students have mastered the content or a skill is to formatively assess them. Formative assessment is, by definition, a way to gauge how well students are doing. If you find that students are doing well, there is no need to provide additional practice; this does not imply, however, that the content or skills should not be subsequently reviewed. If students aren't meeting your expectations, then it is necessary to provide more exposure to the content. In short, let your students' work determine how much practice to provide.

Recommendation 2: Reviewing and revising ideas is an ongoing process. Students should never be done building on and deepening their understanding of science concepts. From a practical standpoint, it is wise to intentionally plan at a minimum one activity per week that specifically allows them to do this.

Environment

Content and understanding strategies contribute in large measure to the instruction we provide. Yet the effectiveness of the most carefully crafted lessons and instruction will be enhanced or undermined by the classroom climate—including relationships among students and between students and the teacher. Therefore, the learning environment is the third essential element of effective science lessons. Strategies that compose this element of the framework help you focus on the question "What's really important in science lessons?" Ultimately, what matters is student learning, and the educational setting of student learning is the classroom environment.

As a result of this chapter, you will

- understand the strategies for creating a positive learning environment and be able to apply them to your own classroom; and

- improve the environment in your classroom and the quality of your science lessons in general.

Table 4.1 provides an overview of six strategies for creating a positive learning environment.

Environment Strategy 1: Believe All Students Can Learn

The Issue

No Child Left Behind (NCLB) legislation requires that all students be proficient in science by 2014. This legislation has caused a shift in thinking for those science teachers who believe that it is not their responsibility if students choose not to learn. Under NCLB, we *are* accountable for all students learning science—even the

Table 4.1
Creating a Positive Learning Environment

Strategy 1: Believe All Students Can Learn Show through your actions that you believe all students have the ability to learn.	
Strategy 2: Think Scientifically Teach students to think scientifically.	
Strategy 3: Develop Positive Attitudes and Motivation Develop positive student attitudes and motivation to learn science.	**What's really important?**
Strategy 4: Provide Feedback Give timely and criterion-referenced feedback.	**How do I create a positive learning environment?**
Strategy 5: Reinforce Progress and Effort Keep students focused on learning by reinforcing progress and effort.	
Strategy 6: Teach Students to Be Metacognitive Involve students in thinking about their ideas and assessing their own progress.	

ones who choose not to learn or believe that it is "way too hard" to learn science. Our attitudes, as well as students' lack of belief in their abilities, contribute to students' difficulties learning science. How can we address both our belief systems and those of our students?

The DESI Approach

Good things happen in every classroom, but do they happen for all students? In other words, are teachers deliberately creating a positive environment that promotes learning for *all* students? All teachers consciously and unconsciously make judgments about their students, and vice versa. The DESI approach is to reflect on current beliefs about how you should interact with students and how students should interact with one another. Articulating these beliefs and addressing both our behaviors and students' behaviors can help promote a positive classroom environment focused on learning for all students. We recognize that this strategy is one of the most difficult to implement because it asks you to take a deep look at your own beliefs and consider their implications for student achievement. We know that changing beliefs can be challenging, but we believe you can make such changes. To help you do so, this chapter presents a number of recommended actions.

Selected Research Related to the Issue

In the research report *Looking Inside the Classroom* (Weiss et al. 2003), trained class-room observers went into science and mathematics classes and recorded data about teacher practices in four areas, one of which was classroom culture. Figure 4.1 (p. 130) captures the elements of high-quality instruction that they observed. A review of the indicators of quality indicates that many of the characteristics of high-quality instruction (e.g., climate of respect for students' ideas, questions, and contributions; intellectual rigor; constructive criticism; and challenging of ideas) are strongly influenced by the climate in the classroom.

1. "Teachers must attend to designing classroom activities and helping students organize their work in ways that promote the kind of intellectual camaraderie and the attitudes toward learning that build a sense of community. In such a community, students might help one another solve problems by building on each other's knowledge, asking questions to clarify explanations, and suggesting avenues that would move the group toward its goal. Both cooperation in problem solving and argumentation among students in such an intellectual community enhance cognitive development." (Donovan, Bransford, and Pellegrino 1999)

2. In a self-fulfilling prophecy, you form an expectation of a student, which is communicated nonverbally through your behavior. The student then responds to your behavior, behaving in ways that conform to your expectation, and the expectation then becomes reality. Self-fulfilling prophecies can be positive or negative. For example, high expectations can lead to high student performance, and low expectations to low performance. (Rosenthal 1998)

3. Whether we are aware of it or not, we all make split-second judgments about people that are affected by physical characteristics, speech, name, and socioeconomics. (Tauber 1997)

4. The four factor theory (Rosenthal 1998) helps explain how teachers convey their expectations to students. The four factors are:

    • *Climate.* Climate is communicated nonverbally by smiling and nodding (or frowning and shaking your head), eye contact, and body position. Climate is the tone you set in which all the teacher-student interactions take place.

Figure 4.1
Elements of High-Quality Instruction

Lesson Design	Lesson Implementation
❏ Available resources contribute to accomplishing the purpose of the instruction.	❏ Teacher appears confident in ability to teach science.
❏ Lesson reflects careful planning and organization.	❏ Teacher's classroom management enhances quality of lesson.
❏ Strategies and activities reflect attention to students' preparedness and prior experience.	❏ Pace is appropriate for developmental levels/needs of students.
❏ Strategies and activities reflect attention to issues of access, equity, and diversity.	❏ Teacher is able to adjust instruction according to level of students' understanding.
❏ Lesson incorporates tasks, roles, and interactions consistent with investigative science.	❏ Instructional strategies are consistent with investigative science.
❏ Lesson encourages collaboration among students.	❏ Teacher's questioning enhances development of students' understanding/problem solving.
❏ Lesson provides adequate time and structure for sense-making.	
❏ Lesson provides adequate time and structure for wrap-up.	

Science Content	Classroom Culture
❏ Content is significant and worthwhile.	❏ Climate of respect for students' ideas, questions, and contributions is evident.
❏ Content information is accurate.	❏ Active participation of all is encouraged and valued.
❏ Content is appropriate for developmental levels of students.	❏ Interactions reflect working relationship between teacher and students.
❏ Teacher displays understanding of concepts.	❏ Interactions reflect working relationships among students.
❏ Elements of abstraction are included when important.	
❏ Students are intellectually engaged with important ideas.	❏ Climate encourages students to generate ideas and questions.
❏ Appropriate connections are made to other areas.	❏ Intellectual rigor, constructive criticism, and challenging of ideas are evident.
❏ Subject is portrayed as dynamic body of knowledge.	
❏ Degree of sense-making is appropriate for this lesson.	

- *Feedback.* Feedback is both affective (e.g., praise or criticism) and cognitive (e.g., detail and quality of the content). Feedback is your response to a student action or communication.

- *Input.* Input is the quantity and quality of information you provide the student. Observations of classrooms have shown that teachers actually teach more (provide greater input) to students of whom they have high expectations.

- *Output.* Output is the responsiveness of the student. You encourage greater or lesser responsiveness through verbal and nonverbal cues.

5. Virtually every aspect of science teaching is influenced by attitudes and beliefs. These aspects include acquiring and interpreting content knowledge, designing and selecting instructional strategies and activities, choosing assessments, engaging in professional development, and interacting with peers, parents, and students (Keys and Bryan 2001).

What Is the Strategy?

More research that addresses the complexities of teacher attitudes and beliefs is needed, but we are convinced that teachers can change their beliefs and use the self-fulfilling prophecy idea to elicit improved performance from students. There are a variety of factors, including the school and department culture, that shape teachers' belief systems (e.g., homework practices and make-up work), but this strategy focuses on actions individual teachers can take to change their beliefs. In our view, if you are cognizant of your beliefs about students and positively change how you behave toward them, you may find that students' performance improves. And when this happens, your beliefs about students' abilities will change. Because beliefs are usually developed over time and are strongly held, the first step is to identify what you believe and why. Second, ask whether the belief has an impact on student learning. If so, then it is important to examine that belief because beliefs influence attitudes, which are revealed in behaviors (Simpson et al. 1994).

If your beliefs result in behaviors that negatively affect student performance, then the third step is to identify and use a different behavior and observe how students respond. Deliberately behaving in a different way can feel "artificial" at first, but with practice, the behavior will seem more natural and become easier to use. Table 4.2 (p. 132) captures the process and is meant to help you reflect on the steps you might take to change a behavior. Specific examples of practices that teachers can implement that will affect their beliefs will be provided in the next section.

Table 4.2
Changing Beliefs by Changing Practices

Identify One Educational Belief: Determine a belief about a classroom practice or policy that affects all of your students. Reflect on the reasons you believe what you believe.

Determine the Affect of the Belief on Student Learning: Are there certain students who benefit from the practice or policy? Who are they and why? Are there some students negatively influenced by this policy or procedure? Who are they and how are they affected?

Identify a Practice or Behavior That Could be Changed to Support Student Learning: What could you do differently that would help all of your students? Take steps to determine a policy or practice that you can change. (You may need to alert your students of the change in practice so that they are not confused by what is expected of them.)

Implement a Change in Practice and Observe the Results: Implement an action or policy where the change supports access to learning for all of your students. Gather some action research data on the effect of the change. If the change supported learning by all students, continue the practice. Think about your change in practice and its impact on the classroom environment.

The procedure for changing beliefs described in the preceding paragraph might seem prescriptive, but it is meant to describe one possible pathway we can use to work on attitudes and beliefs that influence learning. Our point is that beliefs can be changed gradually by new information. When we are open to behaving in new ways and see improvements in students' performance as a result of new behavior, our beliefs will change based on that new information.

Exploring the Strategy

Research studies have found that teachers make hundreds of decisions every day and decisions that teachers make about students are sometimes made unconsciously. The goal is to be self-aware and to make our unconscious thinking conscious so that we can determine why we expect what we expect. From there, we can be more aware of our input and output to our students, focus on practices that build relationships with students, and use this positive energy to create a classroom climate that supports student learning. Read through the information contained in Figure 4.2, which asks, "Are you a good judge of character?" and begin to reflect on your beliefs and the kinds of judgments teachers make all the time.

Figure 4.2
Are You a Good Judge of Character?

Do you feel like you are a reasonably good judge of character? If you have years of teaching experience under your belt, you probably feel that, more often than not, you are able to correctly size up students. Occasionally you may be wrong, but most often you are correct. Right? Many teachers believe that they can judge ahead of time—sometimes by just a glance on the first day of school—how likely certain students are to achieve and behave.

In this activity (Tauber, 1997), what are the thoughts that come to your mind when you think about the following kinds of people? Be honest. No one but you will know what you think. Think about the students you see at your grade level.

Generally, what descriptors might you use to characterize

1. A student from a family that has strong and vocal political ties

2. A significantly overweight girl

3. A student from an affluent family who is an only child

4. A student whose two older siblings you had in class several years ago—each of whom was often a troublemaker

5. An Asian boy who is the son of a respected university math professor

6. A boy who is thin, almost frail, and very uncoordinated for his age

The beliefs and biases that are revealed in this activity are a product of the unconscious, built up over many experiences and messages from your environment. You probably don't want to hold these biases, but being unconscious, they are not subject to rational logic or suppression. Of course, that doesn't mean you shouldn't work on changing your beliefs and biases. On the contrary, by making them conscious, you take the first step to liberation.

For more about the power of unconscious thinking, see *Blink: The Power of Thinking Without Thinking* (Gladwell, 2005).

To implement this strategy, personal reflection is essential. Specifically, it is important to ask yourself, "What beliefs do I have that are *supporting* or *interfering with* my ability to create a positive learning environment for all my students? Which types of students (e.g., who that show hostility) challenge my belief that they can learn?" The scenarios that follow provide examples of teachers' beliefs that negatively impact the learning of some or all of the students in the class. As you read the scenarios, think about the beliefs behind the behaviors and how these beliefs hinder the creation of a positive learning environment.

Scenario 1: Beliefs About Homework

I think my students need to learn the discipline of good study habits, so I assign homework every night. I choose homework of various types—reading their books, answering questions, finishing up class work, doing home experiments, and so on. I'm consistently disappointed in the quality of work they do, because only a few students really do it well. And, of course, I have a few students who never do it. I just record a plus or minus in my grade book indicating whether or not they did it. I don't want to use too much class time correcting homework. I take into consideration whether or not students have shown good effort in their homework when I am deciding their final grade or mark for the class.

Scenario 2: Beliefs About Grading

I want to be fair, so I let my students drop their two lowest marks each quarter. I think this helps them stay motivated because they don't get discouraged by a bad day. Sometimes, it makes a big difference for a kid.

Scenario 3: Beliefs About Classroom Expectations

I just require that students bring materials to class—their books, paper, and pencils. I can't really stand high-control environments, and I have better things to do than spend all my time being the bad guy. I enjoy a relaxed classroom, and we have good discussions and a lot of fun. My students get to know me well because I share a lot about my past and what I do outside school. They get to know me so well that they know what I expect without my having to post a bunch of rules on the bulletin board. It works for me because I know how to relate to the kids, and they respect me for that.

Scenario 4: Beliefs About Inquiry in the Classroom

I feel a real ambivalence about incorporating inquiry into my lessons. I'm worried about covering enough material to enable my students to be well-prepared for the state assessments. On the other hand, I think investigation and working with real things is what really turns kids on to science. So I try not to let a week go by without some kind of hands-on experience. Time is another factor. First, not all investigations fit into a period. Second, I just can't kill myself with so many setups and keeping the inventory for tons of supplies. I don't even have the equipment that I need. I never get out of school until the last minute when I have to rush to pick up the kids from day care. I can only do so much.

Scenario 5: Beliefs About Laboratory Reports

I know this is a really important part of students' learning. I've tried different formats over the years and have found that different formats suit different investigations, so I have pretty much rejected the good old scientific-method style. At the first of the year, I give students written directions with a data sheet to fill out and guiding questions toward the conclusion. I always let them discuss with one another if they want or need to do that—the important thing is that they learn. Then, as the year goes on, I teach them different ways of reporting their data, and the importance of making conclusions based on evidence. Then I can be less supportive with their write-ups and can expect them to apply what I've taught. I "grade" the write-ups by writing comments on them, which takes me about three days. Plus I give a 1 for incomplete or poor, a 2 for complete, or a 3 for impressive. If students want to, they can improve their write-ups by addressing my comments and turning them in again. When I get an "impressive" one, I show it to the class or post a copy.

Figure 4.3 (pp. 136–7) captures these teacher beliefs and the impact of their actions on student success. One recommendation that might improve the teacher's practice is also provided for each scenario. Think about the procedures and policies you have in class. If your school or district already has policies in place for homework and late work, for example, move on to other aspects identified in the four-factor theory findings (Rosenthal 1998). Decide what choices you can make to support learning through clear policies and procedures. Clearly, if we believe that we are able to successfully implement an instructional strategy or policy that supports learning for all students, then this positive belief supports student achievement.

Planning for Classroom Implementation

Our beliefs about student learning and our behaviors toward our students are factors that affect student learning. As you plan to implement this strategy, you will want to consider whether the norms in your classroom support your beliefs about student learning. For example, if you believe that students should be able to share their ideas, reveal their misconceptions, make mistakes, obtain feedback,

Figure 4.3
Analyzing Teacher Beliefs and Actions That Support a Climate of Learning

Scenarios	Teacher Belief	Impact on Learning	Recommendation
1. Homework	The teacher believes that homework every day will develop good study habits among the students.	Since the students are assigned homework every night, it is having a negative effect on their willingness to use homework to improve learning. This negatively impacts all students.	Not all homework is the same and some homework is for practice and some is for preparation or elaboration (Marzano, Pickering, and Pollack 2001). Homework should only be assigned periodically and should be commented on to improve the effect on student learning. Create a homework policy.
2. Grading	The teacher believes that dropping the two lowest grades is fair for students and solves the problem of students with low scores or zeros.	The two lowest scores may represent significant assessments of student achievement. The low-achieving students are affected by having grades that do not adequately align with learning and instead result in grade inflation.	If receiving evidence of student learning is the goal, then devising a strategy that allows for extended time to complete work will maintain rigor and still accommodate personal student issues. Try providing two "oops" passes each marking period to extend deadlines.
3. Classroom Expectations	The teacher believes that they create a positive classroom climate by being the students' friend and sharing personal information.	Students may not be clear about classroom expectations. Trying to be a friend affects all students because the focus is not on a well-managed or learner-centered classroom.	Establishing clear classroom expectations provides order for all students. Providing procedures for students creates a sense of comfort that supports all students. Time spent on telling a personal teacher story is time away from instruction.

and revise their thinking and their work, then you will need to set and follow norms that create an environment of cooperation and camaraderie.

As you consider implementing this strategy, you might also want to examine the belief shared by many teachers that all students can learn. What does this belief look like in practice? What do we do? What do we say? To answer these questions, think about the positive characteristics and actions of the teachers and professors in whose classes you learned the most as a student. Many of us say that we learned most in classes where the teachers liked the subject and showed that they cared about us as people. We also liked teachers who made the learning interesting and even fun sometimes. These teachers gave us chances to think about what we were learning and they didn't give up on us. They were also fair, which means they met

Figure 4.3 (cont.)
Analyzing Teacher Beliefs and Actions That Support a Climate of Learning

Scenarios	Teacher Belief	Impact on Learning	Recommendation
4. Inquiry	The teacher believes that inquiry instruction may be an important strategy, but it just takes too much time to prepare and accomplish in class.	All students are affected by a lack of inquiry instruction in a science class. The first feature of inquiry is to engage students with scientific questions that cause them to think about the concept and their own ideas.	Scientific inquiry refers to the diverse ways in which scientists study the natural work and propose explanations based on evidence. Plan to include inquiries on a regular basis, but share the prep work with other teachers or create a student schedule for set-ups and taking-down of materials.
5. Lab Reports	The teacher believes that laboratory write-ups are important as illustrations of student learning, but any responses from students are accepted and evaluated on a three-point scale.	This affects all students because the criterion for success is not clear for students. There is no way to know if they are progressing or if they understood the concepts unless the comments provide formative feedback.	Provide a rubric for the laboratory write up that includes criteria for proficient work. Provide exemplars for students to refer to and give them opportunities to revise their work based on the teacher comments.

not only our needs but the needs of the other students. Think about the ways in which you demonstrate your belief that all students can learn. What do you think your students would say you do to show that you believe in their ability to learn? Are your responses similar to your students' responses? Self-fulfilling prophecies work both ways: Our performance can reflect our students' beliefs about us just as their performance can reflect what we believe about them.

What Works in Science Classrooms: Implications for Teaching

Recommendation 1: The research on self-fulfilling prophecies shows that if we believe students can learn, then they probably will. When asked, teachers will, of course, say they believe that all students can learn. When probed further, though, there are a number of conditions. All students can learn if they come to school prepared, have the ability, have the opportunities, apply themselves, and so on. Each student should have the opportunity to learn with the support of teachers who believe they *can* learn. Examine your beliefs about student learning and how you demonstrate those beliefs through your actions and classroom policies. Determine if there are students whose learning would improve with a change in those practices or policies. To carry out this recommendation, you can discuss your beliefs with other teachers, plan for a change in practice, or survey other teachers about their effective policies and practices.

Recommendation 2: Take a systematic approach to changing your beliefs. The first step is to accept that it is possible to change your beliefs. Next, acknowledge existing beliefs, identify which of your practices demonstrate beliefs that are interfering with student learning, implement changes in those practices, and see the results of the new practices. As you implement this recommendation, you will benefit from planning how you will interact with students to show them that you believe they can learn science. Add notes to your lesson planner about behaviors you want to try or students you want to specifically interact with to build a positive relationship. Track your results and revise your behaviors as needed.

Recommendation 3: Create a positive climate that fosters camaraderie and collaboration in the classroom by attending to both procedures and interactions. We begin to create a positive climate by teaching procedures that foster student questioning, risk-taking, collaboration, and a mutual focus on learning. Remember, to teach procedures effectively, teachers must teach the steps of the procedure, model them, provide opportunities for students to practice them, and reinforce them. To foster collaboration, encourage interactions that are supportive rather than competitive. Doing so will help you and your students develop a shared belief that everyone in the class can learn. Reviewing the research on collaborative learning and the current research on science teacher beliefs and attitudes can help you incorporate this recommendation into your classroom practices. A summary of the historical and current research on these topics can be found in the *Handbook of Research on Science Education* (Abell and Lederman 2007). From the research, it is becoming clear that our belief systems are embedded in the larger sociocultural environment, which includes students, teachers, parents, administrators, the community, and the political and cultural environment.

Environment Strategy 2: Think Scientifically

The Issue

Understanding the world from a science perspective is different from understanding it from other perspectives. Students may be taught a unit about the nature of science, which addresses thinking and working like a scientist, but these units often do not provide specifics about the daily practices of scientists. In other

Table 4.1
Creating a Positive Learning Environment

Strategy 1: Believe All Students Can Learn Show through your actions that you believe all students have the ability to learn.	
Strategy 2: Think Scientifically Teach students to think scientifically.	
Strategy 3: Develop Positive Attitudes and Motivation Develop positive student attitudes and motivation to learn science.	**What's really important?**
Strategy 4: Provide Feedback Give timely and criterion-referenced feedback.	**How do I create a positive learning environment?**
Strategy 5: Reinforce Progress and Effort Keep students focused on learning by reinforcing progress and effort.	
Strategy 6: Teach Students to Be Metacognitive Involve students in thinking about their ideas and assessing their own progress.	

words, students are not taught *how* scientists go about their work and how they reach scientific conclusions. Students often have misconceptions about scientists. They might think of them only as men in white coats who work in chemical laboratories. As a result, students rarely equate their learning in science classrooms to the work of scientists.

The DESI Approach

From the very first day of class, students should be actively engaged in learning to view the world scientifically. This means they need to have opportunities to ask questions, collect data, and discuss their findings. Every science lesson should provide opportunities for students to share their ideas, ask their classmates to defend their ideas using evidence, communicate data, be creative, critique evidence, and make scientifically based predictions. As students gain experience in working like scientists, they will be able to design and conduct investigations, first with teacher assistance, and then on their own. Ultimately, students should be able to evaluate their own explanations in light of alternative explanations, including those that reflect scientific understanding. The strategy of promoting scientific thinking is critical to establishing a collaborative classroom climate where students can discuss their ideas safely and where challenging each others' ideas is the accepted behavior because it is consistent with the way that scientists work.

Selected Research Related to the Issue

1. "We teach according to how we understand the nature of what we are teaching and according to how we understand the nature of learning.... Science is a major area of human mental and practical activity which generates knowledge that can be the basis of important technological applications as well as of intellectual satisfaction. It is an important part of the education of all, not just of scientists, to be aware of the status and nature of scientific knowledge; how it is created and how dependable it is." (Harlan 1992, p. 2)

2. "Simply telling students what scientists have discovered, for example, is not sufficient to support change in their existing preconceptions about important scientific phenomena. Similarly, simply asking students to follow the steps of 'the scientific method' is not sufficient to help them develop the knowledge, skills, and attitudes that will enable them to understand what it means to 'do science' and participate in a larger scientific community." (Donovan and Bransford 2005, p. 398)

3. "In the long run, no scientist, however famous or highly placed, is empowered to decide for other scientists what is true, for none are believed by other scientists to have special access to the truth. There are no pre-established conclusions that scientists must reach on the basis of their investigations." (AAAS 1990, p. 7)

4. "There can be no future for the human experiment unless a critical mass of involved people understands that the laws of nature constrain our activities and that our solutions to these problems must be based on knowledge and not blind adherence to fads." (Moore 1993, p. viii.)

What Is the Strategy?

Why do we want students to learn to think scientifically? Will learning to do so improve the quality of the science classroom environment? To answer these questions, we have to first define "thinking scientifically." At the simplest level, this means thinking like a scientist thinks. To be able to think like a scientist, students must have a working understanding of the nature of science. If we look at the major characteristics that describe the nature of science (Table 4.3), we can

Table 4.3
The Nature of Science

> **Scientific Inquiry**
>
> Fundamentally, the various scientific disciplines are alike in their reliance on evidence, the use of hypotheses and theories, the kinds of logic used, and much more. Nevertheless, scientists differ greatly from one another in what phenomena they investigate and in how they go about their work; in the reliance they place on historical data or on experimental findings and on qualitative or quantitative methods; in their recourse to fundamental principles; and in how much they draw on the findings of other sciences. Still, the exchange of techniques, information, and concepts goes on all the time among scientists, and there are common understandings among them about what constitutes an investigation that is scientifically valid.
>
> Scientific inquiry is not easily described apart from the context of particular investigations. There simply is no fixed set of steps that scientists always follow, no one path that leads them unerringly to scientific knowledge. There are, however, certain features of science that give it a distinctive character as a mode of inquiry. Although those features are especially characteristic of the work of professional scientists, everyone can exercise them in thinking scientifically about many matters of interest in everyday life.

1.	**Science Demands Evidence** Sooner or later, the validity of scientific claims is settled by referring to observations of phenomena. Hence, scientists concentrate on getting accurate data. Such evidence is obtained by observations and measurements taken in situations that range from natural settings (such as a forest) to completely contrived ones (such as the laboratory). To make their observations, scientists use their own senses, instruments (such as microscopes) that enhance those senses, and instruments that tap characteristics quite different from what humans can sense (such as magnetic fields). Scientists observe passively (earthquakes, bird migrations), make collections (rocks, shells), and actively probe the world (as by boring into the earth's crust or administering experimental medicines). In some circumstances, scientists can control conditions deliberately and precisely to obtain their evidence. By varying just one condition at a time, they can hope to identify its exclusive effects on what happens, uncomplicated by changes in other conditions. Often, however, control of conditions may be impractical (as in studying stars), or unethical (as in studying people), or likely to distort the natural phenomena (as in studying wild animals in captivity). In such cases, observations have to be made over a sufficiently wide range of naturally occurring conditions to infer what the influence of various factors might be. Because of this reliance on evidence, great value is placed on the development of better instruments and techniques of observation, and the findings of any one investigator or group are usually checked by others. <div align="right">(Continued on pages 142 and 143)</div>

Table 4.3 (cont.)
The Nature of Science

2.	**Science Is a Blend of Logic and Imagination**
	Although all sorts of imagination and thought may be used in coming up with hypotheses and theories, sooner or later scientific arguments must conform to the principles of logical reasoning—that is, to testing the validity of arguments by applying certain criteria of inference, demonstration, and common sense. Scientists may often disagree about the value of a particular piece of evidence, or about the appropriateness of particular assumptions that are made—and therefore disagree about what conclusions are justified. But they tend to agree about the principles of logical reasoning that connect evidence and assumptions with conclusions.
	Scientists do not work only with data and well-developed theories. Often, they have only tentative hypotheses about the way things may be. Such hypotheses are widely used in science for choosing what data to pay attention to and what additional data to seek, and for guiding the interpretation of data. In fact, the process of formulating and testing hypotheses is one of the core activities of scientists. To be useful, a hypothesis should suggest what evidence would support it and what evidence would refute it. A hypothesis that cannot in principle be put to the test of evidence may be interesting, but it is not likely to be scientifically useful.
	The use of logic and the close examination of evidence are necessary but not usually sufficient for the advancement of science. Scientific concepts do not emerge automatically from data or from any amount of analysis alone. Inventing hypotheses or theories to imagine how the world works and then figuring out how they can be put to the test of reality is as creative as writing poetry, composing music, or designing skyscrapers. Sometimes discoveries in science are made unexpectedly, even by accident. But knowledge and creative insight are usually required to recognize the meaning of the unexpected. Aspects of data that have been ignored by one scientist may lead to new discoveries by another.
3.	**Science Explains and Predicts**
	Scientists strive to make sense of observations of phenomena by constructing explanations for them that use, or are consistent with, currently accepted scientific principles. Such explanations—theories—may be either sweeping or restricted, but they must be logically sound and incorporate a significant body of scientifically valid observations. The credibility of scientific theories often comes from their ability to show relationships among phenomena that previously seemed unrelated.
	The essence of science is validation by observation. But it is not enough for scientific theories to fit only the observations that are already known. Theories should also fit additional observations that were not used in formulating the theories in the first place; that is, theories should have predictive power. Demonstrating the predictive power of a theory does not necessarily require the prediction of events in the future. The predictions may be about evidence from the past that has not yet been found or studied.

Table 4.3 (cont.)
The Nature of Science

4.	**Scientists Try to Identify and Avoid Bias**
	When faced with a claim that something is true, scientists respond by asking what evidence supports it. But scientific evidence can be biased in how the data are interpreted, in the recording or reporting of the data, or even in the choice of what data to consider in the first place. Scientists' nationality, sex, ethnic origin, age, political convictions, and so on may incline them to look for or emphasize one or another kind of evidence or interpretation.
	Bias attributable to the investigator, the sample, the method, or the instrument may not be completely avoidable in every instance, but scientists want to know the possible sources of bias and how bias is likely to influence evidence. Scientists want, and are expected, to be as alert to possible bias in their own work as in that of other scientists, although such objectivity is not always achieved. One safeguard against undetected bias in an area of study is to have many different investigators or groups of investigators working in it.
5.	**Science Is Not Authoritarian**
	It is appropriate in science, as elsewhere, to turn to knowledgeable sources of information and opinion, usually people who specialize in relevant disciplines. But esteemed authorities have been wrong many times in the history of science. In the long run, no scientist, however famous or highly placed, is empowered to decide for other scientists what is true, for none are believed by other scientists to have special access to the truth. There are no pre-established conclusions that scientists must reach on the basis of their investigations.
	In the short run, new ideas that do not mesh well with mainstream ideas may encounter vigorous criticism, and scientists investigating such ideas may have difficulty obtaining support for their research. Indeed, challenges to new ideas are the legitimate business of science in building valid knowledge. Even the most prestigious scientists have occasionally refused to accept new theories despite there being enough accumulated evidence to convince others. In the long run, however, theories are judged by their results: When someone comes up with a new or improved version that explains more phenomena or answers more important questions than the previous version, the new one eventually takes its place.

American Association for the Advancement of Science (AAAS). 2007. *Science for all Americans*. New York: Oxford University Press. Reprinted with permission.

develop a working definition of what it means to "think scientifically" and an understanding of how a scientific way of knowing and scientific thinking influence science teaching.

Looking at some of the main ideas included in Table 4.3, we see that scientists seek to explain and make predictions that avoid bias. Using logic and imagination they seek to make sense of evidence. There are no predetermined conclusions when developing explanations, and new data contribute to scientific thinking and understanding. Scientists study the natural world by making observations, experimenting, confirming evidence, and thinking about and critiquing other scientists' explanations. They do not rely on beliefs, cultural stories, ethical norms, or social expectations.

What does thinking scientifically look like in the classroom? First and foremost, science is about asking questions, so science instruction that promotes thinking scientifically includes many opportunities for students to ask and answer questions that can be investigated through science. When students act like scientists, they exhibit the following behaviors:

- Using and testing of hypotheses and theories and developing logical explanations

- Thinking creatively and using their imaginations when developing conclusions based on evidence

- Interpreting data and checking for biases in their explanations

- Working on the same problem as other student scientists because having multiple scientists work on the same problem reduces bias

- Recognizing that even with significant amounts of data, scientists and scientific conclusions can be wrong

- Discussing their ideas with other student scientists (because scientists do not always agree, conclusions should be subject to vigorous criticism as explanations are challenged and defended)

If we keep these ideas in mind, then teaching students to think and act like scientists means we need to provide some specific kinds of experiences in the classroom. According to research studies on teaching and learning the nature of science, students need to understand that

1. there is a distinction between hypotheses, facts, and theories, and between laws and theories;

2. scientific data are not the same as scientific evidence;

3. explanations are developed from a combination of collected data and what is already known;

4. scientific thinking includes human imagination and creativity;

5. scientific knowledge is subjective and based upon a scientist's interpretation; and

6. scientific knowledge is never absolute or certain but is subject to change as new evidence makes it possible to advance or modify laws and theories (Lederman 2007, pp. 833–835).

Classroom behaviors that help develop these understandings include asking scientific questions, gathering data and making observations to develop evidence, giving priority to the evidence to develop scientific explanations, communicating and discussing findings with others, and justifying proposed explanations. To help our students get comfortable, we need to model, reinforce, and practice these behaviors every day. You don't need to focus on all of these behaviors at once. Select one to get started, and systematically teach it to your students. Then you can emphasize each of the behaviors in turn until your students become skilled at thinking scientifically.

Exploring the Strategy

We began this section by reviewing information about the nature of science and what scientists do when they conduct scientific investigations. Next, we presented some ideas about what it means to think scientifically and identified some classroom experiences that help students develop their abilities to "think scientifically." Now that we've generated some ideas about the qualities of thinking scientifically, we can address how to create an environment that supports and exemplifies those qualities, while keeping in mind what's really important: learning for all.

One way to start promoting scientific thinking is to use effective questions. Practice using probing questions that require students to think about their thinking to respond. It often is difficult to come up with good probing questions on the spot; preparing some questions ahead of time is one way to be sure that your questions promote thinking. You might start by asking open-ended questions about the investigations your students are conducting. Examples of these types of questions, which were included in Chapter 3, follow.

Questions that help students build confidence and rely on their own thinking and understanding

- How did you reach that conclusion?

- Does that make sense?

- What is the evidence that supports your explanation?

Questions that help students learn to reason scientifically

- What assumptions are you making?

- How would you verify or prove that?

- Would your results hold true for all cases? Explain why.

- Can you think of an alternate procedure?

Questions that help students collectively think about explanations or make sense of science

- What do you think about what _____ said?

- Do the rest of you agree? Why or why not?

- Did anyone get the same data but explain them in a different way?

- Does _____ explanation make sense? Why or why not?

Questions that encourage reflective thinking

- How would you justify your explanation?

- Do your data seem reasonable? Why or why not?

- Can you explain why you got the evidence that you did?

- What additional observations could you make?

- What have you learned or discovered today?

Planning for Classroom Implementation

As you plan to implement this strategy, remember that science provides a way to explain the natural world. In other words, science helps us answer questions about the natural world. As a result, teaching science means helping students understand the difference between questions in general and scientific questions. It also means helping them think about observations to infer, hypothesize, and critique explanations using evidence.

To prepare to use the strategy of promoting scientific thinking, reflect on what you know about the nature of science and ask yourself if you are clear about what makes a question a scientific question. If you have not had many opportunities to think deeply about the nature of science or to develop your own scientific investigations, think about what you would like to learn first to help your students in these areas. To develop your own knowledge and skills, you might read some of the recent studies, many of which relate to elementary teachers and students, designed to test the impact of Nature of Science (NOS) instruction. One finding from these studies is that students' reactions to conflicting evidence are at least partially related to their views on NOS (Sadler, Chambers, and Zeidler 2004).

Improving the quality of your classroom environment by promoting scientific thinking will occur gradually. The strategy will be more effective if we teach our students the procedures involved in thinking scientifically, model those procedures, and provide opportunities for students to use them. In this section, we will investigate two aspects of thinking scientifically: (1) knowing the difference between facts, hypotheses, and beliefs, and (2) using imagination and creativity. You may already have a procedure that you use to help your students with these aspects of thinking scientifically, but we invite you to look at the following ideas as you plan for classroom implementation.

Figure 4.4 (p. 148) explains the difference between fact, theory, law, hypothesis, and belief, and includes a questionnaire for testing understanding of these definitions. To help elementary students understand the differences among these terms, simplify these examples and provide students with opportunities to think about, discuss, and reach consensus on them. These terms also are used in general conversation, so it is particularly important to include explicit vocabulary instruction about the terms and reinforce their correct use throughout the year. In addition, be sure to use the correct terminology yourself to avoid student confusion.

Scientific thinking also requires imagination and creativity. Some ideas to consider as you think about promoting scientific thinking include sponsoring invention conventions or science fairs. With these approaches, once a need or a problem has been identified, students are directed to use problem-solving and creative-thinking skills to invent a product or process to solve or overcome the problem. Communication and research skills are emphasized throughout the invention convention or science fair experience. Another idea is to provide a discrepant event for which the outcome of the inquiry or demonstration is contrary to the students'

Figure 4.4
Definitions and Practice Questionnaire

Belief:	An idea that is accepted as being true based on an observation, opinion, faith (trust), or reason (logic). Beliefs do not require evidence or proof but are frequently passed along from generation to generation and may be part of a person's religious, social, or cultural background.
Facts:	The results of experiments made under carefully controlled conditions. Facts are observations and experimental evidence relating to a question or problem. In science, facts are often referred to as the data or knowledge that is known. The facts that are gathered from direct or indirect observations provide consistent data every time the experiment is conducted.
Hypothesis:	An educated prediction that can be tested and is based on prior observations that can be used as a basis for reasoning or for planning experiments to gather more information. These are frequently written in "If... then..." statements. A tested hypothesis is accepted until and unless it has been disproved.
Theory:	A well-tested model and explanation that makes sense of a great variety of related phenomena and scientific observations and is supported by consistent and extensive evidence. Theories organize knowledge in a field, fit existing data (facts), explain how events or processes are thought to occur, and often predict future discoveries and events.
Law:	A well-established, descriptive generalization that has a history of reliability. Laws state what, under certain conditions, will happen. Scientific laws can change or not hold under some conditions. Theories explain laws and facts.

Is It a Theory, Hypothesis, Fact, or Belief (practice)

1. _____ The Earth is a sphere.

2. _____ An understanding of Earth's magnetic field and animals' migration flight patterns, and finding magnetic materials in some animals' brains, suggest that honeybees, homing pigeons, salmon, and dolphins use Earth's magnetic field to guide them on their migration routes.

3. _____ If pesticide use continues at its present rate, cancer will increase by 50% within the next 10 years.

4. _____ Humans should be vegetarians.

prediction. As a result, students need to create a new explanation using their imagination and creativity. Providing time for students to test their ideas and discuss their thinking will help them learn and practice this aspect of scientific thinking. A wide variety of discrepant events can be found using online resources. Tik Liem's book *Invitations to Science Inquiry* (1987) includes 400 discrepant events that will engage your students in creative thinking. One classic example of a discrepant event follows:

> Stand straight up with your heels against a wall and your feet together. Have someone place a dollar bill about a foot in front of your feet. Can you pick it up without bending your knees?

Students invariably predict that yes, they can. In fact, due to our center of gravity, it is **not** possible without bending our knees. The goal of discrepant events is to get students to think about the scientific explanations related to the event (i.e., to think like a scientist). Since the results do not match student predictions, students immediately start to ask questions and to think about alternative ideas.

Planning for implementation of this strategy means understanding all of the aspects of scientific thinking and creating ways to engage your students in learning about science concepts using scientific thinking. Begin by developing your students' skills in one or two aspects of scientific thinking. As time progresses, you can focus on additional aspects.

What Works in Science Classrooms: Implications for Teaching

Recommendation 1: Teach students what a scientific question is and give students opportunities to convert their questions into scientific questions that can be answered based on background research or observations. Scientific thinking involves answering scientific questions. As science teachers, we teach students that answering a scientific question involves developing explanations that cite evidence, sharing ideas about what the evidence means, and critiquing the evidence to see if the conclusions are valid or if further evidence is needed. For example, if you ask someone to answer the question "Is there global warming?" a nonscientific answer would be based on what that person believes from what they have read or heard from others. Scientific thinking, however, requires examining the evidence, discussing and critiquing the evidence, and generating an answer to the question based on existing science knowledge along with all the current evidence from scientifically designed studies. One way to begin to implement this recommendation is by generating or finding examples of science questions that might be of interest to your students.

Recommendation 2: Leverage the aspects of scientific thinking to create a positive learning environment. For example, one of our challenges is to develop a "safe" classroom environment where students can openly share their ideas and their thinking about science concepts. Class sessions where ideas are shared should not be opportunities to embarrass students or leave them open to ridicule from their peers. One way to ensure that these sessions are positive experiences is to teach students that scientists are most effective when they consider all possibilities, no matter how "outside the box" those possibilities might seem. Many scientific discoveries have resulted from experiments that did not work as planned, and there are a number of examples of when we have learned from unusual findings and creative explanations. For example, Post-Its are the result of an experiment with unexpected findings. To address this recommendation, you can construct a chart that identifies what you would be seen and heard doing with regard to the various aspects of scientific thinking and the expected student responses. There is a template in the Chapter 4 appendix (Environment Strategy 2: Thinking Scientifically) that can be used to capture this information. Use this planning template to record your scripted questions, the procedures you will be teaching your students, or the ways that you will incorporate the features of thinking scientifically into your lesson.

Environment Strategy 3: Develop Positive Attitudes and Motivation

The Issue

When student and teacher attitudes and perceptions about learning science are negative, learning suffers. Conversely, when attitudes and perceptions are positive, learning is enhanced. We all know from personal experiences that different people are motivated by different things. What motivates one student may not motivate another. A number of factors can influence what motivates a person. For example, elementary students usually want to please their teacher, which serves as an external motivator. Middle and high school students, on the other hand, often want to please their peers, which can provide negative motivation to complete in-class work or homework assignments. At any age, attitudes, like beliefs, can persist, even when the conditions that precipitated the negative attitudes no longer exist.

Table 4.1
Creating a Positive Learning Environment

Strategy 1: Believe All Students Can Learn Show through your actions that you believe all students have the ability to learn.	
Strategy 2: Think Scientifically Teach students to think scientifically.	
Strategy 3: Develop Positive Attitudes and Motivation Develop positive student attitudes and motivation to learn science.	What's really important? How do I create a positive learning environment?
Strategy 4: Provide Feedback Give timely and criterion-referenced feedback.	
Strategy 5: Reinforce Progress and Effort Keep students focused on learning by reinforcing progress and effort.	
Strategy 6: Teach Students to Be Metacognitive Involve students in thinking about their ideas and assessing their own progress.	

The DESI Approach

Our goal is to create a classroom environment conducive to learning, where students feel accepted by teachers and peers. Effective teachers are able to assess a student's comfort level and attitudes in ways that enable the student to take risks and share ideas in class. Helping students develop positive attitudes is a two-part process: First, you must help students view the class as worthwhile, and second, you must help students feel confident about their abilities to succeed in the class. You can help students develop positive attitudes in part by engaging them in ways that make learning relevant to their lives. Providing students with tasks that are both valuable and interesting encourages intrinsic motivation for learning. We also can draw upon external motivators, such as grades or group competitions, in ways that support learning.

Selected Research Related to the Issue

1. People are influenced by other people's attitudes and perceptions about their abilities. "In our society, there is a pervasive tendency to equate accomplishment with human value, or put simply, individuals are thought to be only as worthy as their achievements. Because of this, it is understandable that students often confuse ability with worth. For those stu-

dents who are already insecure, tying a sense of worth to ability is a risky step because schools can threaten their ability. This is true because schools typically provide insufficient rewards for all students to strive for success. Instead, too many children must struggle simply to avoid failure." (Covington 1992, p. 74)

"Self-worth theory adds still another perspective to classroom motivation. If the criterion for self-acceptance in the classroom is high academic accomplishment relative to others, then, by definition, only a few high-performing students can obtain a sense of self-worth." (Marzano 2003, pp. 146–147)

2. People are influenced by their own perceptions of their abilities. Attribution theory postulates that how students perceive the causes of their prior successes and failures is a better determinant of motivation and persistence than is a learned success or failure avoidance orientation. In general, there are four causes to which individuals attribute their success: ability, effort, luck, and task difficulty. Of these, effort is the most useful, as the cause of success can translate into a willingness to engage in complex tasks and persist over time. (Marzano 2003, p. 146)

3. Motivation can be awakened in safe and trusting environments where people have the support they need to take risks. The Motivational Framework for Culturally Responsive Teaching includes the following:

   • *Establishing inclusion* refers to employing principles and practices that contribute to a learning environment in which students and teachers feel respected by and connected to one another.

   • *Developing a positive attitude* refers to employing principles and practices that contribute to, through personal and cultural relevance and through choice, a favorable disposition toward learning.

   • *Enhancing meaning* refers to bringing about challenging and engaging learning. It expands and strengthens learning in ways that matter to students and have social merit.

   • *Engendering competence* refers to employing principles and practices that help students authentically identify that they are effectively learning something they value (Ginsberg and Wlodkowski 2000, p. 45).

4. Motivation can be intrinsic or extrinsic and needs to "hook" students into wanting to learn. "Extrinsic motivators include deadlines for research projects, classroom competitions, and tests and quizzes affecting students'

grades. Intrinsic motivation, in contrast, usually stems from intellectual curiosity and a desire to learn. There is some evidence that extrinsic motivation may actually be detrimental, impeding students' intrinsic desire to learn. For example, students doing a research project might focus primarily on completing the task rather than learning the concepts (Moje et al. 2001; Nuthall 1999; 2001). Similarly, a laboratory activity performed only to confirm a previously presented idea is unlikely to deepen students' understanding of that idea; students will likely focus more on finding the 'right' answer than on understanding the underlying concepts." (Banilower et al. 2008, p.6)

What Is the Strategy?

Only two large-scale research studies in recent years have examined teaching inside science classrooms and, in both, attitudes and motivation were key elements. According to the recently released synthesis report on effective science instruction (Banilower et al. 2008), *Teaching Science in Five Countries: Results From the TIMSS 1999 Video Study* (Roth et al. 2006) reported that in eighth-grade classrooms, 32% of instructional time was spent motivating students, and the *Looking Inside the Classroom* (2003) study found that about 40% of lessons included a motivational element. If you talk to most teachers, they will identify motivating students to be one of their biggest and most important challenges. Our ability to motivate students is linked to their attitudes about the class and about the work in the classroom. Thus, this strategy focuses on developing student attitudes and motivation.

Marzano and Pickering (1997) provide guidance on how to address student attitudes and motivation by outlining actions that teachers can take to help students develop positive attitudes and perceptions about classroom climate and classroom tasks. They also address actions for developing students' intrinsic and extrinsic motivation to learn. These actions include the following:

Classroom Climate

- Providing instruction that helps students feel accepted by the teacher and peers

- Establishing classroom procedures and policies that allow all students to experience a sense of comfort and order

Classroom Tasks

- Providing students with tasks that are interesting and relevant to their lives

- Helping students believe that they have the ability and resources to complete tasks

- Helping students understand and be clear about the work they are being asked to complete

Motivation

- Developing intrinsic motivation by using hands-on, inquiry activities, discrepant events, and science mysteries and providing opportunities for students to ask questions and wonder "how" and "why" through investigations and problem-solving activities

- Developing extrinsic motivation through completion of work, grades, and assessments

Restricting motivators to extrinsic types can contribute to negative classroom attitudes. That is why it is important to consider actions that address both intrinsic and extrinsic motivation. Considering both types helps you engage different students in different ways. Clearly, using motivation as a strategy to develop a supportive classroom environment requires reflection and careful planning.

Exploring the Strategy

An important factor in developing positive attitudes and motivation in the classroom is establishing relationships with each student in the class. When students feel accepted, it boosts their confidence, and therefore, they work harder and learn more. Where can you start? Think about this: What do students say about a "good" teacher and a "bad" teacher to the teacher, to their peers, to their parents, or to themselves? What do they say about learning science? Consider what you have personally experienced as a student as well. Figure 4.5 includes common student responses to the question about good and bad teachers.

As a result of these negative attitudes and feelings, students might withdraw, disengage, misbehave, or skip class. To turn these negative attitudes around, we have to think about our own attitudes and reactions. Consider how developing student motivation fits into your perception of your role as a teacher. Do you plan for developing student motivation in your lessons? Also consider how you tend to respond to different student attitudes. What student actions or words "push your

Figure 4.5
Attitudes of Students About Teachers

"Good" Teachers	"Bad" Teachers
• Care about my well-being	• Don't know their subject matter
• Are interested in my progress	• Have expectations that are wretchedly, boringly low
• Provide clear expectations	• Don't care about us or whether we learn
• Treat everyone fairly	• Spend all their time worrying about rules
• Love their subject and love teaching	• Have favorites and don't treat us equally
• Are available outside of class and are there to help us	• Lecture all the time
• Make learning interesting and fun	• Won't help me

buttons"? Think about how you can interact with students in positive ways and what you will say to convey positive expectations.

Positive relationships don't develop by magic—they must be built. There are many ways to establish positive relationships and build mutual respect, including the following (Combs 1982):

- Greet students at the door individually and welcome them to class. Make a personal comment when possible.

- Talk informally with students before, during, and after class about their interests. Whenever you have had a negative interaction with a student, such as asking them why they didn't get their homework turned in or why they did so poorly on a test, it will take seven positive or neutral interactions with that student to rebuild their trust so that they believe you really care about them again.

- Be aware of important events in your students' lives and comment on them (e.g., sports, performing arts, extracurricular activities).

- Include students in classroom planning. Find out what learning experiences they have already had, what they think is important when it comes to rubrics, what expertise they may have, and what questions they would like to have answered as part of the unit.

- Call students by name and do not refer to their siblings. It is important to learn first names as soon as possible and be careful not to mispronounce their name.

- Have students complete a science "autobiography" of themselves or an interest survey related to science and then use that information throughout the school year to connect to student interests.

- Be available to assist and support students both in and out of the classroom. Let them know that you are there to help them.

These examples of how to build relationships with students may not be new to you. Consider them as reminders that can refocus us as we work with all students. Deliberately taking these actions to connect with students on a personal level may seem artificial, but building and rebuilding trust takes time, persistence, and practice.

In addition to building relationships with our students, are there additional ways we can help students develop positive attitudes and perceptions about learning? One action you can take is to provide students with choices about how they demonstrate their learning. This practice acknowledges that not all students have the same needs or react in the same ways. It also provides opportunities for students to use their strengths and interests. For example, you might offer students the option of acting out the science concepts, or writing a poem, or creating an interactive game to provide evidence of their conceptual understanding.

Positive attitudes and perceptions are more likely to develop in an environment where students have the chance to get to know and accept one another. You can create such an environment in your classroom by including structured "working together" activities that encourage students to collaborate. Establishing classroom norms that students discuss and agree upon will provide opportunities for the entire class to practice positive behaviors. Modeling and reinforcing common courtesy and respect also will encourage the development of positive attitudes and perceptions about the classroom and learning.

Planning for Classroom Implementation

There are many different ideas you can consider as you determine what you should implement to help students develop positive attitudes and perceptions. After reading the following ideas and explanations, you can use the tool provided in this chapter's appendix (Environment Strategy 3: Develop Positive Attitudes and Motivation) to plan for implementation in your classroom.

Improve students' sense of comfort and order in your classroom:

- *Use policies and procedures that support a collaborative classroom culture.* Policies and procedures related to turning in work, late assignments, starting and ending class, discussions, leaving class, independent and collaborative work, grading and homework, and laboratory work are ones that will be used again and again. As a result, we need to teach the steps of each procedure, model it, provide time for students to practice it, and reinforce it. Be sure your expectations for how well students will carry out these procedures are realistic when students are first learning them. Depending on the complexity of the procedure and individual student characteristics, students may need as many as 20–24 experiences with the procedure before they master it (Marzano 1992). Developing policies that are schoolwide and consistently enforced by all teachers makes it more likely that students will follow the procedures. To learn more about this approach, see *The First Days of School*, by Harry and Rosemary Wong (2004).

- *Improve your management skills.* The secret to behavior management is having students fully engaged in the learning process and keeping the rules to a minimum. One resource on specific techniques is *Tools for Teaching* (Jones 2000), which is extremely detailed and full of concrete directions.

Make it your responsibility to help students feel accepted by you and their peers:

- *Collect information on preferences that you can use when creating cooperative groups.*

- *Reach out seven times to establish neutral or positive relationships with students.*

- *Learn recommended strategies for high-needs students.* There are many reasons why a student might be designated as "high-needs." Some are designated as high-needs because they are difficult to teach. These students fall into one of the following categories: passive, aggressive, attention problems, perfectionist, or socially inept (Marzano 2003). For more information about these categories, see *What Works in Schools: Translating Research Into Action* (Marzano 2003, pp. 104–105) or *Classroom Management That Works: Research-Based Strategies for Every Teacher*

(Marzano, Pickering, and Pollock 2003). These resources emphasize that the most successful classroom managers employ different strategies for different types of students. Secondary students might have difficulty accepting this concept. To help them understand the concept, explicitly provide examples that illustrate how providing for individual student needs is, indeed, fair. For elementary students, use specific techniques to help students understand the rules and your expectation that they follow them.

Develop students' positive attitudes about classroom tasks:

- *Teach the relationship between effort and achievement.* You might be surprised to learn that not all students realize the importance of believing that effort can lead to achievement (Marzano, Pickering, and Pollock 2001). Fortunately, in their review of the research on instruction, Marzano and his colleagues also found that students can change their beliefs about the role of effort in achievement. Teachers can provide examples from sports, performing arts, and other student activities that illustrate the relationship between effort and achievement. Such examples show students that practice improves performance and that hard work pays off in learning just as it does in other activities.

- *Attend to safety and choice issues that specifically apply to science.* Some students have fears about science—fire, animals, dissection, smells, and such. Many of these fears can be addressed, even on the first day of school, through safety information. Resources for this strategy include the NSTA position statements on safety (*www.nsta.org/about/positions/safety.aspx*) and dissection (*www.nsta.org/pdfs/PositionStatement_LiveAnimalsAndDissection.pdf*). Flinn Scientific provides student safety contracts and other resources that address safety in the science classroom on their website (*www.flinnsci.com/Sections/Safety/safety_contracts.asp*).

As you think about implementing actions to develop students' intrinsic motivation, remember that students are motivated by events that contradict their expectations or that stimulate their curiosity and give them opportunities to solve a mystery. As you plan for implementation, think about discrepant events, mysteries that can be solved through application of science principles, and questions that might be relevant to your students' lives and of interest to them.

Return to thinking about ways that you currently support positive classroom attitudes. Refer to Figure 4.6, Developing Positive Student Attitudes, to decide

Figure 4.6
Developing Positive Student Attitudes

Attitudes and Perceptions	Suggestions to Improve the Classroom Environment
Does each student feel accepted by teachers and peers?	• Establish a relationship with each student in the class. For difficult-to-reach students, aim for one neutral/positive interaction for seven days in a row. • Monitor your own attitudes. Don't hold grudges. • Assist students in gaining acceptance of their peers. • Use cooperative learning strategies in which roles for members of a group are identified, including process observers. • Positively and thoughtfully respond to students' incorrect responses. • Recognize effort and risk-taking in each student's learning.
Does each student experience a sense of comfort and order?	• Focus on creating an environment that is centered around learning—then teach, model, and insist on meeting standards. • Engage students in setting classroom standards. • Establish and communicate classroom rules and procedures. • Establish clear policies about the physical safety of students. • Be proactive about addressing social/emotional issues (e.g., bullying, sexual harassment, racism). • Defuse situations before they become problems.
Does each student perceive tasks as valuable and interesting?	• Communicate learning goals as concepts, and tie them into "real life" situations (e.g., personal decisions, social issues, intriguing questions that don't have one right answer). • Make connections between the knowledge and skills students are learning and the "big ideas" for which they are developing understanding, as well as connections between big ideas. • Involve students in setting goals for their learning, and when possible, link tasks to their personal interests. • Plan an exploratory experience to activate and evaluate prior knowledge on each new topic. • Search for and use hands-on activities that allow students of varied levels of understanding to participate meaningfully.
Does each student believe they have the ability and resources to complete tasks?	• Establish a "we're all here to learn" environment, offer your confidence and assistance, and broker peer support. • Provide examples of good student work, rubrics of proficiency, samples of work products. • Keep learning logs in which students can record what they have learned as well as their ongoing questions. • Support struggling readers by teaching methods of comprehending nonfiction text materials. • Establish timelines and calendars for students to record progress toward learning goals. • Teach students to use positive self-talk.
Does each student understand the tasks?	• Communicate learning goals and descriptions of proficiency for each unit. • Break complex tasks into small steps or parts. • Support English language learners, as well as varied learning styles, by having both oral and written directions, and using consistent carefully chosen vocabulary. • Teach students how and when to ask for help, so they can advocate for themselves.

Adapted from Marzano, R., and D. Pickering. 1997. *Dimensions of learning trainer's manual.* Alexandria, VA: Association for Supervision and Curriculum Development.

where to focus your planning related to student attitudes. Begin by scanning the left-hand column to assess your current challenges. Think about particular students and the kinds of outcomes you would like to see. Scan the suggestions column for strategies to address your desired outcomes. Use the planning template provided in the appendix of this chapter (Environment Strategy 3. Develop Positive Attitudes and Motivation) to describe how you will incorporate these ideas in your lesson plans.

What Works in Science Classrooms: Implications for Teaching

Recommendation 1: Analyze your own attitudes about students and check your perception of your ability to create a positive classroom climate. Research suggests that the goal is not only to identify your own attitudes related to learning but also to help students identify theirs. In addition, it is important to determine what students need to feel comfortable and have a sense of order in the classroom. By working together and building relationships with and among students, you can set the stage for positive classroom behavior that will result in improved learning.

Recommendation 2: Create classroom tasks that relate to students' interests and help them meet the learning goals. When tasks are perceived as too easy, students get bored and disengage. When they perceive tasks as too difficult, they frequently give up. Tasks must be both rigorous and relevant to keep students on track and help them succeed (NASSP 1996). As you address this recommendation, keep in mind that, as teachers, we are also responsible for helping students understand that we will support them by providing the tools and resources they need to complete tasks successfully.

Recommendation 3: "Hook" students with the learning and find ways to engage them intellectually with the content. Think about the many ways to use the wonder, mystery, and investigations that are part of science to develop students' intrinsic motivation. Too often, teachers complain that their students aren't motivated by anything but grades; that if they don't grade everything, students won't do any work. That response may stem, in part, from students' perceptions that the work is uninteresting and has nothing to do with them and their lives. We can change that.

Environment Strategy 4: Provide Feedback

The Issue

For many students, particularly those who learned little or no science in elementary school, science seems like a foreign language, because their science experiences were neither rooted in the ways of science nor focused on developing understanding. This lack of experience with "doing science" is compounded by superficial exposure to an abundance of science topics. Generally, students do not receive the type of feedback that would help them understand the extent of their science knowledge and skills or make progress in learning science. The result is frustration for students and teachers.

Table 4.1
Creating a Positive Learning Environment

Strategy 1: Believe All Students Can Learn Show through your actions that you believe all students have the ability to learn.	
Strategy 2: Think Scientifically Teach students to think scientifically.	
Strategy 3: Develop Positive Attitudes and Motivation Develop positive student attitudes and motivation to learn science.	**What's really important?**
Strategy 4: Provide Feedback Give timely and criterion-referenced feedback.	**How do I create a positive learning environment?**
Strategy 5: Reinforce Progress and Effort Keep students focused on learning by reinforcing progress and effort.	
Strategy 6: Teach Students to Be Metacognitive Involve students in thinking about their ideas and assessing their own progress.	

The DESI Approach

Providing meaningful feedback to students is essential in helping students understand science concepts. The DESI approach focuses on planning for and providing feedback that is corrective, timely, criterion-referenced, and clear. In other words, feedback goes beyond grading assignments using a "right/wrong" or "minus-one-point-for-each-error" model. Feedback needs to be corrective so that students can learn from their work. The feedback must be timely to provide the best opportunity for students to assimilate the information into their learning framework. And, the feedback needs to be criterion-referenced and communicated clearly so that students know what high-quality work looks like, what they have done correctly, and what they still need to learn.

Selected Research Related to the Issue

1. Feedback that is formative in nature supports learning. "Effective feedback should help the learners know where they are and where they should go next: the focus is improvement.... Comments are the most common way for the teacher to have a dialogue with everyone in the class.... In many cases, an effective comment relates back to the success criteria or descriptions of quality that have been shared with or devised by the students before they attempt a task. In this way, students work towards success or quality by considering the criteria as their work progresses. The feedback is then the teacher's judgment, which can be matched against the student's own judgment of quality." (Black and Harrison 2004, pp. 11–12)

2. One of the most general strategies a teacher can use is to provide students with feedback relative to how well they are doing. In fact, feedback seems to work well in so many situations that it led researcher John Hattie (1992) to make the following comment after analyzing almost 8,000 studies: The most powerful single modification that enhances achievement is feedback. The simplest prescription for improving education must be "dollops of feedback."

3. Marzano, Pickering, and Pollock's (2001) meta-analysis of K–12 instruction revealed nine categories of instructional strategies with the highest expected student achievement gains. These categories include "Setting Objectives" and "Providing Feedback." Additional information about this research will be provided in the following "What Is the Strategy?" section.

What is the Strategy?

First, let's look at the recommendations regarding feedback provided in *Classroom Instruction That Works* (Marzano, Pickering, and Pollock 2001). As you read the research summary on "Providing Feedback," note the information that speaks specifically to what a teacher should do and the numerical information in the charts that indicates a relatively strong likelihood for a positive effect on students' achievement. Findings from some of the studies that have synthesized research on the general effects of feedback are reported in Figure 4.7 (p. 164). Perhaps one of the more interesting findings regarding feedback was reported by Bangert-Drowns et al. (1991). They report an overall effect size of only .26. However, it is important to note that their study focused on feedback that takes the form of a test or, as they prefer, "test-like events." Their findings are reported in Figure 4.8 (p. 165), which highlights research that emphasizes the points that feedback should be corrective in nature and timely.

Summarizing from the research, this strategy suggests that you provide feedback to students after assessments of learning (i.e., summative assessments such as tests, laboratory write-ups, and projects). For these student products the feedback must be timely, criterion-referenced, clear, and corrective in nature. Providing feedback one day after a test is more effective than after each item, or immediately after the test. Additionally, providing right or wrong answers is not as effective as providing opportunities for students to correct their answers. A combination of verification and elaboration is most effective so that students have an idea of what they need to do next (Shute 2008). The complexity of the elaboration is best determined by the teacher in each teachable moment. Since the effectiveness of feedback depends on its utility for a particular student with a particular learning goal, teachers need to be mindful about what information each student needs and when, as each of their students makes progress in learning science.

As long as the feedback is not perceived as an interruption by students, feedback can be provided in the moment, at predetermined junctures in the learning, or whenever you need to check whether students are ready to move forward and need help with what to work on next. As described in Chapter 3 (Understanding), feedback on formative assessment is most effective if provided after a period of learning, using descriptive comments that probe a students' thinking to reveal what they are doing well and what they should do to progress. When providing formative assessment feedback, using only points ("marks") or points plus comments doesn't seem to help students (Butler 1987) and is a waste of our time. This practice is not effective because students tend to look only at the score and ignore the comments. Using points to provide feedback can have negative effects on low achievers' motivation and, at the same time, it fails to challenge high achievers to improve. Using descriptive comments seems to motivate low achievers because they receive information about how to improve (Black and Wiliam 1998). Research also suggests that teachers provide opportunities for students to self-assess and provide some of their own feedback. Student self-assessment can be guided by use of goal-setting, rubrics, checklists and/or self-monitoring questions, allowing

Figure 4.7
Research Results for Providing Feedback

Synthesis Study	Focus	Number of Effect Sizes	Average ES	Percentile Gain [b]
Lysakowski & Walberg, 1982 [a]	General effects of feedback	22	.92	32
		7	.69	25
		3	.83	30
		9	.71	26
Lysakowski & Walberg, 1981 [a]	General effects of feedback	39	1.15	37
		19	.49	19
		49	.55	21
		11	.19	7
Walberg, 1999	General effects of feedback	20	.94	33
Tennebaum & Goldring, 1989 [a]	General effects of feedback	15	.66	25
		7	.80	29
		3	.52	20
		3	.51	19
		2	.67	25
Bloom, 1976	General effects of feedback	7	.54	21
Haller, Child, & Walberg, 1988	General effects of feedback	20	.71	26
Bangert-Drowns, Kulik, Kulik, & Morgan (1991)	General effects of feedback	58	.26	10

[a] Multiple effect sizes are listed because of the manner in which they were reported.
    Readers should consult those studies for more details.

[b] These are the maximum gains possible for students currently at the 50th percentile.

Note that some of the effect sizes reported are .90 and even higher.
Generally, feedback that produces these large effect sizes are "corrective" in nature.

From Marzano, R., D. Pickering, and J. Pollock. 2001. *Classroom instruction that works: Research-based strategies for increasing student achievement.* Alexandria, VA: Association for Supervision and Curriculum Development. Copyright 2001 by McREL. Reprinted with permission.

Figure 4.8
Feedback Study Results

Synthesis Study	Focus	Number of Effect Sizes	Average ES	Percentile Gain [a]
Type of Feedback	Right/wrong answer	6	-.08	-3
	Correct answer	39	.22	9
	Repeat until correct	4	.53	20
	Explanation	9	.53	20
Timing of Feedback	Immediately after item	49	.19	7
	Immediately after test	2	.72	26
	Delayed after test	8	.56	21
Timing of Test	Immediately	37	.17	6
	One day	2	.74	27
	One week	12	.53	20
	Longer	4	.26	10

[a] These are the maximum gains possible for students currently at the 50th percentile.

students to compare their performances with their own or another's expectations (Bangert-Drowns et al. 1991).

When it comes to feedback on summative assessments, the advice is also clear. From the research, we know that this type of feedback must be provided in a timely fashion and be based on clear criteria. In addition, it must provide students with information about what they have done correctly in relation to those criteria. Providing feedback after students complete projects, laboratory write-ups, or any other summative assessment is yet another strategy that contributes to increased student achievement.

Exploring the Strategy

Criterion-referenced feedback, which provides students with feedback in terms of specific levels of performance relative to the learning objectives, is better than feedback in the form of percentage scores. Providing criterion-referenced feedback involves

- using well-developed rubrics that are based on quality of performance, not quantity of work. Remember that rubrics should be specific to the project and that levels of performance should be written in clear language that students can understand;

- using exemplars to help students know what quality work looks like and how their work compares to high-quality work. Numerous online and print resources are available to help identify the characteristics of high-quality science work;

- informing students whether their work is proficient and what advanced work looks like.

Teachers should provide students with feedback throughout a unit of instruction and **as soon after individual assessment events as possible**. The more delayed the feedback, the less improvement there is in achievement. If it takes a month to evaluate laboratory write-ups and get them back to students, the feedback will not support students' achievement. Make this aspect of providing feedback a priority by providing formative feedback for projects, performance assessments, laboratory write-ups, and other classroom assignments along the way. This will help students improve the quality of their work throughout the unit. As a result, you will need to spend less time reviewing final student work. This means you can return students' work quickly and students can connect the feedback they have received to improved understanding.

Simply telling students their answer is right or wrong has a negative effect on achievement. The best feedback involves an **explanation** of what is correct and incorrect about the response. If teachers provide students with this type of feedback, and ask them to keep working on a task until they succeed, they will achieve at higher levels. To practice this aspect of providing feedback, ask students to work in pairs or teams to research the correct answers to an assessment you have given them and to explain why those answers are correct. Also ask them to explain why the incorrect answers are wrong. This approach works even with multiple-choice questions.

Students benefit from participating in **peer and self-assessment.** Engaging students in peer and self-assessments develops students' abilities to recognize quality and gaps in their work and the work of others. As they get better at comparing their level of work, and the work of others, to the criteria for quality work, they can discuss strengths and weaknesses of a sample of work with clarity. As with any procedure, you need to help students learn how to be effective self-assessors and peer-assessors. You may want to start by having students assess their own work using the criteria for success and then add some descriptive comments yourself to their self-assessments. After students have practiced assessing the quality of their own work, you can ask them to assess the work of their peers. The practice with self-assessment is important because it provides students with some knowledge of what to look for and how to provide constructive comments. To help students overcome their tendency to provide only positive comments to their peers, show them how providing constructive comments helps them and their peers improve their learning.

Planning for Classroom Implementation

The appendix for Chapter 4 (Environment Strategy 4) provides a template on which you can record reminders as you plan ways to implement the "Providing Feedback" strategy. Start by selecting an aspect of this strategy that you consider as your top priority. As you think about using this strategy, remember that the purpose of feedback is to advance learning and that there are many ways to provide feedback to students. Some teachers rely on teacher-student conferencing and others provide written comments to let students know what to focus on next in their learning. In either case, including probing questions in your feedback will prompt students to think and encourage them to act on the information about what they should do next.

What Works in Science Classrooms: Implications for Teaching

Recommendation 1: Establish feedback systems that work. There is rigorous research evidence that providing students with feedback promotes student achievement. Remember, students have to do their own learning; we can't do it for them. Our job is to make the learning targets clear and then help students understand and meet the criteria for quality work. An effective feedback system provides students with information about their performance that helps them progress in their learning. Without feedback, learning won't progress.

Recommendation 2: Use both formative and summative feedback, relative to established criteria for quality work, to help students progress. "Grading" every assignment teaches a student how to get points, not how to learn and demonstrate learning of science concepts. Grades and points should be given only on work that is summative in nature. Formative feedback should replace points or grades on some of the assignments that lead up to the summative assessment. To ensure that feedback on summative work supports increased student learning, clearly identify the criteria for success, share these criteria with students, and base feedback on those criteria.

Environment Strategy 5: Reinforcing Progress and Effort

The Issue

Some students don't succeed in science because they don't put enough effort into learning. This lack of effort occurs for a variety of reasons. For example, some students feel that they are just not "good at science" so they stop trying to learn. Other students don't exert effort to learn because there is an atmosphere of competition in the classroom. In these classrooms, it seems that students are pitted against one another and challenged to be the first to come up with an answer or solution. Students know, if they just bide their time, someone else will provide the answer and they won't have to exert any effort to learn. They know that as soon as the "right" answer is found and shared with the class, the teacher will move on. In other cases,

Table 4.1
Creating a Positive Learning Environment

Strategy 1: Believe All Students Can Learn Show through your actions that you believe all students have the ability to learn.	
Strategy 2: Think Scientifically Teach students to think scientifically.	
Strategy 3: Develop Positive Attitudes and Motivation Develop positive student attitudes and motivation to learn science.	**What's really important?**
Strategy 4: Provide Feedback Give timely and criterion-referenced feedback.	**How do I create a positive learning environment?**
Strategy 5: Reinforce Progress and Effort Keep students focused on learning by reinforcing progress and effort.	
Strategy 6: Teach Students to Be Metacognitive Involve students in thinking about their ideas and assessing their own progress.	

students do not have adequate time to put in the effort required to learn. We need to consider all of the reasons why students do not exert effort and help students understand the importance of effort.

The DESI Approach

Students often do not realize the impact of effort on learning (Marzano, Pickering, and Pollock 2001). They try once to complete activities, and if they are not successful, they often give up rather than keep trying. To address this problem, teachers need to develop strategies to reinforce effort. Reinforcing effort does not mean telling students the "right" answers; rather, it means teaching students how to practice and struggle to make sense of what they are learning.

Selected Research Related to the Issue

1. "[P]eople generally attribute success at any given task to one of four causes: ability, effort, other people, or luck (Covington 1983; Harter 1980). On the surface, a belief in ability seems relatively useful—if you believe you have ability, you can tackle anything. However, regardless of how much ability you think you have, there inevitably will be tasks for which you do not believe you have the requisite ability. In fact, Covington's research (1983; 1985) indicates that a belief on the part of students that they do not possess the necessary ability to succeed at a task will cause them not to even try to succeed at the task. Belief that other people are the primary cause of success also has drawbacks, particularly when an individual finds himself or herself alone. Belief in luck has obvious disadvantages—what if your luck runs out? Belief in effort is clearly the most useful attribution." (Marzano, Pickering, and Pollock 2001)

2. One study found that students who were taught about the relationship between effort and achievement increased their achievement more than students who were taught techniques for time management and comprehension of new material (Van Overwalle and De Metsenaere 1990).

3. A number of researchers have synthesized the studies on the effects on student achievement of reinforcing effort. As explained in *A Different Kind of Classroom: Teaching With Dimensions of Learning* (Marzano 1992) and *Classroom Instruction That Works* (Marzano, Pickering, and Pollock 2001), studies have shown that simply teaching students that added effort will pay off in terms of enhanced achievement actually increases student achievement. The results from some of those syntheses are reported in Figure 4.9 (p. 170).

Figure 4.9
Synthesis Results

Synthesis Study	Number of Effect Sizes	Average ES	Percentile Gain [c]
Schunk & Cox, 1986	3	.93	32
Stipek & Weisz, 1981 [a]	98	.25	10
Hattie, Biggs, & Purdie, 1996 [b]	8	1.42	42
	2	.57	22
	2	2.14	48

[a] These studies also dealt with students' sense of control.

[b] Multiple categories of effect sizes are listed for the Hattie, Biggs, and Purdie study because of the manner in which effect size was reported. Readers should consult that study for more details.

[c] These are the maximum gains possible for students currently at the 50th percentile.

From Marzano, R., D. Pickering, and J. Pollock. 2001. *Classroom instruction that works: Research-based strategies for increasing student achievement*. Alexandria, VA: Association for Supervision and Curriculum Development. Copyright 2001 by McREL. Reprinted with permission.

What Is the Strategy?

Given that some students might not understand the importance of a belief in the power of effort, we need to provide them with basic information about the effects of effort. One way to do this is by sharing examples. You might challenge students to think of people, especially scientists, who persevered despite great challenges. Bob Ballard, for example, conducted a 12-year search for the wreck of the *Titanic* and developed state-of-the-art visual imaging technology, in addition to using geologic, oceanographic, and historic information, before his dream was realized in 1985. You can also personalize examples by giving your own story of perseverance or by asking students to recall times when they completed a project or achieved a personal goal because of persistence and hard work. In various fields—sports, music, performing arts, science—practice, with the help and support of a coach, is key to success. As teachers, we must coach students, by encouraging them and creating opportunities for them to practice what they're learning.

You might have noticed the connection between this strategy and the strategy on getting the content correct from Chapter 2. For students to make progress in their learning, teachers must identify clear learning goals and the criteria for achievement. Doing so helps students know where to direct their efforts. Effort, in and of itself, should be taught and reinforced as it is a factor that can move students from novice learners toward mastery of science concepts.

Exploring the Strategy

Rubrics are one way to provide students with the criteria for achievement; however, students often think of rubrics as checklists. When they "check off" everything on a rubric, they think they have finished learning. So, we need to create rubrics that expect high-quality performance and focus on higher cognitive demand. This means that rubrics should focus on quality indicators (e.g., students will critique the claims presented in their hypothesis by citing significant, appropriate evidence) rather than solely on quantity indicators (e.g., students will provide three pieces of supporting evidence).

It is sometimes difficult to include the criteria for all aspects of the expected learning in a rubric. One option is to couple the rubric with samples of student work that illustrate how students have met the criteria. Discussing such examples with students helps them understand why one piece is exemplary and illustrates advanced work and another is basic and indicates that more effort is needed. This strategy can be linked with the previous one on feedback. Rubrics help students understand the evidence needed to demonstrate understanding of the content and provide a way to give feedback to students. Students can use feedback on their performance to think about where they are in the learning process and where they need to exert more effort to perform at higher levels on the rubric.

Figure 4.10 (p. 172) provides a general description of the achievement characteristics of performance at five levels (including zero). Note that level three is the "acceptable" level of performance. This level is often called "proficient" performance.

In addition to using a progress (achievement) rubric, or other method to show students the criteria that must be met to master learning goals, teachers can use an effort rubric to assess students' persistence in learning. Involving your students in creating effort and achievement rubrics will make the learning goals more relevant to them. Students can gauge their level of effort by self-assessing or by receiving feedback from peers or the teacher. Depending on your grade level, helping students self-assess and peer-assess might take some practice. Younger students

Figure 4.10
Performance Rubric

4		Exemplary performance that exceeds the targeted level of performance. Students are able to apply their learning to new situations, going beyond what was taught in class and demonstrate high levels of cognitive learning.
3	**Acceptable level of Performance**	Solid performance that meets the targeted level of performance. Students are able to demonstrate conceptual understanding and demonstrate knowledge and skills based on what was presented in class. No major errors or gaps in student work products.
2		Performance that is emerging or developing toward the targeted level of performance. Students can demonstrate mastery of knowledge and skills, but their conceptual understanding of the materials is not at the depth of understanding expected.
1		Performance in which an attempt was made but there are some serious misconceptions or errors. With teacher support, students can show some knowledge and skills.
0		No judgment can be made about the students' level of performance. Even with teacher support, students cannot demonstrate understanding of the science ideas.

Adapted from Marzano, R. 2006. *Classroom assessment and grading that work.* Alexandria, VA: Association for Supervision and Curriculum Development.

might have more difficulty recognizing how their work compares with expected performance levels. Middle school students often perceive that completion demonstrates competency. And peer assessment can be confusing for students who want to give positive feedback to their friends and will resist making recommendations for improvement. Self-assessing effort also should be discussed and practiced.

Effort scores can then be matched with the progress rubric scores or criteria to emphasize the impact of persistence and hard work. A blank effort rubric that you can use with your students when you discuss the characteristics of effort is provided in this chapter's appendix for Environment Strategy 5.

Don't forget to post the rubric (but not individual student scores) in the classroom for students to refer to as they work or when they provide feedback to peers.

A new tracking sheet can be used each quarter (marking period) or for each unit, whichever works for you and your students. You can keep track of the performance of the class as a whole and illustrate this graphically for the class to see. For elementary students, you might want to complete a tracking form each day. Once middle and high school students learn about the impact of effort, it might not be necessary to have every student complete a self-assessment. Some teachers use this method on a student-by-student basis. You may want these students to record their effort for each unit and then set goals for themselves for the next unit. Because teachers and students have different perceptions of the learning environment and their effort, feedback from students about the classroom and their participation should be collected. We can then use that data as we strive to create productive, positive learning environments that are more cohesive and goal oriented and where there is less overall friction.

Planning for Classroom Implementation

Reinforcing effort and progress in the classroom takes time. Just telling students that they can succeed is not enough. Asking them to work harder is also not a strategy that yields achievement gains. Teaching about effort, practicing it, monitoring it, and reflecting on the results that are achieved with effort are all proactive ways that we can help students as we address this strategy.

Reflect on the following ideas for your practice:

1. Teach students about the research on effort to make them self-aware.

2. Help students believe that they can succeed by providing the resources they need (including time), encouraging and reinforcing their efforts, and providing support so they can complete tasks (this doesn't mean telling them the answer).

3. Ask students to set goals for both effort and achievement and track their effort compared to achievement.

4. Engage the class in group goal setting around effort that supports learning. At the completion of difficult learning experiences, discuss with students what they learned about effort as they participated in the learning activities.

As mentioned earlier, a powerful way to exemplify the impact of effort is to implement a system by which students track their effort in relationship to achievement. Students can track their own effort and achievement using record sheets. Then, students can plot the relationship between their effort and achievement in

Figure 4.11
Sample Tracking Sheet

Student _____

Date(s) of Work	Assignment	Due Date	Effort Rubric	Achievement Rubric
October 6—7	Design an experiment	October 7	2	2
October 8—9	Conduct the experiment	October 9	3	3
October 10—13	Develop explanations and communicate to the class	October 13	3	3
October 15	Laboratory write-up completed	October 15	4	3.5

Adapted from Weiss, I., J. Pasley, S. Smith, E. Banilower, and D. Heck. 2003. *Looking inside the classroom: A study of K–12 mathematics and science education in the United States.* Chapel Hill, NC: Horizon Research, Inc.

a chart or graph so that they can visualize the relationship. A student example is provided in Figure 4.11, which shows a tracking sheet for students to record their assignments, when it was assigned, their effort score, and their achievement progress score from the rubric designed with class input.

In addition to charting the relationship between the two variables (effort and achievement), students might be asked to tell us what they learned from the experience. For example, teachers might periodically ask students to describe what they noticed about the relationship between the effort they put into a project or task and their achievement. Reflecting on their experiences in this way helps students heighten their awareness of the power of effort.

To build students' confidence in their learning abilities, we have to help them set reasonable, attainable goals. Figure 4.12 provides a self-assessment tool that can be used by students to determine their effort and what they want to work to improve. Conferencing with students one-on-one will give you a chance to see what each student needs. This may sound impractical if you have 150 plus students, but targeting a few students each day while they are working on other learning experiences can make this approach work. Conferencing provides opportunities to discuss with students what they believe about themselves and how those beliefs align with the behaviors you observe in class. Students are generally very honest in their self-assessments so the conference provides a chance to promote positive improvement in behaviors. When students develop positive work habits their behavior contributes to the overall positive classroom climate.

Figure 4.12
Student Self-Assessment and Goal Setting Template

Put an X on the scale to indicate your self-assessment.
Write a sentence below the scale to explain your response.

1. I always listen to the teacher in class and follow instructions.

Never   Sometimes   Always

2. I contribute to class discussions and readily share my ideas about the science concepts.

Never   Sometimes   Always

3. I turn in my assignments when they are due.

Never   Sometimes   Always

4. My work is always done to the best of my ability.

Never   Sometimes   Always

5. I get help when I need it from both my teacher and my classmates.

Never   Sometimes   Always

6. I contribute fully during group work and help the others in my group with the learning.

Never   Sometimes   Always

7. I use class time wisely and make sure that I clearly know what is expected of my work.

Never   Sometimes   Always

8. I contribute to a positive classroom environment through both participation and supporting the efforts of others.

Never   Sometimes   Always

Goals that will help me improve:

What Works in Science Classrooms: Implications for Teaching

Recommendation 1: Teach students about the relationship between effort and achievement. Effort is a key characteristic of people who succeed. Just like the Little Engine That Could ("I think I can, I think I can, I think I can"), when students believe that they can succeed, they are more likely to persevere and push the limits of their cognitive abilities. Learning about the research that supports effort helps students realize that their capabilities are linked to their motivation to learn, the effort they put into the process, and the belief that their teachers will scaffold the learning to close their gaps in understanding.

Recommendation 2: Ask students to track their progress with learning. Tracking their progress is the simplest way for students to know if they are learning. To track their progress, students must be clear about the learning goals, where they are in relation to those goals at the beginning of a unit of study, and the learning progression that will take them from where they are to the learning goals. You can help students determine their starting point in the learning progression by eliciting their existing thinking about concepts in the unit. Next, explain the learning progression (how ideas within the unit are linked) and share the criteria for success and examples of quality work that provides evidence of learning. It is important to help students develop the belief that with effort and support, they can master the next step in the learning progression. To help students develop this belief, break the learning targets into manageable next steps. Doing so helps students believe that the bigger learning goal is attainable. Without this assistance, students might give up, thinking that the learning goal is just too hard to achieve.

Environment Strategy 6: Teach Students to Be Metacognitive

The Issue

In their efforts to address the vast array of content included in most science curricula, teachers often use a direct teaching approach rather than an inquiry approach. As a result, student learning is frequently limited to knowing definitions and a few facts or details. This race through the curriculum also means that students rarely have opportunities to think about what they are learning. Lack of processing time results in few opportunities for students to make sense of the science concepts embedded in the learning experiences or to learn the information at a deep level. If we want students to think about their thinking, then we need to teach them the processes associated with metacognition and provide time for them to put those processes to use.

Table 4.1
Creating a Positive Learning Environment

Strategy 1: Believe All Students Can Learn Show through your actions that you believe all students have the ability to learn.	
Strategy 2: Think Scientifically Teach students to think scientifically.	
Strategy 3: Develop Positive Attitudes and Motivation Develop positive student attitudes and motivation to learn science.	**What's really important?**
Strategy 4: Provide Feedback Give timely and criterion-referenced feedback.	**How do I create a positive learning environment?**
Strategy 5; Reinforce Progress and Effort Keep students focused on learning by reinforcing progress and effort.	
Strategy 6: Teach Students to Be Metacognitive Involve students in thinking about their ideas and assessing their own progress.	

The DESI Approach

To develop deep understanding of science concepts, students need to think critically and creatively, reason scientifically, and monitor their own thinking and progress with achieving learning goals. In other words, students need to use mental procedures associated with metacognition. It is important for science students, in particular, to be able to use metacognitive processes; these processes are useful as students process information from their observations, analyze their data, and develop conclusions based on their scientific evidence. Teachers can help students develop skills for metacognition by modeling metacognitive strategies, providing opportunities for students to practice those strategies, and reinforcing students' use of them. The DESI approach is to ensure that students have skills and opportunities to think about their thinking so that they can identify what they understand about the science concepts in their units of study, what they think they might understand but aren't sure, what they clearly don't understand, and what they will do to learn what they don't understand.

Selected Research Related to the Issue

1. "Students need to be able to self-assess. This is not a simple task as it requires the student to have a sufficiently clear picture of the targets in the learning trajectory ahead of them and a means of moving forward to close the learning gap. In some classrooms, students do not have this clear picture and respond to lessons as a set of exercises to be completed. In this scenario, the students are not engaged with the learning and are not aware of the rationale behind specific tasks…. Peer assessment helps students develop and hone their self-assessment skills. Students have the ability to recognize both quality and inadequacies in others students' work even if the level of competence that they themselves are performing at is different from the level of work that they are reading." (Black and Harrison 2004, pp. 15–16)

2. "The habits of mind identified in the Dimensions of Learning model fall into three general categories: critical thinking, creative thinking, and self-regulated thinking.

   If you have mental habits that exemplify *critical thinking*, you tend to

   • Be accurate and seek accuracy

   • Be clear and seek clarity

   • Maintain an open mind

- Restrain impulsivity

- Take a position when the situation warrants it

- Respond appropriately to others' feelings and level of knowledge

If you have mental habits that exemplify *creative thinking*, you tend to

- Persevere

- Push the limits of your knowledge and abilities

- Generate, trust, and maintain your own standards of evaluation

- Generate new ways of viewing a situation that are outside the boundaries of standard conventions

If you have mental habits that exemplify *self-regulated thinking,* you tend to

- Monitor your own thinking

- Plan appropriately

- Identify and use necessary resources

- Respond appropriately to feedback

- Evaluate the effectiveness of your actions" (Marzano and Pickering 1997)

3. "The metacognitive system [of thought] includes processes that address goal specification, process monitoring, and disposition monitoring." (Marzano, Pickering, and Pollock 2001, p. 56)

Objectives for metacognition include the following:

- Goal Specification: The student can set a plan for goals relative to the knowledge.

- Process Monitoring: The student can monitor the execution of the knowledge.

- Monitoring Clarity: The student can determine the extent to which he or she has clarity about the knowledge.

- Monitoring Accuracy: The student can determine the extent to which he or she is accurate about the knowledge. (Marzano, Pickering, and Pollock 2001, p.57)

4. "A 'metacognitive' approach to instruction can help students learn to take control of their own learning by defining learning goals and monitoring their progress in achieving them." (Donovan, Bransford, and Pellegrino 1999, p. 13)

What Is the Strategy?

There are two ideas for you to think about in this strategy. The first idea is related to assessment: Teach students to peer-assess and self-assess. Such involvement in assessment will help students recognize, based on the criteria for achievement, what they are uncertain about or not understanding in relation to the learning goals. As a result, they will know what they need to do next to make progress toward the learning goal. The second idea is related to habits of mind: Teach students the habits of mind that encourage the development and use of critical thinking, creative thinking, and self-regulated thinking aspects of metacognition. Connecting the habits of mind with peer assessment helps students develop the thinking they need to objectively self-assess.

These two ideas form our metacognition strategy. This strategy contributes to the development of a positive classroom climate because it builds relationships among students and sets expectations that students will support one another's learning and use habits of mind—such as seeking accuracy and clarity, keeping an open mind, responding appropriately to others' feelings and level of knowledge— that make students feel accepted and capable in the classroom.

The first step in using peer assessment is to teach students the steps in the peer assessment process. For this instruction to be effective, it must help students understand how to recognize quality work and how to provide feedback that highlights both accomplishments and deficiencies demonstrated by the work. We need to explain to students what they should look for in samples of student work and model the process of examining work for evidence of those indicators. We also need to guide discussions of samples of work that include formative feedback to help students learn what to look for as evidence of learning and how to provide comments that will help their peers take the steps they need to improve their work. Finally, we need to help students learn how to discuss their work with one another in class. Discussion allows students to share their ideas and reveal their thinking. This two-way sharing can help students clarify their own ideas and, occasionally, lead them to revise their thinking to include the viewpoints of others.

The first step in using habits of mind is to call explicit attention to these skills, define them, and explain how they relate to learning. In addition, teachers should discuss how the habit of mind is associated with specific behaviors that help students be more metacognitive. You can explain to students that metacognition is sometimes described as having an internal conversation with yourself about what you are doing and how well you are doing it. To use ideas about metacognition and habits of mind in the classroom, teach students how to predict outcomes (critical thinking), activate their background knowledge, plan ahead, note when their thinking does not lead to comprehension, and explain to themselves how to improve their understanding of the content (all of which are aspects of self-regulated thinking). Students and teachers need to discuss and practice the actions associated with habits of mind to learn how to use them. With practice, students—even very young ones—should be able to monitor their own thinking and comprehension without teacher support.

Exploring the Strategy

To develop their abilities to assess their peers, students need examples of significant work that is intellectually engaging. Examples of such work result from engaging students in inquiries in which they explore a scientific question. Inquiries, whether guided or open-ended, involve students with gathering and analyzing data, formulating explanations from the evidence, connecting their explanations with scientific knowledge, and communicating and justifying their explanations. In most classrooms, students gather this information in science notebooks. Some teachers ask the students to place their work into portfolios.

One way to start using peer assessment is to ask the students to trade science notebooks or portfolios and simply check one another's work, looking for specific indicators of performance. For example, are charts and graphs labeled? Do the measurements use the correct units? Are the key vocabulary words included? Do the explanations make sense on the first read and does the student cite evidence? After checking for these indicators, students can practice writing comments that point out one thing that was done well and provide one suggestion for what to look out for in future work. Many students do not want others, including the teacher, to write directly on their work; ask students to provide their comments on sticky notes or a comment sheet where comments can be added each time there is a peer review opportunity. Peer assessment can be used even with young students. They can review pictures and diagrams and ask about the meaning of various parts of the representations.

The feedback from peer review is only valuable if students use the feedback they receive. Small groups or the whole class can discuss the comments they received to determine if they agree with the feedback or not. If there is consensus, then students need to respond to the feedback by writing a summary of what they will do to improve the quality of their work. Through repeated experiences with the peer-assessment process, students will become more objective about the feedback they receive, which will help them be better self-assessors.

There are many approaches to teaching the habits of mind, which include critical thinking, creative thinking, and self-regulated thinking (Marzano and Pickering 1997). One simple approach is to model the process, using an appropriate example. To help students consciously think about these metacognitive processes, you will want to provide multiple opportunities for them to practice using the habits of mind. For example, to help students think critically, you can ask them to conduct an error analysis when the results of their investigations don't match their predictions. Asking students to be accurate and clear about their findings when they present and discuss their evidence provides another opportunity to think critically. They also practice thinking critically when they keep an open mind to others' ideas and proposed explanations as they seek clarity about what happened.

Another way to ask students to think critically in science class is to ask them to debate a science issue related to the concepts in a particular unit. For example, should we use antibacterial soap? Some say this is creating resistant bacteria that hospitals can't fight. Or try discussing the question "Which is better, tap water or bottled water and why?" These kinds of debates ask students to provide evidence to support their claims and use evidence to critique the claims and predictions of others (Banilower et al. 2008). You can teach formal debate procedures or use a simple "fish bowl" format. In the "fish bowl" format, several students sit in a small circle in the middle of the room with the rest of the students in chairs outside of the circle. There are a few empty chairs in the inner circle that provide space for students outside the circle to join the discussion on a short-term basis. The students seated in the circle are asked to take a position on a question and use evidence to support their claims. The students outside the circle listen to the discussion and join in if they have points to add to the conversation. Those in the circle can similarly cycle out to the perimeter. Some students will need to remain in the circle to carry on the discussion. These students should be designated ahead of time or, at some point, there may not be a sufficient number of students inside the fish bowl to sustain the discussion. Designated students on the outside of the circle could serve as process observers, noting when students in the circle demonstrated the attributes of critical, creative, or self-regulated thinking. At the end of the debate, ask these students to give feedback on the metacognitive practices that were demonstrated.

Planning for Classroom Implementation

Implementation of this strategy requires that you plan how you will provide students with the criteria for quality work. It is important to provide these criteria so that students become aware of what success looks like. That will enable them to recognize and articulate problem areas in their own work and the work of others. Be sure you understand, and can explain to students and parents, the benefits of peer assessment. Peer assessment helps students learn about the characteristics of quality work and use this information to improve their own work. Consider how you will provide opportunities for students to verbalize their own thinking. Doing so will help them monitor their understanding. The more they do this, the more they will be able to understand whether new information is consistent with what they already understand. At the same time, they will become adept at identifying what they don't understand conceptually.

Habits of mind refer to mental processes that students use consciously, not behaviors that student do without thought. Our goal is that students apply these mental processes when they are learning science or any other content. In the science classroom, critical thinking includes analyzing errors and weighing evidence to be used in decision making. Thinking creatively in science class involves thinking abstractly and being inventive. To encourage the development and use of habits of mind in your classroom, you will need to present students with activities that require them to analyze errors and weigh evidence (critical thinking), wrestle with abstract concepts and be inventive (creative thinking), and master the art of self-assessment with the help of feedback (self-regulated thinking). Planning for implementation of habits of mind includes determining how and when you will model these habits, provide students with opportunities to practice using them, and reinforce their use.

To plan lessons that support teaching and learning about the habits of mind, think about upcoming learning activities that you might do with your students. Determine what kinds of outcomes you would like students to achieve as a result of these activities and determine how those outcomes relate to the habits of mind. Scan the characteristics for critical, creative, and self-regulated thinking. Use the suggested methods contained in Figure 4.13 (p. 184) to find strategies that will address your desired outcomes.

Figure 4.13
Habits of Mind

Habits of Mind	Methods
Critical Thinking • Be accurate and seek accuracy. • Be clear and seek clarity. • Maintain an open mind. • Restrain impulsivity. • Take a position when the situation warrants it. • Respond appropriately to others' feelings and level of knowledge.	**Help students understand productive habits of mind.** • Facilitate classroom discussion. • Use examples from literature and current events of people who are using the habits in different situations. • Share personal anecdotes. • Notice and label student behavior that demonstrates a habit. • Ask students to identify personal heroes or mentors and describe the extent to which they exemplify specific habits of mind. • Have students create posters that illustrate their understanding of the habits.
Creative Thinking • Persevere. • Push the limits of your knowledge and abilities. • Generate trust, and maintain your own standards of evaluation. • Generate new ways of viewing a situation that are outside the boundaries of standard conventions.	**Help students identify and develop strategies related to the habits of mind.** • Use think-aloud to demonstrate specific strategies. • Ask students to share their own strategies. • Encourage students to find examples of strategies mentioned in literature and current events. • Ask students to interview others to identify strategies. • Each quarter or semester, ask students to identify and focus on a habit of mind they would like to develop.
Self-Regulated Thinking • Monitor your own thinking. • Plan appropriately. • Identify and use necessary resources. • Respond appropriately to feedback. • Evaluate the effectiveness of your actions.	**Create a culture in the classroom and the school that encourages the development and use of the habits of mind.** • Model the habits. • Integrate the habits into the daily routines and activities of the classroom. • Develop and display posters, icons, and other visual representations to express the importance of productive habits of mind. • When appropriate, cue students to focus on specific mental habits or ask them to identify habits that would help them while working on difficult tasks.
	Provide positive reinforcement to students who exhibit the habits of mind. • Appoint "process observers," students who watch for positive examples of other students who are demonstrating the habits. • Ask students to self-assess their use of specific habits. • Give students feedback on a report card or progress report.

Adapted from Marzano, R., and D. Pickering. 1997. *Dimensions of learning trainer's manual*. Alexandria, VA: Association for Supervision and Curriculum Development.

Determine how you will teach, model, practice, and emphasize the type of thinking (critical, creative, self-regulated) that will support your learning goals. Remember, if we want students to be metacognitive, we must first model and teach metacognitive strategies. Then students need opportunities to practice and discuss the strategies. With time, students will develop their self-regulation skills and be able to have productive internal conversations with themselves without teacher support.

What Works in Classrooms: Implications for Teaching

Recommendation 1: Teach students how to engage in peer and self-assessment. Teaching students to peer and self-assess helps them recognize what quality work looks like. For these processes to contribute to student learning, the tasks you assign must be robust enough to reveal student progress toward conceptual understanding. Your role in these processes is to ensure that students know how to write appropriate comments and discuss work with peers and to facilitate discussions about how to examine work against a set of criteria. These practices will help students become more aware of the quality of their own work, when they are on track with their learning, and when they need help and feedback to move forward.

Recommendation 2: Teach students metacognitive strategies that help them construct new knowledge, monitor their own progress, and contribute to the positive climate in the classroom. Students construct new understandings based upon their current knowledge and how that knowledge is connected to new experiences. Given that, one of the first tasks you will want to accomplish when introducing new content is to make visible students' current thinking about the content. Metacognitive strategies that help students engage in creative, critical, and self-regulated thinking prompt learners to elaborate on their existing ideas by incorporating new learning into a set of coherent ideas. To ensure that students are able to use such strategies, model the strategies and provide opportunities for students to practice them and receive feedback on how well they are using them. As part of implementing this recommendation, involve students in collaborative learning experiences that provide opportunities for them to share and clarify their understanding of content.

Teacher Learning: A Beginning

Growing up, I was always amazed that my father had the ability to fix just about anything. He was the ninth of ten children who lived on a farm in northern Minnesota, and that was just what you did when he was growing up. There wasn't money to buy new things so you had to be pretty handy to keep the farm equipment in working order. He kept our old car (a Plymouth Fury!) and the cars of my four brothers running. He kept *everything* in working order—refrigerator, radio, household appliances, and other items—well past their expected life spans. He delighted in teaching me, his only daughter, the names of the tools he used and what they were for. I learned from watching him that the key to a successful fix-it project was a little bit of know-how and the right tools. (A couple of his favorite expressions didn't hurt either.) As I got older and finally had fix-it projects of my own, I did not possess the same confidence that he did when it came to repair jobs. While I will attempt minor ones, I am just as happy calling in my favorite handyman, Ron, to come and do it right. I refuse to tackle any electrical projects since I worry that I will burn the house down. However, despite my fear of some repair jobs and tools, I am comfortable fixing some things, and use those tools that I am comfortable with.

In my years as a high school science teacher, I came to rely on a different box of tools. I still applied what my father taught me, which is that a little bit of know-how and the right tools can do the trick for most fix-it projects. And unlike the hesitancy that I have with pipe wrenches and socket sets, I had no qualms about using the tools at my disposal to fix a problem related to my teaching job.

A great deal of my time was spent helping students learn and solve problems that they encountered in class. One of my many jobs was to advocate for students who needed assistance. Whenever I could, I tried to give my students the tools that they needed to solve problems themselves. As teachers, we know how important it is to give our students the skills they need to be successful learners.

I was often amazed, however, at the number of times I forgot to give students the tools that they needed and I just expected them to have the necessary skills required to solve problems. After all, shouldn't they have learned the skills from one of their other teachers? Sometimes, even if they had the tools at their disposal, they didn't use them. Just like our students, the same can be said about teachers. (I suppose I shouldn't be surprised given my own aversion to the use of some tools or to some fix-it projects. I am sure it all boils down to the confidence and comfort level we each have.)

As teachers, sometimes the tools that we use just don't work. We know that it is time to look for a better, more appropriate tool. It is usually at this junction that teachers, myself included, will manifest their fears about using a different tool. Maybe it won't work. Maybe it will make matters worse. After all, the one that I was using was still perfectly good and I was comfortable using it.

So what are some of these new "tools" designed to help students learn? Research into children's ideas in science is one such tool. With this tool we can better understand how students think about the content and where they are likely to struggle. Some content areas—e.g., force and motion—have a rich research base on student preconceptions and misconceptions. Armed with this information, we can use other tools to help move student thinking forward. Tools like investigations and discrepant events, which confront students with phenomena that make students think. Tools like analogies that link new content to experiences that are already familiar to students. Or questions, that if asked at the right junctures in the instruction, can get them to reflect on their thinking and grasp the new idea.

The C-U-E instructional framework presented in this book is meant to add some tools to your toolbox. Many of the tools are ones that you already use, but others may be sitting on your workbench waiting for a chance to be put to good use or may be brand-new to your toolbox. My message to you (even though I don't practice what I preach when it comes to electrical fix-it projects or using pipe wrenches for plumbing projects) is to try to use the right tools to help reach out to your students and solve your instructional problems. Using the right tool may require expanding the box of tools at your disposal as well as getting additional outside help. Whatever the case, ignoring the problem and hoping it will go away is almost always a sure recipe for a bigger fix-it project down the road.

Unfortunately, my father passed away when I was only 24, just as I was starting my teaching career. At that time he was working as a rocket mechanic and still working with tools—although very sophisticated tools compared to what he used for home repairs. I think he would be happy to know that his ability to fix anything, given time and the right tools, inspired me to continue to learn and add tools to my "educational" toolbox. Because of my love of learning new ideas and strategies, most of my summers were spent going to workshops or participating in educational travel trips. My philosophy was, and still is, if you want to learn about something and how it works, you need to experience the learning, not just read about it. This is part of what I did for myself to regain my enthusiasm and energy to teach and to continue to add new tools to my educational toolbox. I discovered that it wasn't just the learning, but my confidence and competency using the tools that mattered. Ultimately, my attitudes, beliefs, and dispositions had and continue to have a powerful influence on why I went into teaching and why I now work as a professional developer in support of school improvement.

Just like our students, we learn in different ways. In the February 2009 edition of *Educational Leadership* there are several featured articles that discuss how teachers learn. One such article is "From Surviving to Thriving" by Sonia Nieto. She makes some strong recommendations about the climate that teachers need to remain enthusiastic and committed to their work. The bottom line is teachers need environments that promote meaningful learning. She includes three simple suggestions that clearly connect to the purpose of this book:

- First, learn about yourself. Reflect on your teaching beliefs and practices. Become self-aware and reassess what you do and can do to be an effective teacher. Some self-assessment tools are included in the appendix to get you started.

- Second, learn about your students. Find out what happens in their world. Build relationships with them and make connections. When students believe we care about them and their learning they start to trust us. Positive environments make a huge difference no matter what level we teach.

- Finally, Nieto recommends developing allies. New teachers need the support of other teachers to survive. Working as a community alleviates the loneliness some teachers feel. When we work with a "buddy," friend, or mentor, we become energized and hopeful.

I, like most teachers, continue to learn. This book brings together many of the ideas and tools that I have acquired and added to my own toolbox. My goal was to share with you some of the research-informed practices that are changing instruction—for the better. The key to this work is to take from it what is useful to you. I encourage you to get comfortable with the strategy tools and use them to create a positive environment for yourself and your students that promotes learning—

learning and thinking about the content we teach, learning about content-specific strategies that move students' thinking forward, and learning how to keep our lives in balance while still maintaining the energy to teach.

Content References

American Association for the Advancement of Science (AAAS). 1993. *Benchmarks for science literacy.* New York: Oxford University Press.

American Association for the Advancement of Science (AAAS). 2001. *Designs for science literacy.* New York: Oxford University Press.

American Association for the Advancement of Science (AAAS). 2007. *Atlas of science literacy, volume 2.* New York: Oxford University Press.

American Association for the Advancement of Science (AAAS). 2001. *Atlas of science literacy, volume 1.* New York: Oxford University Press.

Banilower, E., K. Cohen, J. Pasley, and I. Weiss. 2008. *Effective science instruction: What does research tell us?* Portsmouth, NH: RMC Research Corporation, Center on Instruction.

Barton, M. L., and D. L. Jordan. 2001. *Teaching reading in science: A supplement to the Second Edition of Teaching Reading in the Content Areas Teacher's Manual.* Aurora, CO: Mid-continent Research for Education and Learning.

Bell, A.W., and D. Purdy. 1985. *Diagnostic teaching.* Nottingham, England: University of Nottingham.

Black, P., and C. Harrison. 2004. *Science inside the black box: Assessment for learning in the science classroom.* London: nferNelson [sic] Publishing Co. Ltd.

Black, P., C. Harrison, C. Lee, B. Marshall, and D. Wiliam. 2003. *Assessment for learning: Putting it into practice.* New York: Open University Press.

Black, P., and D. Wiliam. 1998. Inside the black box: Raising standards through classroom assessment. *Phi Delta Kappan, 80* (2): 139–148.

Bransford, J., A. Brown, and R. Cocking, eds. 1999. *How people learn: Brain, mind, experience, and school.* Washington, DC: National Academy Press.

Bybee, R. 2002. In *Learning science and the science of learning: Science educator's essay collection,* ed. R. W. Bybee, 31–33. Arlington, VA: NSTA Press.

Carey, S., and R. Gelman. 1991. *The epigenesis of mind: Essays on biology and cognition.* Hillsdale, NJ: Erlbaum.

Catley, K., R. Lehrer, and R. Reiser. 2005. Tracing a prospective learning progression for developing understanding of evolution. Paper Commissioned by the National Academies Committee on Test Design for K–12 Science Achievement.

Dean, C., and J. Bailey. 2003. *A report documenting the process for developing an integrated standards-based instructional unit.* Aurora, CO: Mid-continent Research for Education and Learning.

Dewey, J. 1916. *Democracy and education: An introduction to the philosophy of education.* New York: Macmillian.

Donovan, S., and J. Bransford, eds. 2005. *How students learn: Science in the classroom.* Washington DC: National Academy Press.

Donovan, S., J. Bransford, and J. Pellegrino, eds. 1999. *How people learn: Bridging research and practice.* Washington, DC: National Academy Press.

Doran, R., F. Chan, and P. Tamir. 1998. *Science educator's guide to assessment.* Arlington, VA: NSTA Press.

Driver, R., A. Squires, P. Rushworth, and V. Wood-Robinson. 2005. *Making sense of secondary science: Research into children's ideas.* New York: Routledge Falmer.

Druker, S. L., H. Garnier, M. Lemmens, C. Chen, T. Kawanaka, D. Rasmussen, S. Trubacova, et al. 2006. *Teaching science in five countries: Results from the TIMSS 1999 Video Study.* U.S. Department of Education. Washington, DC: National Center for Education Statistics.

Gooding, D. 1990. *Experiment and the making of meaning.* London: Kluwer Academic Publishers.

Goodwin, C. 2000. Practices of color classification. *Mind, Culture and Activity* 7: 19–36.

Hazen, R. M., and J. Trefil. 1991. *Science matters: Achieving science literacy.* New York: Anchor Books

Heritage, M. 2008. Learning progressions: Supporting instruction and formative assessment. Research brief from the Council of Chief State School Officers, The FAST SCASS—Formative Assessment for Teachers and Learners. Los Angeles.

Hyerle, D. 1996. *Visual tools for constructing knowledge.* Alexandria, VA: Association for Supervision and Curriculum Development.

Keeley, P. 2005. *Science curriculum topic study: Bridging the gap between standards and practice.* Thousand Oakes, CA: Corwin Press.

Keeley, P, and F. Eberle. 2008. Using standards and cognitive research to inform the design and use of formative assessment probes. In *Assessing science learning,* eds. J. Coffey, R Douglas, and C. Stearns, 206–207. Arlington, VA: NSTA Press.

Keeley, P, F. Eberle, and C. Dorsey. 2008. *Uncovering student ideas in science, vol. 3: Another 25 Formative assessment probes.* Arlington VA: NSTA Press.

Keeley, P, F. Eberle, and L. Farina. 2005. *Uncovering student ideas in science, vol. 1: 25 formative assessment probes.* Arlington VA: NSTA Press.

Keeley, P., F. Eberle, and J. Tugel. 2007. *Uncovering student ideas in science, vol. 2; 25 more formative assessment probes.* Arlington VA: NSTA Press.

Keeley, P., and J. Tugel. 2009. *Uncovering student ideas in science, Vol. 4, 25 new formative assessment probes.* Arlington VA: NSTA Press.

Kesidou, S., and J. E. Roseman, 2002. How well do middle school science programs measure up? Findings from Project 2061's curriculum review. *Journal of Research in Science Teaching, 39*(6): 522–549.

Marzano, R. 1997. *Dimensions of learning.* 2nd ed. Alexandria, VA: Association for Supervision and Curriculum Development.

Marzano, R., D. Pickering, and J. Pollock. 2001. *Classroom instruction that works: Research-based strategies for increasing student achievement.* Alexandria, VA: Association for Supervision and Curriculum Development.

Mid-continent Research for Education and Learning (McREL). 2005. *Classroom instruction that works: Facilitator's manual.* Aurora, CO: McREL.

National Assessment Governing Board. 2005. *National Assessment of Education Progress 2009 Science Framework* (September 30, 2005 Draft for Public Review). *www.nagb.org.*

National Research Council (NRC). 1996. *National science education standards.* Washington, DC: National Academy Press.

National Research Council (NRC). 1999. *Selecting instructional material: A guide for K–12 science.* Washington, DC: National Academy Press.

National Research Council (NRC). 2007. *Taking science to school: Learning and teaching science in grades K–8.* Committee on Science Learning, Kindergarten Through Eighth Grade, eds. R. A. Duschl, H. A. Schweingruber, and A. W. Shouse. Washington, DC: National Academies Press.

Nuthall, G. 1999. The way students learn. *The Elementary School Journal 99*(4): 303–341.

Pellegrino, J. W., N. Chudowsky, and R. Gleser. 2001. *Knowing what students know.* Washington, DC: National Academies Press.

Reynolds, D., R. Doran, and S. Agruso. 1996. *Alternative assessments: A teacher's guide.* Buffalo, NY: University of Buffalo Press.

Roberts, L., M. Wilson, and K. Draney. 1997. *The SEPUP assessment system: An overview.* BEAR Report Series, SA-97-1, University of California, Berkeley.

Robertson, W. C. 2003. *Light: Stop faking it! Finally understanding science so you can teach it.* Arlington, VA: NSTA Press.

Rovee-Collier, C. 1995. Time windows in cognitive development. *Developmental Psychology* 31: 147–169.

Schmidt, W. H., D. D. McKnight, R. T. Houang, H. D. Wang, D. E. Wiley, L. S. Cogan, and R. G. Wolfe. 2001. *Why schools matter: A cross-national comparison of curriculum and learning.* San Francisco: Jossey-Bass.

Smith, C., M. Wiser, C. W. Anderson, J. Krajcik, and R. Cooppola. 2004. *Implications of research on children's learning for assessment: Matter and atomic molecular theory.* Committee on Test Design for K–12 Science Assessment, Center for Education, Washington, DC: National Research Council.

Stigler, J. W., and J. Heibert. 1998, Winter. The TIMSS Videotape Study. *American Educator.* Washington, DC: American Federation of Teachers.

Vitale, M. R., N. R. Romance, and M. F. Dolan. 2006. A knowledge-based framework for the classroom assessment of student understanding. In *Assessment in science: Practical experiences and education research,* eds. M. McMahon, P. Simmons, R. Sommers, D. DeBaets, and F. Crawley, 1–13. Arlington, VA: NSTA Press.

Weiss, I., J. Pasley, S. Smith, E. Banilower, and D. Heck. 2003. *Looking inside the classroom: A study of K–12 mathematics and science education in the United States.* Chapel Hill, NC: Horizon Research.

Wiggins, G. 2008. What is a Big Idea? *www.authenticeducation.org/bigideas/article.lasso?artId=99*

Wiggins, G., and J. McTighe. 2005. *Understanding by design.* 2nd ed. Alexandria, VA: Association for Supervision and Curriculum Development.

Williamson, B. 2000. The floating leaf assay for investigating photosynthesis. *http://home.earthlink.net/~bioteacher/LeafDisk.htm.*

Wilson, M. 2005. *Constructing measures: An Item response modeling approach.* Mahwah, NJ: Lawrence Erlbaum Associates.

Wilson, M., and K. Sloane. 2001. From principles to practice: An embedded assessment system. *Applied Measurement in Education* 13 (2): 181–208.

Understanding References

Arizona State University. Modeling Instruction Program. Motion maps and the modeling method: A synopsis. *http://modeling.asu.edu.*

Atkin, J. M., and J. E. Coffey, eds. 2003. *Everyday assessment in the science classroom.* Arlington, VA: NSTA Press.

Banilower, E., K. Cohen, J. Pasley, and I. Weiss. 2008. *Effective science instruction: What does research tell us?* Portsmouth, NH: RMC Research Corporation, Center on Instruction.

Black, P. 1993. Formative and summative assessment by teachers. *Studies in Science Education* 21: 49–97.

Black, P., and D. Wiliam. 1998a. Assessment and classroom learning. *Assessment in Education* 5 (1): 7–74.

Black, P., and D. Wiliam. 1998b. Inside the black box: Raising standards through classroom assessment. *Phi Delta Kappan* 80 (2): 139–148.

Bransford, J., A. Brown, and R. Cocking, eds. 1999. *How people learn.* Washington, DC: National Academy Press.

BSCS. 2006. *Why does inquiry matter: Because that's what science is all about!* Dubuque, IA: Kendall/Hunt Publishing Co.

Bybee, R. W. 2000. Teaching science as inquiry. In *Inquiring into inquiry learning and teaching in science,* eds. J. Minstrell and E. H. VanZee, 37–38. Washington DC: American Association for the Advancement of Science.

Colburn, A. 2004. Inquiring scientists want to know. *Education Leadership* 62: 63–66.

Cothron, J., R. Giese, and R. Rezba. 1989. *Students and research.* Dubuque, IA: Kendall/Hunt Publishing Co.

Cowie, B., and B. Bell. 1996. Validity and formative assessment in the classroom. Paper presented at the International Symposium on Validity in Educational Assessment, University of Otago, Dunedin, New Zealand.

Crooks, T. 2001. The validity of formative assessments. Paper presented at the Annual Meeting of the British Educational Research Association, Leeds, UK.

Donovan, S., and J. Bransford, eds. 2005. *How students learn: Science in the classroom.* Washington DC: National Academies Press.

Donovan, S., J. Bransford, and J. Pellegrino, eds. 1999. *How people learn: Bridging research and practice.* Washington, D.C: National Academy Press.

Driver, R., A. Squires, P. Duck, and V. Wood-Robinson. 1994. *Making sense of secondary science: Research into children's ideas.* London: Rutledge.

Duckworth, E. 1996. *The having of wonderful ideas and other essays on teaching and learning.* New York: Teachers College Press.

Gallas, K. 1995. *Talking their way into science: Hearing children's questions and theories, responding with curricula.* New York: Teachers College Press.

Grall Reichel, A. 1994. Performance assessment: Five practical approaches. *Science and Children* 32 (2): 21–25.

Hattie, J. A. 1992. Measuring the effects of schooling. *Australian Journal of Education* 36 (1): 5–13.

Harvard-Smithsonian Center for Astrophysics, Science Education Department, Science Media Group. 1987. *A private universe.* Available from Annenberg Media at *www.learner.org/resources/series28.html.*

Harvard-Smithsonian Center for Astrophysics, Science Education Department, Science Media Group. 1997. *Minds of our own.* Available from Annenberg Media at *www.learner.org/resources/series26.html.*

Heritage, M. 2008. Formative assessment: What do teachers need to know and do? *Kappan* 89 (2): 140–145.

Hunter, M. 1982. *Mastery teaching.* El Segundo, CA: TIP Publications.

Jensen, E. *Teaching with the brain in mind.* 1998. Alexandria, VA: Association for Curriculum and Supervision Development.

Johnson, D., and R. Johnson. 1988. Cooperative learning: Two heads learn better than one. *Transforming education* (winter): 34.

Johnson, D., and R. Johnson. 1994. An overview of cooperative learning. In *Creativity and collaborative learning,* eds. J. Thousand, A. Villa, and A. Nevin, 31–44. Baltimore: Brookes Press.

Johnson, D., R. Johnson, and M. Stanne. 2000. Cooperative learning methods: A meta-analysis. Retrieved December 12, 2005, from the University of Minnesota, the Cooperative Learning Center website: *www.co-operation.org/pages/cl-methods.html*

Keeley, P. 2008. *Science formative assessments: 75 Practical strategies for linking assessment, instruction, and learning.* Arlington VA: NSTA Press.

Keeley, P., F. Eberle, and L. Farrin. 2005. *Uncovering student ideas in science, vol. 1: 25 formative assessment probes.* Arlington VA: NSTA Press.

Keeley, P., F. Eberle, and J. Tugel. 2007. *Uncovering student ideas in science, vol. 2: 25 more formative assessment probes.* Arlington VA: NSTA Press.

Keeley, P., F. Eberle, and C. Dorsey. 2008. *Uncovering student ideas in science, vol. 3: Another 25 formative assessment probes.* Arlington VA: NSTA Press.

Keeley, P., and J. Tugel. 2009. *Uncovering student ideas in science, vol. 4: 25 new formative assessment probes.* Arlington VA: NSTA Press.

Kelley, G. J., D. Brown, and T. Crawford. 2000. Experiments, contingencies, and curriculum: Providing opportunities for learning through improvisation in science teaching. *Science Education* 84: 624–657.

Kirwan, G. 2004. *Matter circus activity.* Department of Physics and Astronomy: Louisiana State University.

Klentschy, M., and M. De La Torre. 2003. Students' science notebooks and the inquiry process. In *Crossing borders in literacy and science instruction: Perspectives on theory and practice,* ed. W. Saul, 340–354. Arlington, VA: NSTA Press.

Layman, J., G. Ochoa, and H. Heikkinen. 1996. *Inquiry and learning: Realizing science standards in the classroom.* New York: National Center for Cross Disciplinary Teaching and Learning.

Lederman, N. G., and J. S. Lederman. 2004. Revising instruction to teach nature of science. *The Science Teacher* 71 (9): 36–39.

Legleiter, E. 2005. Modeling: Changes in traditional physics instruction. In *Exemplary science in grades 9–12: Standards-based success stories,* ed. R. Yager, 73–81. Arlington, VA: NSTA Press.

Lowery, L. F. 1990. *The biological basis of thinking and learning.* Berkeley, CA: University of California Press.

MacIsaac, D. 2004. *Using whiteboards.* Department of Physics: SUNY Buffalo State College.

Magnusson, S., and A. Palinscar. 2005. Teaching to promote the development of scientific knowledge and reasoning about light at the elementary school level. In *How students learn history, mathematics, and science in the classroom,* eds. M. Donovan and J. Bransford, 425. Washington, DC: National Academies Press.

Martin, M. O., I. V. S. Mullis, E. J. Gonzalez, and S. J. Chrostowski. 2004. *Findings from IEA's trends in international mathematics and science study at the fourth and eighth grades.* Chestnut Hill, MA: TIMSS & PIRLS International Study Center, Boston College.

Marzano, R. J., D. J. Pickering, and J. E. Pollock. 2001. *Classroom instruction that works.* Alexandria, VA: Association for Supervision and Curriculum Development.

McLaughlin, M. 1994. Using KWL to introduce inquiry. Presented at the Association of Science-Technology Centers Annual Conference, Portland, OR. *www.exploratorium.edu/ifi/resources/lifescienceinquiry/usingkwl.html*

Minstrell, J. 1989. Teaching Science for Understanding. In *Toward the thinking curriculum: Current cognitive research,* eds. L. B. Resnick and L. E. Klopfer,

129–149. Alexandria, VA: Association for Supervision and Curriculum Development.

Mortimer, E. F. 1998. Multivoicedness and univocality in classroom discourse: An example from theory of matter. *International Journal of Science Education* 20: 67–82.

Mortimer, E. F., and P. Scott. 2003. *Meaning making in secondary science classrooms.* London: Open University Press.

National Research Council (NRC). 1996. *National science education standards.* Washington, DC: National Academy Press.

National Research Council (NRC). 2000. *Inquiry and the national science education standards: A guide for teaching and learning.* Washington, DC: National Academy Press.

National Research Council (NRC). 2005. *How students learn: Science in the classroom.* Washington, DC: National Academies Press.

O'Brien Carlson, M., G. E. Humphrey, and K. S. Reinhardt. 2003. *Weaving science inquiry and continuous assessment: Using formative assessment to improve learning.* Thousand Oaks, CA: Corwin Press.

Özdemir, G., and D. B. Clark. 2007. An overview of conceptual change theories. *Eurasia Journal of Mathematics, Science & Technology Education* 3 (4): 351–361.

Powell, J. C., J. Short, and N. Landes. 2002. Curriculum reform, professional development, and powerful learning. In *Learning science and the science of learning,* ed. R. Bybee, 121–136. Arlington, VA: NSTA Press.

Public Broadcasting System (PBS) Teacherline (Producer). 2004. *Developing mathematical thinking with effective questions.*

Sadler, D. R. 1989. Formative assessment and the design of instructional systems. *Instructional Science* 18: 130.

Shepard, L. 2001. The role of classroom assessment in teaching and learning. In *The handbook of research on teaching,* 4th ed., ed. V. Richardson, 1066–1101. Washington, DC: American Educational Research Association.

Sousa, D. A. 1995. *How the brain learns.* Reston, VA: National Association of Secondary School Principals.

Strike, K., and G. Posner. 1985. A conceptual change view of learning and understanding. In *Cognitive structure and conceptual change,* eds. L. West and A. Pines, 6. Orlando, FL: Academic Press.

Thier, M. 2002. *The new science literacy: Using language skills to help students learn science.* Portsmouth, NH: Heinemann.

Thorndike, E. L. 1898. Animal intelligence: An experimental study of the associative processes in animals. *Psychological Review Monograph Supplement* 2 (4): 8.

van Gog, T., K. Anders Ericsson, R. M. J. P. Rikers, and F. Paas. 2005. Instructional design for advanced learners: Establishing connections between the theoretical frameworks of cognitive load and deliberative practice. *Educational Technology, Research and Development* 53 (3): 73–81.

Vygotsky, L. 1978. *Mind in society.* Cambridge, MA: Harvard University Press.

Wheeler, G. F. 2000. The three faces of inquiry. In *Inquiring into inquiry learning and teaching in science*, eds. J. Minstrell and E. H. Van Zee, 14–19. Washington, DC: American Association for the Advancement of Science.

Wiggins, G., and J. McTighe. 2005. *Understanding by design.* 2nd ed. Alexandria, VA: Association for Supervision and Curriculum Development.

Zimmerman, T. D., and E. K. Stage. 2008. Teaching science for understanding. In *Powerful learning: What we know about teaching for understanding*, eds. G. N. Cervetti, J. L. Tilson, L. Darling-Hammond, B. Barron, D. Pearson, A. H. Schoenfeld, E. K. Stage, and T. D. Zimmerman, 170–176. San Francisco: Jossey-Bass.

Environment References

American Association for the Advancement of Science (AAAS). 1990. *Science for all Americans.* New York: Oxford University Press.

American Association for the Advancement of Science (AAAS). 1993. *Benchmarks for science literacy.* New York: Oxford University Press.

Bangert-Drowns, R. L., C. C. Kulik, J. A. Kulik, and M. T. Morgan. 1991. The instructional effect of feedback in test-like events. *Review of Educational Research* 61 (2): 218–238.

Banilower, E., K. Cohen, J. Pasley, and I. Weiss. 2008. *Effective science instruction: What does research tell us?* Portsmouth, NH: RMC Research Corporation.

Black, P., and C. Harrison. 2004. *Science inside the black box: Assessment for learning in the science classroom.* London: nferNelson [sic] Publishing Co. Ltd.

Bransford, J., A. Brown, and R. Cocking. 2000. *How people learn: Brain, mind, experience, and school.* Washington, DC: National Academy Press.

Combs, A.W. 1982. Affective education or none at all. *Educational Leadership* 39 (7): 494–497.

Covington, M. V. 1983. Motivation cognitions. In *Learning and motivation in the classroom,* eds. S. G. Paris, G. M. Olson, and H. W. Stevenson, 139–164. Hillsdale, NJ: Erlbaum.

Covington, M. V. 1985. Strategic thinking and the fear of failure. In *Thinking and learning skills: Vol.1, Relating instruction to research,* eds. J. W. Segal, S. F. Chipman, and R. Glaser, 389–416. Hillsdale, NJ: Erlbaum.

Covington, M. V. 1992. *Making the grade: A self-worth perspective on motivation and school reform.* New York: Cambridge University Press.

Donovan, S., and J. Bransford. 2005. *How students learn.* Washington, DC: National Academy Press.

Donovan, S., J. Bransford, and J. Pellegrino. 1999. *How people learn: Bridging research and practice.* Washington, DC: National Academy Press.

Doran, R., F. Chan, and P. Tamir. 1998. *Science educator's guide to assessment.* Arlington, VA: NSTA Press.

Eaker, R., R. DuFour, R. Burnette DuFour. 2002. *Getting started: Reculturing schools to become professional learning communities.* Bloomington, IN: Solution Tree.

Ginsberg, M., and R. Wlodkowski. 2000. *Creating highly motivating classrooms for all students: A schoolwide approach to powerful teaching with diverse learners.* San Francisco: Jossey-Bass.

Gladwell, M. 2005. *Blink: The power of thinking without thinking.* New York: Little, Brown.

Harlan, W. 1992. *The teaching of science.* London: David Fulton Publishers.

Harter, S. 1980. The perceived competence scale for children. *Child Development* 51: 218–235.

Hattie, J. 1992. What works in special education. Presentation to the Special Education Conference, Auckland, NZ. Available online at *www.arts.auckland. ac.nz/FileGet.cfm?ID=C302783E-1243-4B65-AC54-B7FD4A5B7EF7*

Jensen, E. 1998. *Teaching with the brain in mind.* Alexandria, VA: Association for Curriculum and Supervision Development.

Jones, F. 2000. *Tools for teaching.* Santa Cruz, CA: Fredric H. Jones & Associates.

Jones, M., and G. Carter. 2007. Science teacher attitudes and beliefs. In *Handbook of research on science education*, eds. S. Abell and N. Lederman, 1067–1104. Mahwah, NJ: Lawrence Erlbaum Associates

Keys, C. W., and L. A. Bryan. 2001. Co-constructing inquiry-based science with teachers: Essential research for lasting reform. *Journal of Research in Science Teaching* 38: 631–645.

Lederman, N. G. 2007. Nature of science: Past, present, and future. In *Handbook of research on science education,* eds. S. Abell and N. Lederman, 832–835. Mahwah, NJ: Lawrence Erlbaum Associates.

Liem, T. 1987. *Invitations to science inquiry.* Placerville, CA: Science Inquiry Enterprises.

Marzano, R. 1992. *A different kind of classroom: Teaching with dimensions of learning.* Alexandra, VA: Association for Supervision and Curriculum Development.

Marzano, R. 2003. *What works in schools: Translating research into action.* Alexandria, VA: Association for Supervision and Curriculum Development.

Marzano, R. 2006. *Classroom assessment and grading that work.* Alexandria, VA: Association for Supervision and Curriculum Development.

Marzano, R., and D. Pickering. 1997. *Dimensions of learning trainer's manual.* Alexandria, VA: Association for Supervision and Curriculum Development.

Marzano, R., D. Pickering, and J. Pollock. 2001. *Classroom instruction that works: Research-based strategies for increasing student achievement.* Alexandria, VA: Association for Supervision and Curriculum Development.

Marzano, R., D. Pickering, and J. Pollock. 2003. *Classroom management that works: Research-based strategies for every teacher.* Alexandria, VA: Association for Supervision and Curriculum Development.

Mid-continent Research for Education and Learning (McREL). 2005. *A participant's manual for classroom instruction that works.* Aurora, CO: McREL.

Moore, J. 1993. *Science as a way of knowing: The foundations of modern biology.* Cambridge, MA: Harvard University Press.

National Association of Secondary School Principals (NASSP). *Breaking ranks II.* Available online at *www.principals.org/s_nassp/bin.asp?TrackID=&SID=1&DID= 46539&CID=1237&VID=2&DOC=FILE.PDF*

Nieto, S. 2009. From surviving to thriving. *Educational Leadership* 66 (5): 8–13.

Rosenthal, R. 1998. Covert communication in classrooms, clinics, and courtrooms. *Eye on Psi Chi* 3 (1): 18–22.

Roth, K. J., S. L. Druker, H. E. Garnier, M. Lemmens, C. Chen, T. Kawanaka, D. Rasmussen et al. 2006. *Teaching science in five countries: Results from the TIMSS 1999 video study (NCES 2006-011).* U.S. Department of Education, National Center for Education Statistics. Washington, DC: U.S. Government Printing Office.

Sadler, T. D., F. W. Chambers, and D. Zeidler. 2004. Student conceptualizations of the nature of science in response to a socioscientific issue. *International Journal of Science Education* 26 (4): 387–409.

Shute, V. 2008. Focus on formative feedback. *Review of Educational Research* 78 (1): 153–189.

Simpson, R. D., T. R. Koballa, J. S. Oliver, and F. Crawley. 1994. Research on the affective dimension of science learning. In *Handbook of research on science teaching and learning,* ed. D. Gable, 211–234. New York: Macmillan.

Tauber, A. 1997. *Science and the quest for reality.* New York: New York University Press.

Van Overwalle, F., and M. De Metsenaere. 1990. The effects of attribution-based intervention and study strategy training on academic achievement in college freshmen. *British Journal of Educational Psychology* 60: 299–311.

Weiner, B. 1972. Attribution theory, achievement motivation and the educational process. *Review of Educational Research* 42: 203–215.

Weiner, B. 1983. Speculations regarding the role of affect in achievement-change programs guided by attributional principles. In *Teaching and student perceptions: Implications for learning,* eds. J. M. Levine and M. C. Wang, 57–73. Hillsdale, NJ: Erlbaum.

Weiss, I., J. Pasley, S. Smith, E. Banilower, and D. Heck. 2003. *Looking inside the classroom: A study of K–12 mathematics and science education in the United States.* Chapel Hill, NC: Horizon Research.

Wilson, T. D., and P. W. Linville. 1982. Improving the academic performance of college freshman: Attribution theory revisited. *Journal of Personal and Social Psychology* 42: 367–376.

Wong, H. K., and R. T. Wong. 2004. *The First Days of School.* Mountain View, CA: Harry K. Wong Publications.

Appendixes

Appendix Chapter 1.
Designing Effective Lessons

Get the Content Right	
What is the important key concept that the student should learn? (Include facts and vocabulary, skills, and processes.)	How will you know the students understood the key concept? (Formative and/or summative)
Develop Student Understanding	
How is student understanding developed? (Discourse, inquiry, problem solving, etc. What strategies will you use?)	What opportunities are provided in the lesson to help students make sense of the concepts? (Sense-making and/or wrap-up activities)
Develop Student Understanding	
How did this lesson support learning by all students? (Individualization and/or differentiation)	What feedback did the teacher provide to support student learning? (Peer review, self-assessment, timely, criteria for evaluation, collaboration)

Appendix Chapter 2.
Content Strategy 1. Sample Unit Planning Template

Title:	Grade:	Length:
Step 1. Content		
Big Idea		
Key Concepts		
Knowledge		**Skills**

Appendix Chapter 2.
Content Strategy 2. Steps in the Pruning Process

Pruning the Curriculum

 Step 1 Identify the big idea(s) for your unit and write a paragraph that elaborates on what this big idea means or draw a concept map that details the relationship between the key concepts and knowledge embedded in this statement.

 Step 2 Determine the unit of study or topic and, using whatever resources you have, create a list of related standards and benchmarks that could be included in the unit.

 Step 3 Using the district curriculum guide for your course, previous unit plans, and/or the textbook resources available, create a list of key concepts for a unit.

 Step 4 Using the two lists previously generated, add lesson objectives that would address specific facts, vocabulary, and skills included in the unit.

 Step 5 Using the paragraph or concept map as your guide, identify which statements you will keep and which you will consider for pruning. Remember, you may choose to keep some vocabulary statements, ideas that engage students, or ones that are relevant to students.

 Step 6 Using your pruning criteria, go through the list again and decide which additional statements to keep and which will be deleted from the unit, covered in another unit, covered in a different course, or pruned as unnecessary repetition since it was or will be covered elsewhere.

Appendix Chapter 2.
Content Strategy 4a. Steps in Identifying Prior Knowledge and Preconceptions

Steps in Identifying Prior Knowledge and Preconceptions
Build Your Content Understanding—take stock of what you know and what you don't know about the science concepts using resources to build your own content understanding.
Identify Prior Conceptual Understandings and Common Preconceptions—Identify the concepts students should already understand and the common preconceptions (possible misconceptions) identified through cognitive research.
Assess for Prior Student Knowledge—Devise a way to find out about students' ideas to determine their prior knowledge and preconceptions.
Plan Instruction That Connects to Students Ideas—Figure out a way to connect student ideas with the scientific concepts you will be teaching. Make the connection of student ideas and science concepts explicit.

Appendix Chapter 2.
Content Strategy 4b. Prior Knowledge and Preconceptions

Unit Topic _____   Big Idea(s) _____

Prior Knowledge	Key Concept	Possible Misconceptions	Tips for Planning
What students are expected to understand already. This can be determined by looking at references that identify learning trajectories to see what students should have learned in earlier science classes.	A broad idea that can be understood only by linking several ideas into a more comprehensive framework of ideas. Scientific concepts unify ideas within a discipline into general principles of understanding.	These are student preconceptions that have been identified through cognitive research into students' ideas. Teacher experiences also will provide clues to student preconceptions.	How will you elicit prior student knowledge? What preconceptions will you address? How will you plan to connect student ideas to the lesson objectives?

Appendix Chapter 2.
Content Strategy 5a. Criteria for Success for Key Concepts

Key Concept *(What the student should understand)*	Knowledge, Skills, and Understanding Embedded in the Key Concept		
	Knowledge of Benchmark ideas *(Identify correct patterns and representations)*	Inquiry *(Raise questions, classify, measure, identify patterns in date)*	Application *(Use scientific patterns to describe, explain, predict, design)*

Appendix Chapter 2.
Content Strategy 5b. Blueprint for Planning Summative Assessments

Key Concepts and Learning Targets	Selected Response	Essay	Performance Assessment	Personal Communication	Inquiry	(Other)

Adapted with permission from: C. Dean and J. Bailey. (2003) "A Report Documenting the Process for Developing an Integrated Standards-Based Instructional Unit." © Copyright 2004 McREL

Appendix Chapter 2.
Content Strategy 6. Sequencing Learning Targets Into Progressions
With Learning Activities Identified

Big Ideas	Key Concepts	Learning Targets	Learning Activities

Appendix Chapter 3.
Understanding Strategy 6. K-W-L Student Handout Template

What I Know	What I Want to Know	What I Think I Know What Is My Evidence How I Would Find Out	What I Learned

Adapted from McLaughlin, M. 1994. Using K-W-L to introduce inquiry. Presented at the Association of Science-Technology Centers Annual Conference, Portland, OR. *www.exploratorium.edu/ifi/resources/lifescienceinquiry/usingkwl.html.*

Appendix Chapter 4.
Environment Strategy 1. Changing Practices to Change Beliefs

Analyzing Teacher Beliefs and Actions That Support a Climate of Learning			
Current Belief or Behavior *(Inputs, outputs, climate, and feedback)*	Impact on the Class or on Student(s)	Action or Procedure You Will Change	Expected Change in Student Behavior

Appendix Chapter 4.
Environment Strategy 2. Thinking Scientifically

When this quality of thinking scientifically is being taught, modeled, or used...			
You would see teachers...	You would hear teachers...	You would see students...	You would hear students...

Appendix Chapter 4.
Environment Strategy 3. Develop Positive Attitudes and Motivation

Record Notes to Youself on...	
What specific things to try, or do more of	What issues remain as dilemmas
Does each student feel accepted by teachers and peers?	
Does each student experience a sense of comfort and order?	
Does each student perceive tasks as valuable and interesting?	
Does each student believe he or she has the ability and resources to complete tasks?	
Does each student understand the tasks?	

Adapted from Marzano, R., and D. Pickering. 1997. *Dimensions of learning trainer's manual.* Alexandria, VA: Association for Supervision and Curriculum Development.

Appendix Chapter 4.
Environment Strategy 4. Providing Feedback

1. Feedback Should Be "Corrective" in Nature.
What does the research say? Summarize the finding(s)—the "big idea."
What would this look like in practice? Generate some classroom examples of "dos" and "don'ts."

2. Feedback Should Be Timely.
What does the research say? Summarize the finding(s)—the "big idea."
What would this look like in practice? Generate some classroom examples of "dos" and "don'ts."

Appendix Chapter 4.
Environment Strategy 4. Providing Feedback (cont.)

3. Feedback Should Be Specific to a Criterion.
What does the research say? Summarize the finding(s)—the "big idea."
What would this look like in practice? Generate some classroom examples of "dos" and "don'ts."
What is the students' role? Generate some strategies for involving the students in addressing feedback.
Providing Feedback
Write some reminders to yourself about how and when providing feedback increases student learning.

Appendix Chapter 4.
Environment Strategy 5. Effort Rubric

	What Teachers Would Be Doing	What Students Would Be Doing
Advanced **4**	In addition to including the "Proficient" indicators:	In addition to including the "Proficient" indicators:
Proficient **3**		
Beginning **2**		
Not in Use **1**		

Index

Note: **Boldface** page numbers indicate figures.